10
DOWNING STREET
THE ILLUSTRATED HISTORY

To meet General of the Army and Mrs. Dwight D. Eisenhower

The Prime Minister and Mrs. Churchill

request the honour of the company of

at Dinner at 10, Downing Street

on Thursday, the 15th May, 1952, at 8.15 p.m. for 8.30 p.m.

An answer is requested to :
The Private Secretary.

Evening Dress

10
DOWNING STREET

THE ILLUSTRATED HISTORY

ANTHONY SELDON

with photography by **Mark Fiennes**

HarperCollins*Illustrated*

To my young family: Jessica, Susannah and Adam Seldon

First published in 1999 by HarperCollins*Illustrated*
an imprint of HarperCollins*Publishers*
77-85 Fulham Palace Road
London W6 8JB

The HarperCollins website address is:
www.**fireandwater**.com

A CIP catalogue record for this book is available from the British Library

ISBN: 0 00 414073 7

Designer: Caroline Hill
Copy Editor: Caroline Taylor
Proofreader: Carole McGlynn
Indexer: Susan Martin

99 01 03 02 00
2 4 6 8 9 7 5 3 1

Colour reproduction by Colourscan Pte.
Printed and bound in the UK by Bath Press Colourbooks Ltd

Introduction & Acknowledgements

Number 10 has always fascinated me. Book and diaries about prime ministers and tales of how they used the buildings would be lapped up. Yet it was not until the mid-1990s that I first set foot inside that front door, with a biography of John Major.

This has been a strange book to research and write. I anticipated that it would be based exclusively on secondary sources, written and pictorial, but in fact over 60% of the book has been based on primary research. I imagined that the voluminous biographies of prime ministers since Walpole would be full of details of how their subjects interacted with the building in which they lived and worked. Not a bit of it. Finding little within such books, I wrote to many biographers of prime ministers for help. The responses were always warm, but there was a common strand in the replies: 'I really know very little about which rooms my prime minister lived in and used, or indeed how they organised their day,' was a standard response. To my surprise, very few biographers had ever visited Number 10. One book alone was outstanding, by R J Minney.

This book was begun at West Buckland School in North Devon in mid-April on our annual A-Level reading party, and finished in early June at Walberswick in Suffolk. At the former I would like to thank John Vick, the Headmaster, and Terry Meadows, the Bursar, for providing such an excellent environment for serious study. At the latter I would like to thank Jean Pappworth for hospitality and the best writing retreat on the Suffolk marshes that I know. Over the six weeks of writing the book, I have been sustained by my colleagues and History classes at the wonderful Brighton College.

My thanks go first to Prime Minister Tony Blair for allowing this book to go ahead. Many figures in the Blairs' Number 10 have been very helpful, above all John Holroyd, Anji Hunter, John Holmes, Alastair Campbell, Jonathan Powell, Carol Allen and Janice Richards. Indeed, I acknowledge the dedication and professionalism of all who have worked at Number 10.

To John and Norma Major I will always owe a considerable debt. From their years in office I would above all like to thank Jonathan Hill, whose delight in the building first inspired me to write the book, Andrew Turnbull, Alex Allan, Howell James and Norman Blackwell. I acknowledge the support of the ESRC for my research into Number 10.

I have been fortunate to have had help from an outstanding group of researchers, including Daniel Collings, Peter Snowdon, Alexander Sabine, Andrew Spencer and Richard Hooper, who also compiled the bibliography.

The following individuals provided invaluable help and advice. Lewis Baston, Robert Blake, Bryan Burrough, Trevor Burridge, Neil Cairncross, David Carlton, Lord Carr of Hadley, Geoffrey Cass, Sir Robin Catford, Catherine Charlton, Michael Cockerell, John Collings, John Derry, David Dilks, John Ehrman, Richard Garnier, Norman Gash, Ken Godbeer, John Grigg, Joe Haines, Alistair Horne, Simon Hurst, Roy Jenkins, Dennis Kavanagh, Sarah King, Richard Lamb, H C G Matthew, Sir Guy Millard, Kenneth O Morgan, Jane Parsons, Ben Pimlott, Philip Reid, Malcolm Reid, Lilian Rhodes, Robert Rhodes James, Jasper Ridley, Andrew Roberts, Alan Robson, Lorne Roper-Caldbeck, Lady Soames, Quinlan Terry, John Vincent, Lady Williams of Elvel, Muriel Williams, Sir Oliver Wright, Philip Ziegler, and many others too numerous to list.

HarperCollins were an ideal publisher. I would like to thank Eddie Bell for backing the project, Fiona Screen, as able, quick and gentle an editor as I have met, Caroline Hill for her excellent designs and her willingness to accommodate my suggestions, and especially Polly Powell, a model of tact and good judgement. I enjoyed working with Mark Fiennes on his photographs.

Annemarie Weitzel and Linda Hudson and, above all, Mary Anne Brightwell, proved first-rate typists of my illegible script.

Finally, I would like to thank the following for reading particular passages: John Barnes and Hugh Berrington in particular, Christopher Collins, Jane Parsons, Sir Robin Catford, Sue Goodchild, Simon Hurst, Alan Robson, Janice Richards, Joanna Seldon and Paul Thomas. The errors that remain are entirely my own.

Number 10 is in flux: it is a living building and the interiors change. The photographs and text thus capture it only as it was at the end of this century. All profits from this book will go to educational charities of my choice.

Anthony Seldon
Brighton, June 1999

CONTENTS

THE BUILDING IN HISTORY

WALPOLE TO BALFOUR 1735-1902

A HOUSE IN THE HEADLINES

BALFOUR TO HOME 1902-64

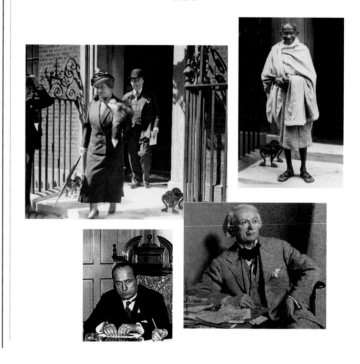

Wilson to Blair 1964-
152

Art, Artefacts & Entertaining
170

Below Stairs
204

4 Departures & an Arrival
214

The Building in History

Britain's, perhaps even the world's, most famous address lies on ground once marshy and undulating. The River Tyburn flowed down from the hills of Hampstead Heath, four miles to the north, splitting into two tributaries before it joined the River Thames. This boggy, inhospitable land was known as Thorney Island, or the Island of Thorns, and comprised a 30-acre site on the Northern Channel of which Downing Street was later to be built.

▶ The Entrance Hall, with its distinctive black and white chequered floor. In the cramped Number 10, visitors are often made to wait on these hard wooden chairs.

◀ Sir George Downing, founder of Downing Street, whose portrait can be seen in the photograph opposite.

The Romans selected this unpromising ground on which to place a settlement. The River Thames in Roman times was much shallower and wider than it is now, and could be forded close by the settlement, the ford being roughly where Westminster Bridge is now located. The Romans started a vogue. The Danish King, Canute, chose Thorney Island to build his royal palace, and in the eleventh century, Edward the Confessor (r. 1042-66) and William I (r. 1066-87), later consolidated Westminster as centre of the church and government.

In the centuries that followed, Westminster, with its great abbey, the adjacent church of St Margaret, and Westminster Hall to their east, rose or fell in importance in step with the fluctuating fortunes of the English monarchy. The earliest building known to have stood on the site of Downing Street was a brewery called the Axe, owned by the Abbey of Abingdon, but by the early 1500s it was falling into disuse.

Henry VIII (r. 1509-47) moved his centre of government a few hundred yards to the north when he confiscated York House from the disgraced Cardinal Wolsey in 1530 and renamed it Whitehall Palace; the avaricious king speedily set about making his fallen minister's residence into his own pleasure palace. Tennis courts, for 'real' or royal tennis, a tiltyard for jousting and a cockpit for cock-fighting were among the structures erected to entertain the King. Whitehall Palace was an enormous and sprawling affair, stretching from St James's Park to the Thames, and from Westminster half a mile northwards to Charing Cross. It became the monarch's official residence, serving remaining Tudor monarchs as well as Stuart kings after 1603, until the destruction by fire, in 1698, of all but Inigo Jones's Banqueting House of 1622, which still stands elegantly on the east side of the road, itself known as Whitehall. Remains of the Tudor buildings, as well as those from the Roman settlement, lie just below the surface, and very occasionally above it, today.

TWO EARLY BUILDINGS: 1670-1732

The evolution of Number 10 to the building we now see has been uneven and, at times, confusing. Parts of the story are still obscure; historians cannot be certain about some phases of the house's past. As most of the evidence has already come to light, it seems likely that parts of the history of Number 10 will remain shrouded in mystery. To try to bring sense to the house's chequered past our history will be divided into nine phases.

The first phase in the emergence of the Number 10 that we see today is historically the most uncertain. But the facts seem to be as follows. The first domestic house known to have been built on the site of Number 10 was a large dwelling leased to Sir Thomas Knyvet, a parliamentarian and Justice of the Peace. It was Knyvet who arrested Guy Fawkes for the Gunpowder Plot of 1605, when Fawkes and his accomplices tried to blow up James I and the Houses of Parliament with 36 barrels of gunpowder placed in the vaults under the buildings.

Elizabeth I (r. 1558-1603) first leased the house to Knyvet in 1581. The property was built of timber and brick, and contemporary drawings show it as having a large, L-shaped garden adjacent to Henry VIII's cockpit (later converted into a theatre for Charles I [r. 1625-49] by Inigo Jones).

On Knyvet's death in 1622, the house passed to his wife and then, on her death a few weeks later, to his niece, the formidable Mrs Hampden, whose son, John, was one of the leaders of the Parliamentary opposition to Charles I; when he and four fellow MPs eluded arrest by Charles's men in 1642, the hapless King proclaimed, 'the birds have flown'. Elizabeth Hampden lived in the building, which became known as 'Hampden House', for forty years, residing there throughout the period of the Commonwealth. Charles I's execution in 1649 took place on a scaffold in front of Banqueting House in Whitehall, within earshot of the house, and her nephew, Oliver Cromwell, then became Lord Protector (or head of state). Mrs Hampden was still living in the house when Charles II (r. 1649-85) was restored to the throne in 1660. She died in 1662.

SIR GEORGE DOWNING

The man who itched to gain control of the valuable land, in such a prime site in London, and of Hampden House in particular, was one Sir George Downing, by all accounts a disagreeable and unpleasant man. Brought up in New England, Downing had become one of the first graduates of the newly founded Harvard University, and came to England at the time of the Civil War in the 1640s. By 1650, he had become Cromwell's Scoutmaster-General (or chief of intelligence) and was subsequently Ambassador at the Hague. His fortunes flourished during the Cromwell years, and he continued worrying away at gaining title to this prize land in Westminster. In 1654, he acquired the crown interest in the land. However, the Restoration of the monarchy in 1660 created problems for someone so identified with the old regime, and it required time and patience for Downing to ingratiate himself at Charles II's court, and for the land to become fully available. The demolition of the dilapidated Cockpit Theatre helped create space for his plans, but it was not until 1682 that he finally secured the leases and, now an old man, began to build a string of 15 houses, with 40-year leases, along the north side of what became known as Downing Street. Existing properties were pulled down, and in their place came not well-built dwellings but the cul-de-sac of terraced houses put up purely for profit; they were of poor quality, erected on inadequate foundations for the water-logged ground beneath, and laid down major problems for future generations. Downing himself, who died in July 1684, gained little

▲ Sir George Downing. By all accounts a 'disagreeable and unpleasant man'.

personal benefit from his speculative enterprise, so, in one sense, justice could be said to have been done.

Drawings dating from about 1749 show the cul-de-sac of houses with Numbers 2, 3, 4 and 5 standing where 10, 11 and 12 stood after they were renumbered in 1779. The present Number 10 in fact consists of two houses, connected in two places, the larger of which is not Downing's, but the one behind. A plan by the great architect, Christopher Wren, the surveyor general, shows a drawing of a building just to the north of what was originally Number 5. This larger building was erected in about 1677, but it is unclear how much, if anything, of the earlier Hampden House it incorporated. Its frontage faced north, into Horse Guards Parade, from which it was separated by a railing. What is certain is that this building, which became the home of the Earl and Countess of Lichfield, consisted of grander rooms and was better built than Downing's subsequent buildings to its immediate south. The Countess, who was married at the age of 12 and bore an exceptional 18 children, was, not unsurprisingly, disconcerted by having her nest overlooked by the new jerry-built Downing houses. They were, moreover, built on slightly higher ground and so literally overshadowed her home. The Countess duly complained to her father, as daughters do. Her father, Charles II replied as above left.

> 'I think it is a very reasonable thing that other houses should not look into your house without your permission, and this note will be sufficient for Mr Surveyor [Christopher Wren] to build up your wall as high as you please'
>
> CHARLES II TO HIS DAUGHTER THE COUNTESS OF LICHFIELD

History does not record whether the Countess of Lichfield's domestic problems were happily resolved. But, in 1690, the Lichfields ceased to live there and Lord Overkirk, Master of the Horse to William III (r. 1689-1702), moved into what now became known as Overkirk House. In 1720, his widow died, and the house was renamed Bothmar House, after its new resident, Count Bothmar, an eccentric Hanoverian who had been *éminence grise* to George I (r. 1714-27). The street was described in a survey of London in the year Bothmar moved in (1720) as 'a pretty open place, especially at the upper end, where are four or five very large and well-built houses, fit for persons of Honour and Quality, each House having a pleasant Prospect in to St James's Park'.

TWO BUILDINGS BECOME ONE: 1732-1780

On Bothmar's death, a new phase in the history of the building began. The King, George II (r. 1727–60), offered the property to Sir Robert Walpole, who bore the title 'First Lord of the Treasury'. Walpole is generally accepted to be the country's first prime minister, and it is in their role as First Lord of the Treasury that prime ministers today occupy Number 10. Walpole turned the house down as a personal gift, but accepted it in his capacity as First Lord on condition that it remained in the possession of subsequent First Lords. The brass letter box on the black front

▶ Downing Street and Westminster as seen from the air today. St James's Park is to the west and Horse Guards Parade to the north. Number 10 can be clearly seen at the heart of government, with Number 11 to the immediate west, the Foreign Office to the south and the Cabinet Office to the east.

door is still inscribed with the title 'First Lord of the Treasury'. Walpole never himself used the title 'Prime Minister', and his emergence as the pre-eminent figure in British politics was due less to any official post than to his mastery of the House of Commons, from which he extracted a favourable financial settlement. Like his father before him, George II was first and foremost a German prince, and he, too, came to rely heavily on his experienced First Lord.

It was the distinguished Palladian architect William Kent who ushered in the second and important phase of the house's development. Walpole, a man of some wealth, had already engaged Kent to enhance the interiors of his Norfolk home, Houghton Hall. Now he called on Kent to make the London house fitting for the First Lord. Kent was a man in demand: at the same time as he was working on the First Lord's house he was busy on a much more ambitious London project – the new Treasury building at the east end of Downing Street, on the site of the old Cockpit Theatre. This extensive and imposing building runs along Whitehall and is now occupied by the Cabinet Office. Downing Street was at this time still a pleasant cul-de-sac, offering lodgings to MPs, though there were also signs of it falling victim to some of the seedier sides of the area including drinking houses and brothels. Little changes at Westminster.

RENOVATIONS FOR WALPOLE

Kent's work took a full three years to complete, from 1732 to 1735; work at Number 10 was apt to take longer to complete than expected. The buildings were linked on two stories, forming a courtyard facing west. Kent seems to have made no important alteration to the interior of the Downing Street building, which became little more than a passageway from the rear of the house, where the Walpoles lived and where the First Lord worked, to the street outside.

History does not record how Kent viewed his assignment for Walpole, but he set about the work with gusto. He joined both houses together at the eastern end, making one grander house with the front facing southwards into Downing Street, convenient for the First Lord's journeys to Parliament.

Comparison of Kent's plans of c.1735 with Wren's of 1677 reveal that the staircases in Bothmar House were replaced by a grand, three-sided staircase. Central rooms were also created to the north of the stairs, with larger rooms on either side on both stories. As the ground slopes away from south to north, the ground floor of the Downing Street building becomes the first floor of the grander Bothmar House building behind. In time, the large rooms at the rear of the Bothmar building became the Cabinet Room and the Private Secretaries' Room, while above them, the rooms that had been used for living quarters by successive premiers became the three inter-linked State Drawing Rooms of today.

The oldest surviving drawings of the interior are to be found in New York's Metropolitan Museum, which holds the scrapbooks of Walpole's son, Horace, a celebrated man of letters. These drawings show the ground and first-floor

Then and Now *The Garden*

The earliest garden dated back to Knyvet's house in the late sixteenth century. In its present form, the garden came into existence in 1677, when the house at the rear of Downing's terrace was probably erected. The garden was added to in 1736, at the completion of Kent's major reconstruction. Today, the garden measures half an acre. It still wraps around Numbers 10, 11 and 12, but belongs wholly to Number 10. The garden wall may also have been erected in the 1730s.

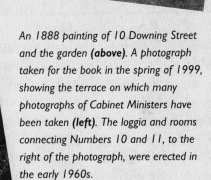

An 1888 painting of 10 Downing Street and the garden (above). A photograph taken for the book in the spring of 1999, showing the terrace on which many photographs of Cabinet Ministers have been taken (left). The loggia and rooms connecting Numbers 10 and 11, to the right of the photograph, were erected in the early 1960s.

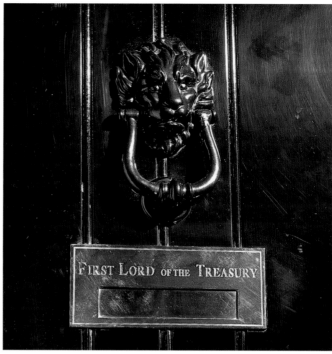

▲ The seven-petal window above the front door and the famous lamp with its elaborate metal support, the crowning features of countless doorstep shots. The lamp, knocker and letter box are thought to date from the 1770s.

▲ The lion door knocker and letter box. It was as 'First Lord of the Treasury' that Walpole occupied Number 10 in 1735, and it is in this capacity that Prime Ministers still inhabit the house.

elevations, including the fireplaces and door surrounds, still recognisable today. These decorative details are thought to be the principal surviving examples of Kent's work, although some ascribe the fireplaces to Kent's colleague, Henry Flitcroft, then clerk of works in Whitehall. On the north-facing roof line, to help enhance the building's importance, Kent erected a shallow, triangular pediment, a typical Palladian motif. The cost of the Kent conversion is unknown, but the sum may have been subsumed within the final cost of the Treasury building – £20,000, as against the estimate of £8,000 – revealing another trait of Downing Street building: actual cost usually exceeding estimates.

Walpole resigned in 1742, and by the mid-1760s, after the house had been rented out mostly to lesser beings, serious rebuilding and redecoration were considered necessary. Colourful inhabitants of Downing Street came and went. James Boswell had lodgings in the street in 1762, and in 1774 the writer Tobias Smollet tried to establish a surgeon's practice there. They would have seen the largely rebuilt Downing Street frontage. As Simon Hurst, the most authoritative source on the history of the building, records: 'The neat Downing Street facades belie the shoddiness of the brickwork behind. Once built, lines of lime putty were applied to give the impression of symmetrical quality brickwork and, in places, false joints have been cut across whole bricks to complete the artifice!'

By the mid-1770s, the building had been refronted, and it is thought likely that the front doorways also date from this period (Number 10 has two separate doorways: the one in use, and 10A, between Numbers 10 and 11, which is a now a false door). The hallmark features of the lion's head knocker, the letter box, and the electric light (originally oil, then gas) above the door, mounted on the wrought-iron overhang surround, would also appear to date from the 1770s. Inside, the black and white chequer-patterned marble floor of the Entrance Hall can be traced to this period. By the conclusion of this second phase in the house's development, a unified house had emerged and the present footprint of the house had more or less been defined.

PHASE THREE: KITCHENS, CORRIDORS AND PILLARS

In the early 1780s, William Pitt (the 'Younger'), the longest serving inhabitant of the building (1783-1801, 1804-6), moved in, and further building work was

◀ Downing Street, Westminster, in 1827, before the government offices were built on the south side of the street. From a water-colour by C Buckler.

▼ An illustration of how Downing Street looked in the 1880s, following the pulling down in the 1860s of the old buildings on the south side. The buildings at the top (west) end were destroyed by fire in 1879.

deemed necessary to what he described as his 'vast, awkward house'. This work, the third phase of the rebuilding, was carried out between 1781 and 1783, probably under the direction of another distinguished architect of his day, Sir Robert Taylor. The foundations, which had never been strong, were strengthened, a great vaulted kitchen was installed on the eastern side of the building facing Treasury Green, and the narrow connecting corridor on the house's central axis, that is still in use today, was either built or strengthened, creating an inner, closed-in courtyard. Kent's pediment on the north side of the building was also removed at this time, and a tall parapet was added. Pitt complained in 1783 that the repairs had cost the country £11,000.

The final development of the third phase in Number 10's history was the creation of the present Cabinet Room in 1796. This was achieved by knocking down the end wall and extending the room to the east, using two double Corinthian columns to support the structure above. This took space away from what was designated the Waiting Room but provided 3.6m/12ft of extra space in the Cabinet Room, and a much more usable public room. It is probable also that the mid-1790s saw a similar extension of the first-floor room upstairs at the north-east corner of the building, again made possible by the use of supports – this time, two single Ionic columns; it is today the Pillared Drawing Room.

SIR JOHN SOANE SPLENDOUR: 1820S

Pitt's 20-year tenure, which ended in 1806, with a short break of 3 years when Addington became Prime Minister from 1801-4, left its mark, if an untidy one, on Number 10. A bachelor, with a liking for port, Pitt had little interest in cleanliness. When its new occupants, Lord and Lady Grenville, pronounced Number 10 uninhabitable, Charles Craig, who had been foreman in charge of the repairs 20 years before, was detailed to restore the house to pristine condition. Number 10 was smartened up but, like so much work then, it was largely cosmetic.

▼ Sir John Soane's 1825 designs for the State Dining Room. The design first from left on the second row was chosen.

Then and Now *The State Dining Room*

Soane's great work was the State Dining Room. From several possible designs (opposite), he chose a star vault pattern for the double height room, and again knocked two rooms together, to create a grand room with small indentations in both west corners. A third, central window was added, while the external walling had to be adapted to take the re-routed flues that used to run up from the kitchens below, through the dismantled central wall of the room. The State Dining Room had similar stained oak panelling to his smaller Breakfast Room, which is adjacent, and is today the most architecturally satisfying (and unified) room in Number 10.

The State Dining Room in a painting by Charles Flower, early 1900s (above). The State Dining Room today (left).

The principal nineteenth-century alterations to Number 10 took place in the 1820s, on the crest of a great wave of public prosperity and building, a wave that saw the building of the British Museum, the foundation of the National Gallery and extensions to Windsor Castle. The incumbent of Number 10 from 1823 to 1828, the Chancellor of the Exchequer, Frederick John Robinson (who later, as Viscount Goderich, became Prime Minister) had a taste for the arts and wanted to see Number 10 bask in the national prosperity. He called in John Soane, the most celebrated architect of his day, to spruce up the house. Soane duly created the State Dining Room and the smaller Dining or Breakfast Room above Taylor's vaulted kitchen, in a space which was previously used for bedrooms. This work constitutes the fourth phase in the emergence of the modern house.

The smaller Dining Room, or Breakfast Room, was created, as the surviving plans reveal, by removing an internal wall, and knocking a double door through the south wall into what became the State Dining Room. This door displaced the fireplace and flue from the kitchen below, which meant that this essential device had to be relocated. Soane repositioned it under the east-facing, central window, cunningly running the flue up either side of the window aperture. The walls were given dark stained oak panelling and the ceiling a simple, flat cornice.

A CENTURY OF TINKERING: 1830-1930

Little changed in Number 10 over the next century – the fifth phase in the emergence of the modern house. In 1829, His Majesty's Office of Works reported (a comment that echoed down unchanged throughout the years): 'This is a large, old building which has been altered, and added to, at many different periods, and though in a substantial condition requires very frequent repairs.'

▼ The Entrance Hall in 1927. Note the extraordinary antlers which adorn the walls.

The nineteenth century was, however, a time of great change in Britain: the industrial and transport revolutions altered forever the face and prosperity of the nation, while imperial expansion and the growth of government intervention created new demands on the seat of government. Plans were also afoot for dramatic changes to Whitehall: one such plan, of 1839, envisaged the demolition of all existing buildings on the north side of Downing Street, including Number 10. The area had been becoming steadily more seedy since the eighteenth century, and by

▲ An 1885 photograph
of Number 10. The
terrace resembles a run-
down row of tenement
flats, and the single-
storey building, where
Number 12 stands today,
looks rather like a
workman's hut.

1846, the year Robert Peel ceased to be Prime Minister and his Tory party tore itself apart over the repeal of the Corn Laws, debauchery had reached a high point. In that year, parish records reveal that there were an estimated 170 brothels and 145 gin parlours in the area, which was renowned for its squalor and desperate poverty. Despite this sleaze and hardship, Downing Street itself had been expanding as the centre of government. The Foreign Office was thriving across the road, based in Number 16; the Colonial Office had moved into Number 14 in 1798; the West Indies Department was in Number 18; the Tithe Commissioners were in Number 20; and in 1846-7 the distinguished architect, Sir Charles Barry, was employed to refront and heighten Soane's Treasury building to the east of Number 10. To the immediate west of Number 10, Number 11 had been bought by the Crown in 1805 for use as the Home Secretary's Office, but in 1828 it became the official home of the Chancellor of the Exchequer (the Second Lord of the Treasury). Nearly £4,000 of government money was spent in 1847 to make it more habitable both for the Chancellor's official duties and for

Then and Now *The Cabinet Room*

Number 10's most celebrated and historically most important room is the Cabinet Room. Its size is surprising, barely 12m/40ft long and 5.7m/19ft wide. The dominant feature, visible in photograph upon photograph, is the white marble fireplace, located immediately behind the Prime Minister's chair. The room was created in its present form in 1796, when the pillars (visible in the photographs below and below right) were erected at the east end of the room.

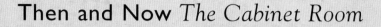

The Cabinet Room in 1927, which Prime Minister Baldwin used as a study **(above)**. *A 1907 painting by Charles Flower* **(left)**. *The Cabinet Room today, with the famous boat-shaped table* **(below)**.

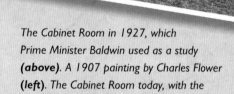

his private use. Number 12, meanwhile, was bought by the Crown in 1803 for the Judge Advocate General's official residence; it later became the office of the Government Whips.

In the late 1860s, the buildings on the south side of Downing Street were pulled down to make way for George Gilbert Scott's imposing and monumental government offices. His Victorian pile utterly overshadowed Number 10. It boasted a fine archway and inner court, sumptuous conference rooms, ornate corridors and state rooms, grand staircases and painted ceilings, and its own cabinet room and foreign secretary's room. Number 10 in comparison seems like a gatehouse to a grand mansion. The arrival of the Scott building summoned some florid defences of Number 10, such as that of writer Charles Eyre Pascoe.

> 'The First Lord's residence is overshadowed by the statelier glories of the Foreign Office opposite . . . but not one of its grand rooms has a tithe of interest that belongs to the smallest chamber in that little house fronting it.'
>
> CHARLES EYRE PASCOE

The impression of a forlorn north side of Downing Street was heightened when a fire in 1879 destroyed Number 12: the c.1885 photograph of Numbers 10 and 11 (see page 21) makes the houses look like unprepossessing Victorian tenement dwellings in a run-down area of London. Little is known about the fire at Number 12, but the charred walls were pulled down to first-floor level and a new roof constructed, making a single-storey building, with a door which faced back down Downing Street, clearly visible in photographs and sketches.

Yet Number 10 survived both redevelopment plans and its overshadowing by the Foreign Office. This fifth phase of Number 10's evolution saw a smattering of minor modifications, most precipitated by the requirement to keep pace with technology and the need for frequent repairs. Benjamin Disraeli moved into the house in 1877, and promptly put in requests for £2,350 to 'improve' his drawing room and bedroom and to provide a bath 'with hot and cold water' (cost £150). The Treasury tried to cut back such extravagant proposals, but they did consent to £1,550. 5s. 0d. for furniture for Numbers 10 and 11 in 1880. Electric lighting, at a cost of £425, was introduced in 1894, replacing the gas and candlelight that had hitherto been the source of illumination. The first telephones were introduced around this time; the exact date is elusive. Around the 1880s, the first-floor room in the north-west corner (then the principal bedroom) had the window sills lowered (these were replaced in the late 1930s by sills of ordinary height). In 1906, a lift for access to the first floor was installed for the new Prime Minister's wife, Lady Campbell-Bannerman, who was an invalid and could not climb stairs. It was placed not in its present location but off the corridor in the inner courtyard well. In 1906, Campbell-Bannerman requested two baths to be installed at public expense. On the eve of the First World War, a light-weight extension was erected on the north-east corner of the building to create extra bedrooms at the request of the new Prime Minister Asquith's wife, Margot (later Lady Oxford and Asquith), who occupied the house from 1908 to 1916. In 1917, to facilitate catering, a service lift was built.

A PRIVATE FLAT FOR THE PRIME MINISTER

The sixth phase saw more substantial building work. In 1936, an undistinguished single-storey ground-floor annexe was added to the building at the eastern end of Number 10, parallel with Downing Street (an addition that was mercifully to be knocked down in the early 1960s). In 1937 came central heating, replacing coal fires throughout the building. 'Dreadful stuff, central heating,' said a departing Mrs Baldwin. 'You'll all have colds in the head. Mark my words!' Further rebuilding was also begun at the top of the north end of the building, to accommodate a private flat for the Prime Minister in a warren of attic-space rooms hitherto occupied by servants. The First Commissioner of Works, Sir Philip Sassoon, directed these modifications while Neville Chamberlain (1937-40) was away on summer holiday. A substantial piece of work, it included building a new formal staircase from the second floor to the attic, hitherto served only by a functional stairway. The Sassoon staircase ate significantly into the Ante Room outside what later became the State Drawing Rooms. Sassoon also reinstated the pediment on the north elevation of the Kent block, and added Dormer windows and a replacement roof to make space for a quite extensive new flat. Soane's Dining Room oak panels were painted over at the same time, to mixed reception. The Chamberlains had major plans for Number 10, in what they hoped would be a long stay. In 1938, they were supplied by the government with new wine glasses, and the following year records in the Public Record Office reveal they received a fresh supply of furniture. The last of a distinguished political family, Neville was in fact to be out of the prime ministerial home within a year of his furniture arriving.

With war in Europe looming ever closer, air-raid shelters were created by erecting extensive steel girders under the Cabinet Room, in the two ground-floor Garden Rooms occupied by the Number 10 secretaries. Heavy sliding metal shutters were attached to the outside of the building for protection during bombing raids, the possibility dreaded by all London.

▼ Downing Street in the 1930s, still with a rather unprepossessing feel.

Then and Now *The Pillared Room*

The Pillared Room is the largest of the three inter-linked State Drawing Rooms. The room takes its name from the pillars, visible in all three pictures, and is thought to have been installed in 1796 as a means of extending the space. It is in this room that guests congregate during Number 10 receptions. The room as depicted by Charles Flower (below right) shows the new, lighter furniture chosen by the Campbell-Bannermans, following the Liberal election victory of 1906.

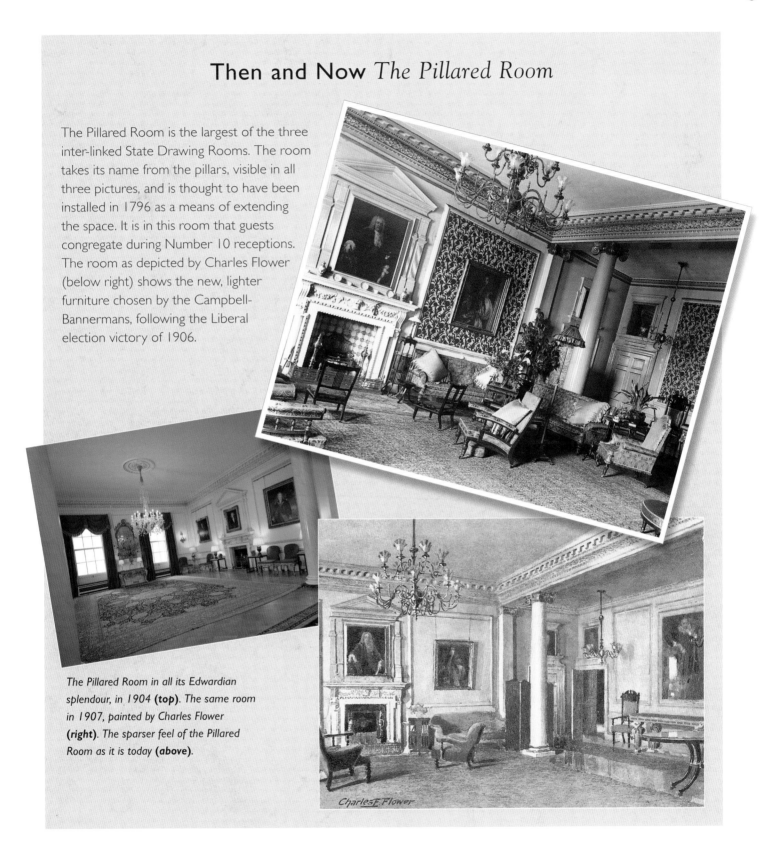

The Pillared Room in all its Edwardian splendour, in 1904 (top). The same room in 1907, painted by Charles Flower (right). The sparser feel of the Pillared Room as it is today (above).

Then and Now *The Green Drawing Room*

The Green Drawing Room is the middle room of the three first-floor drawing rooms. It is in this room that guests are traditionally received by the Prime Minister. Through the open doors in the photograph below left. Through the central doors in the photograph below right is the White Drawing Room.

*The Green Drawing Room photographed in 1927, in all its Edwardian splendour, during Baldwin's second government **(top)**.*
*The Green Drawing Room in 1902-5 **(above)**.*
*As it looks today **(right)**.*

NUMBER 10 UNDER SIEGE: 1940-60

In the seventh phase of Number 10's history, its very existence came under threat first from Hitler's bombs and then from the grandiose schemes of planners.

By the late 1930s, serious consideration was being given to moving the nerve centre of British government in the event of war. RAF planners told Neville Chamberlain that 600 tons of bombs could fall on London, causing 200,000 casualties, in the first week alone of a war with Germany. The race was on to find a site for the Central War Rooms, to act as a hub for the military and political leaders directing the war; they needed to be close to the centre so that the government could not be accused of abandoning London, but safe from falling bombs. A location was eventually found in the basement chambers of the Office of Works building (now the Treasury) facing St James's Park, conveniently close to Downing Street and Parliament. The site was duly agreed in June 1938, the strengthening of the rooms, just 3m/10ft underground, with steel girders, was ready by August 1939, and the first Cabinet meeting was held in the rooms, with Chamberlain in the chair, on October 21st of that year. In 1940, an underground walkway linking Number 10 to the Admiralty was completed.

During the blitz on London by the Luftwaffe in 1940, damage was caused on September 13th when a (British) anti-aircraft shell exploded on Horse Guards Parade, damaging windows and roof tiles. On September 18th Number 10 was again under attack from 'friendly fire' when a trailing cable from a barrage balloon went out of control and damaged a chimney stack and roof tiles. More seriously, on September 21st, 36 panes of glass and three sashes were broken in Number 10 by a nearby bomb. Then, on October 14th, a high-explosive bomb fell just to the east of Number 10 on Treasury Green, the green area between Number 10 and the Kent Treasury block, just missing both buildings. But, as the photographs on pages 28 and 82 reveal, the internal damage was extensive.

Churchill, Prime Minister since May, had been concerned even before the bombs fell that he and his personal staff should move out of the vulnerable Number 10, and, in the last two weeks of September 1940, a long suite of rooms was adapted to become the Number 10 Annexe, on the ground floor of the Office of Works building,

▼ The Downing Street roof in need of repair, following bomb damage.

▲ The Middle (now Green) Drawing Room as it was after the Blitz damage in late 1940. Plaster had fallen over the ground, and extensive damage done to the east end of the building. Through the open door can be seen the Pillared Room with piano and disturbed painting.

immediately above the Central War Rooms. The Number 10 Annexe was hastily adapted to provide office space and also living quarters for the Prime Minister and Mrs Churchill. Number 10 itself was stripped of its valuable furniture, paintings and carpets, and only the reinforced basement Garden Rooms and a few of the offices above ground remained in use.

With peace in 1945 came a Labour government, and the new Prime Minister, Clement Attlee (1945-51), moved back into Downing Street with his staff. Mrs Attlee wanted the conversion work in the attic flat completed so that the family could move in; it proved an extensive operation, creating a sitting and dining room, a study, and up to six bedrooms. At the same time, Attlee ordered the basement vaulted kitchens to be closed, and the first-floor reception rooms to be used only on 'important' occasions; this meant a cutback of staff running Number 10 from six to two. The office rooms were redecorated in 1949, and the Cabinet and State Rooms in

▶ Sketch of the interiors of the north end of the building in 1949. On the left (east) side can be seen the kitchens, with dining rooms above. Along the north wall are the offices and Cabinet Room on the ground floor, and the three drawing rooms on the first floor.

▶ The inner courtyard of Number 10, showing the lift shaft at the top right-hand corner, the interconnecting corridors and overflow office space. The image, which resembles a hospital building, can be compared to the photograph of the cleaned-up courtyard on page 46, after the early 1960s reconstruction.

1950. But with repairs being carried out for most of his premiership, Mr Attlee's Number 10 was a spartan place, little used for entertaining.

When the Churchills returned in October 1951, they had no time for such parsimony, and ordered the State Rooms and kitchens to be renovated in time for Queen Elizabeth II's coronation in June 1953. In the 1950s, under three flamboyant Conservative Prime Ministers – Churchill (1951–55), Anthony Eden (1955-57) and Harold Macmillan (1957-63) – Number 10 again became a centre of entertainment and social activity.

THE ERITH RENOVATION: 1960-63

The eighth phase in Number 10's history saw the most radical changes to the building since Kent's alterations in the eighteenth century.

Bomb damage had caused structural weaknesses in Number 10, and for years it had been known that major surgery rather than incremental changes would be needed if it was to survive. An annual repair bill of up to £8,000 was already required and, because of subsidence, a carpenter was based permanently on site to ease windows and doors as the building groaned and slumped on its sinking foundations. Many of the internal walls were out of line, while the blackened wall on the Downing Street frontage bulged outwards by several inches. Everyone knew something had to be done. But what?

In 1954, R L Rothwell, architect to the Ministry of Works, was called in to conduct a survey. Inevitably superficial, as the building was busily in use throughout, his report landed on the Prime Minister's desk in March 1955. The following month, Churchill was succeeded by Anthony Eden and, 21 months later, by Harold Macmillan, to whom fell the task of deciding Number 10's future. In July 1957, Macmillan set up a committee to 'consider the report of the Ministry of Works on the present condition of Numbers 10, 11 and 12 Downing Street and the proposals for reconstruction'.

The Crawford Committee, as it was known, concluded that the buildings needed drastic and urgent attention: walls were in danger of collapse; fire, due to timber construction, was a serious hazard, and the building's historic features were in danger. Four options were put forward for consideration:

a Demolition, and replacement by modern buildings
b Demolition, but retaining the external design and transferring or
   copying internal historical features (such as the Soane Dining Room)
c Minimum repairs, limited only to making the building
   structurally sound
d A course between options b and c, including strengthening but also
   internal replanning while retaining historic features

▼ Raymond Erith, the architect of the major reconstruction of 1960–63, standing in the street outside the front door.

Option a was dismissed because of the historic associations of the building; option b was rejected because it would create a replica with 'little historical or sentimental significance'; option c was similarly discarded on the grounds that it would create 'a museum piece'; so the decision fell on option d, which would include the wholesale rebuilding of Number 12 from the ground up, including the demolition of the late nineteenth-century single-storey stump.

The Ministry of Works was appointed supervisory agent for the work, and the hunt began for a suitable architect. An early suggestion, Sir Albert Richardson, was rejected by Macmillan on the grounds that, in his late seventies, the distinguished architect was 'too old' as well as perhaps too rigid. In May 1958, the selection fell on Raymond Erith, a devout classicist out of favour with the burgeoning number of modernists, but with the experience and sensitivity to work with the grain of the existing buildings. Operating from a small office in the Constable-country village of Dedham, in Essex, Erith was charged with the whole operation, including the rebuilding of Number 12; altogether, it was one of the most significant government contracts awarded to an architect in the twentieth century.

Erith set about his privileged assignment with relish. By September 1958, he had reached his conclusions. He wrote: 'Although Number 10 is old, it is surprisingly well suited to its present purpose. The arrangement of the rooms, which has evolved naturally over the years, is essentially right . . . My aim is, therefore, to repair the building by working within its established framework.'

Number 11, however, he found less satisfactory ('a makeshift affair'), and therefore planned only to retain the best of the State Rooms, including the State Dining Room, and strip the rest of the house. Number 12 he planned to rebuild to its original height, continuing the roofs of Numbers 10 and 11 without a break over Number 12. He further stated, with characteristic modesty, that: 'I do not intend to leave my mark on these additions in Downing Street, nor on Number 12. I attach no importance at all to originality and modernity.'

He possessed, however, a lively and even mischievous sense of humour. He inserted a window into the kitchen yard, and invented a story that it was 'Pitt's window' through which the hedonistic Premier used to peer longingly to see where his next meal was coming from. When Erith introduced pillars under the central corridor (see page 46) connecting the Downing building to the house behind, he designed them to look as if there was more of the pillar buried underground, and would tell people that Number 10 was built on the site of a Roman temple.

▼ A view of the main corridor leading towards the front door, with the black and white square flooring in the Entrance Hall protected by boards.

▼ The hallway as it is today.

The work was scheduled to take a maximum of two years, at a cost of £500,000. Macmillan and his staff moved out in July 1960, and settled into Admiralty House, between Trafalgar Square and the Mall, a quarter of a mile away from Number 10 beyond the opposite corner of Horse Guards Parade. Macmillan and his Number 10 staff rapidly adapted to their new surroundings, as Churchill had done 20 years earlier to his own temporary Number 10. Macmillan in fact preferred Admiralty House: it was grander and the private space was less cramped.

But the work at Downing Street soon began to go awry. Underlying currents of water had affected the original wooden foundations, which had deteriorated badly, and many of the walls had to be underpinned to a depth of up to 3m/10ft with solid concrete. The internal and external walls and floors were also found to be of poor quality and inadequate to the task. Further delays were caused by archaeological excavation, with significant Roman, Saxon and medieval remains found, dating back to the Thorney Island days. Another worry was labour unrest. Trade unions were nearly at the height of their power and, as early as January 1961, disputes erupted over the important issue of tea breaks. Numerous strikes, often over similar matters, punctuated progress. Completion was delayed by over a year, to late September 1963, and the final cost, of £1,000,000, was double the initial estimate. It should not be overlooked, however, that it was a formidable undertaking: the three houses contain a total of over 200 rooms, spread over five floors.

THE REFASHIONED DOWNING STREET

Erith's work at Number 10 did indeed appear, as he had promised, largely devoid of the architect's individual personality. The unsuspecting visitor would have seen little outward change, apart from the rebuilt Number 12, from the three years of work. Yet the fabric was almost all gutted, many of the wooden floors were replaced by concrete, and the walls were stripped to bare brick before being completely rebuilt. Some walls and floors were found to be entirely rotten. In the Soane Dining Rooms, Erith removed the panels, stripped off the ill-considered white paint, and restored the wood to its natural oak colour before replacing them.

Among the visible changes, the most important were the extension of the building on each floor by two windows to the east, facing Whitehall, including the addition of the bay-windowed room now occupied by the Press Secretary, and the removal of the 1930s ground-floor annexe to make way for it. The floor in the Garden Room basement was lowered, the ceiling raised, and windows altered, creating a better working environment for the secretaries. The internal courtyard was remodelled, with the crumbling lift shaft and temporary walkways removed and more space created within the building for circulation. New wooden floors, of rather uncertain modern patterned-wood tile design, were introduced to cover the concrete floors in the State Drawing Rooms, but the original black and white

◄ A rooftop view of Downing Street during the 1960–63 rebuilding, looking eastwards. In the background is the Ministry of Defence and, beyond it, the River Thames. The photograph reveals how substantial the renovation was.

chequered floor tiles in the Entrance Hall and the wooden floorboards with a distinctive grain in the Cabinet Room were preserved. The elaborate cornices in the principal rooms were stripped of up to 40 coats of paint, revealing details hidden, in some cases, for two hundred years. Beams above the columns in both the Cabinet and Pillared Rooms were sagging and rotten in part, and so had to be replaced. A lift was built off the Inner Hall and an extra staircase removed, increasing space by a third in the first-floor Ante Room beside the State Drawing

33

Rooms. The outside brickwork was stained black to give it the familiar sooty 'London' look that the external walls had acquired over the years. The front door was painted black rather than the dark green described by Asquith's daughter, Violet Bonham Carter, in *Country Life* magazine in March 1941. Erith's work also allowed Number 10 a major piece of empire-building; it took over most of the basement space under the three houses, part of Number 11, and all of the third floor, except for several rooms over Number 12 allotted to the Chancellor for private use. The extra space was needed for the Prime Minister because, even under Macmillan in the early 1960s, the Number 10 staff numbered 70 in total.

Number 11, in contrast to much of Number 10, was gutted of all its internal floors and walls. A new sweeping staircase behind the false 10A street door was created in Soane style, and Soane's Small Dining Room in Number 11 was taken apart, then put back and extended by about 2.4m/8ft to be more in sympathy with its creator's original plans. A verandah was added, clearly visible on the west wall where Number 11 joins Number 10, providing more space for the Chancellor of the Exchequer's State Dining Room. Number 12, meanwhile, was built afresh from the basement up, with a spectacular staircase at the centre of the building. Much new office space was provided for the Whips, while living space for the Chancellor of the Exchequer was created on the upper floors. For the brickwork, Erith chose a red colour, which provides a contrast with the stolid blackened bricks of Numbers 10 and 11.

Erith removed the pediment Sassoon had put on the north-facing elevations of Number 10, considering it historically unsatisfactory. On the west-facing wall, the distinctive first-floor loggia between Numbers 10 and 11 accommodated extensions to Number 11 and the reconstruction of the Dining Room in the Chancellor's house. Where possible, he reused Soane's work, including two of his doors. Some elements, such as the Number 11 fireplace, Erith redesigned in the style of Soane. Although external walls were straightened as far as was possible, those in Number 11 were left bulging by as much as seven inches out of vertical.

Overall, Erith's designs were a triumph: every bit as much as Kent, Soane, Taylor and Sassoon, he deserves to be celebrated as a key artist in creating the largely successful Downing Street complex in Georgian style. His achievement was all the greater because he met government parsimony head on. As one of his young office staff remembers: 'The principal point Macmillan impressed on Mr Erith was that the rebuilding should not look expensive.' Time and again, Erith found his designers and work under attack from Ministry of Works officials: his stone staircases were criticised for not being in the original plans, while, more trivially, his wooden toilet seats were

> *'I am heart broken by the result . . . the whole project has been a frightful waste of money because it just has not been done properly. The Ministry of Works has insisted on economy after economy. I am bitterly disappointed with what has happened . . . there will be woven rayon coverings to the walls of the state rooms instead of the damask and gold leaf I felt ought to grace the historic official residence of the Prime Minister of England.'*
>
> RAYMOND ERITH

dismissed as being an unmitigated extravagance. Most significantly, his plans to create a pleasant internal courtyard with a water feature in Number 10, were cut away from under him. At the conclusion of the project, Erith was left deeply disillusioned, as seen in his statement opposite.

MODIFICATIONS AND ELABORATIONS: 1960-2000

Macmillan had been back from Admiralty House only days before he resigned for reasons of ill-health, and within a year a Labour government was back in Number 10. The new incumbent, Harold Wilson, had barely begun to enjoy his new house before serious dry rot became evident. Blamed generally on inadequate waterproofing during the three-year refurbishment, it seems more likely that a pierced water pipe was responsible, which had flooded the new concrete floor above the Pillared Drawing Room. Further dry rot soon came to light in those parts of Number 10 which Erith had left largely untouched; cornices had to be replaced, the damask wall linings remounted on plaster board, and the brick wall between the Pillared and Middle Drawing Rooms, along with the landing wall leading on to the main stairwell, had to be rebuilt. As the work had to be fitted around the bustling activities of Number 10, it was not until 1969 that the State Drawing Rooms were finally completed. Those who worked there recall the ubiquitous presence of dust in the atmosphere and dust sheets covering the furniture.

▲ Margaret Thatcher taking a keen interest in Quinlan Terry's work on the White Drawing Room in the summer of 1989.

When Ted Heath became Prime Minister in June 1970, he determined to recapture the house's former glory. Further renovation in 1970-71 due to more dry rot gave him the chance to demand some fresh work. The Drawing Room walls were given a covering of figured silk, and new furniture, paintings and carpets were introduced to enhance the house's appearance. In the late 1970s, prior to the completion of the Thames Barrier, there were great fears about the River Thames flooding, and alternative accommodation was prepared in Chancery Lane in the event of an evacuation being necessary.

Heath's successor, Margaret Thatcher, thought the Drawing Rooms needed something more in keeping with Britain's renewed status as a world power, and initiated a more fundamental attempt to recapture some of Britain's past glory. Thus was ushered in the ninth and final phase in the house's evolution.

Mrs Thatcher looked for a suitable architect, and found Quinlan Terry, recommended by her friend Olga Palozzi, and a classicist even more out of favour with modernists than had been his mentor, Raymond Erith. Terry worked in the same small architectural firm in the Essex village of Dedham and was pleased to accept the prestigious assignment. He examined the three State Drawing Rooms closely, and concluded that while they probably retained some of William Kent's original fireplaces, door surrounds and cornices, the three inter-connecting rooms had lost their distinctive features through the haphazard interventions of successive incumbents and indeed bomb damage. As Terry said: 'Mrs Thatcher liked ornament and she liked Kent. I felt it would be a good idea to do a Kentian-style restoration. I was not, in truth, very interested in historical precedent. I was interested in doing something that was architecturally fairly lively – especially because so much of Downing Street was rightfully restrained. She thought the rooms were boring. The best of the three was the Pillared Room, and she wanted the rooms to be more imposing. She wanted pictures of achievers, like Nelson, Wellington, and she felt that, after the Falklands War, the time had come to do something mildly triumphalist and confident.'

THE TERRY TOUCH

Terry began work on the Pillared Room in 1988, and the following summer worked on the other two drawing rooms. He picked up the motif of the two Ionic columns in the Pillared Room, creating an Ionic overmantle above the fireplace, and introduced Ionic motifs on door surrounds and panelling. But he left the ceiling unadorned. By 1989, however, he had become bolder. In the middle room he changed the colour from blue to green, thus creating the Green Drawing Room. Here, Terry emphasised the Doric order and designed a very large Palladian overmantle to the fireplace: its double columns with the royal arms above were deemed suitable for this more formal room in which guests were received. In the White Drawing Room, he used the Corinthian order, complete with swan-neck pediment. The Green and White Drawing Rooms boast highly enriched ceilings, in ornate Baroque style; in the White Room, he placed in the four corners of the ceiling the four national flowers of Britain: rose (England), shamrock (Ireland), thistle (Scotland) and daffodil (Wales). In the Green Room, he used a rich four-lobed pattern of solemn and formal style.

Terry's work was poorly received by the architectural establishment. Part of this was no doubt motivated by the fact that Mrs Thatcher was considered to be a scourge of the arts and a woman of little artistic sensitivity. But Terry was also criticised because it was considered that, unlike Erith, he had not made his work and personality invisible. He was thought by critics to have departed from the historical traditions of the building and introduced fussy elaborations inappropriate for a town house of the comparatively small size of Number 10. His failure to consult the arbiters of taste and decorum, English Heritage, no doubt

◀ One of Terry's ornate ceiling mouldings in the White Drawing Room. Terry was intrigued by Mrs Thatcher and by her deep love of Baroque: 'Behind the exterior beats a sensitive and romantic heart,' he said.

a tactical error, engendered further mistrust. Yet one should remember that the rooms are intended for use by the top political figure in Britain, and they give Number 10 a grandeur which at least matches that experienced by overseas visitors to the Foreign Office, Lancaster House and Buckingham Palace.

As has so often happened after a major change at Number 10, the incumbent Prime Minister departed shortly after the work was completed. Mrs Thatcher made way, in November 1990, for John Major. Again, the house was temporarily partly closed for restoration, while essential strengthening work was carried out following the IRA mortar bomb attack in February 1991; in the autumn of 1992, Major and some of his staff decamped, as Macmillan had done 30 years before, to Admiralty House. The summers of 1993 to 1995 saw further work on windows, and the installation of computer cabling, as Downing Street embraced the IT age. In 1995, the ceiling of the Cabinet Room was replastered amidst concern that it might detach itself from the concrete floor above, and fall down on the Cabinet's heads. While the Prime Minister remained in situ in his flat, many of the Number 10 staff decamped, with understandable reluctance, to portacabins in Horse Guards Parade.

Tony Blair's arrival in May 1997 led to further work, as extra space had to be found for the greatly increased staff in Number 10. The Prime Minister and his family swapped flats with the Chancellor, Gordon Brown, who gave up his accommodation over Numbers 11 and 12 for the more confined Number 10 flat.

A GUIDED TOUR TODAY

The geography of the house as it is today will, to a large extent, have become apparent from the nine phases in its history, outlined above.

Behind the heavy black door, now made of metal, with 'First Lord of the Treasury' inscribed on the letter box, is the formal Entrance Hall. The Prime Minister does not carry keys: a security guard always opens the door smartly as he and other visitors approach. The floor of the Entrance Hall is covered with black and white marble chequered tiles, and up until 1999 the walls were painted a distinctive red. The most striking feature is the covered Chippendale black leather hall-porter's seat in the north-east corner.

◄ The Tour begins...

► The Entrance Hall, facing south-west. Prime ministers and their guests often pose in front of the fireplace for official photographs.

◄ The interconnecting front corridor from the Number 10 hall towards Numbers 11 and 12.

A corridor to the left (opposite) takes one through to Numbers 11 and 12. Straight ahead one enters the Inner Hall, to the left of which is the small Erith lift (above). Off to the right are the press rooms, including the distinctive bow-windowed front room built by Raymond Erith. The role of the press began to grow early this century, as a reflection of the need for Number 10 to respond to newspaper requests for information. But it has been with the proliferation of broadcast and other media outlets since the 1960s that the Press Office has become one of the largest and busiest areas of Number 10.

▲ The lift, installed in the early 1960s, off the main corridor. The lift is very small, and visitors can find themselves squashed shoulder to shoulder with their illustrious host.

◄ The main corridor looking north. Through the open door at the end is the Cabinet Room, and in between is the interconnecting corridor erected probably in the 1780s to link the two houses that make up Number 10. Off to the left of the corridor is the 'Henry Moore' alcove (see page 180).

The main corridor continues through the narrow passage connecting the Downing house, which one now leaves, to Bothmar House behind it. To the left of the corridor is an alcove with a reclining Henry Moore sculpture; to the right, windows allow a glimpse of the inner courtyard.

Ahead is the Cabinet Ante Room, where ministers assemble before Cabinet meetings; the Prime Minister always enters first, before the lesser mortals are summoned. In the Ante Room have hung paintings of Whitehall Palace and the great post-war Labour leader, Clement Attlee. To the left are two rooms, used at one time as dressing then waiting rooms, but now highly prized offices, strategically placed for senior political staff. A tiled gentlemen's lavatory nearby is truly a room where more political gossip has been exchanged than in any other comparable space in the UK. Regrettably for historians, and perhaps for the Prime Minister, no hidden microphones have recorded the hushed ministerial conversations.

▲ The Cabinet Ante Room, with bust of Disraeli in the foreground. The painting is a view of Whitehall by Rendrick Danckerts from the mid-seventeenth century. Downing Street is on the extreme right of the painting.

43

▲ The Cabinet Room today, taken from the west end looking east towards the twin pillars and the door to the Private Secretaries' inner sanctum. The table top is twentieth century, but its tripod legs date from the time of William IV.

Beyond the Ante Room lies the Cabinet Room, in which every Cabinet has met, with exceptions, such as during the Second World War. The room was altered in the late eighteenth century, and two sets of distinctive double pillars allowed the room to be extended eastwards. It now measures 12m/40ft x 5.7m/19ft, which is not large considering the historic importance of the room. In the early 1960s, on Macmillan's instructions, an earlier rectangular table was replaced by the coffin, or boat-shaped table we see today. The new arrangement allows the Prime Minister to see and hear every member of his Cabinet, including those on the same side of the table, without having to lean forward. The 23 chairs

▲ The Prime Minister's chair, positioned in front of the fireplace. It is permanently turned out, and is the only chair in the room with arm rests. The Cabinet Secretary always sits to the Prime Minister's right.

around the table are the very chairs used in the time of Gladstone and Disraeli. Cabinet Ministers always sit in the same chair, according to seniority. The Prime Minister sits with his back to the fireplace, and when Cabinet is not is session, his chair is left permanently half out from under the table. Attlee, a pipe-smoker, left his mark in 1946 by starting a self-sacrificing no-smoking policy, a good 30 years ahead of the trend.

Until 1856, the Cabinet Room was also Number 10's library, and contained a good stock of maps. Most of the books have now been moved elsewhere, to lighten the room, and only two bookcases remain, on either side of the door at the east end. On the brown baize-covered table are items of silver, including some given as presents to Mrs Thatcher by President Reagan. At the time of Erith's 1960–63 restoration, the existing brownish-pink hand-knotted carpet was replaced, and curtains of dark emerald-green damask were hung at the windows. The room has two clocks: the more prominent one is on the mantelpiece behind the Prime Minister, under the portrait of the first Prime Minister, Walpole; the other is on the small table opposite. The clocks have a disconcerting habit of chiming at different times. No one looks to these ancient devices for correct time-keeping, which is provided by the 'world clock' in the Private Secretaries' room. Until Mrs Thatcher's time, the inner doors were covered in green baize; now they have a dark blue covering.

▲ The double doors at the east end of the Cabinet Room, leading to the nerve centre of Number 10: the Private Secretaries' rooms.

45

◄ The Inner Courtyard. This area was cleaned up enormously by Raymond Erith in the early 1960s. The columns are an architectural joke which appealed to Erith's sense of humour: as Roman remains had been found on the site, he wished to create the impression of much taller columns which travelled far down below the ground.

► The garden seen from the north-west corner. To the right is Number 11 and, disappearing from view, Number 12. The L-shaped garden is little used, but is beautifully kept. In its soil are buried several Number 10 pets.

On the way back to the Cabinet Ante Room, one sees the elegant three-sided grand staircase (see page 48), the most arresting feature in the house (with the possible exception of the State Dining Room). Downstairs are the now disused kitchens, storage, 'confidential filing', and the Garden Rooms, where secretaries work around the clock. As the north side of the house is on lower ground than the Downing Street house, the basement leads onto the garden; the French windows in the Cabinet Room lead one to a terrace and, via steps, down into the garden (opposite). The garden is used for social occasions, for press conferences and for photographing visiting statesmen. The L-shaped plot is almost half an acre and runs behind Numbers 11 and 12. A flowering cherry, a magnolia and an evergreen oak survived the disruption of the early 1960s. The garden is mainly lawn, with one flower border, and is looked after by a single gardener; it is regrettable that it cannot be enjoyed more fully, though both Major and Blair liked to work there in summer.

◄ The grand staircase, taken from the ground floor near the Cabinet Room door. One looks up to the first-floor landing alongside the State Dining Rooms, and down to the basement corridor and the Garden Rooms. Lining the wall is the sequence of Prime Ministers' portraits, and at the bottom are group photographs of Cabinets and imperial conferences.

► The Ante Room outside the first-floor Drawing Rooms. The corridor leads through to offices at the front of the building, and the open door leads to the Prime Minister's flat. The art was selected after Tony Blair became Premier.

The grand staircase leads up to the State Rooms on the floor above the Cabinet Room. Portraits of every prime minister since Walpole line the wall, regardless of whether or not they lived at Number 10. Lady Dorothy Macmillan had the portraits removed, but the Wilsons, in a fine example of adversarial politics for which the British system is renowned, had them moved back. All are black and white; Callaghan's (1976-79), which was originally in colour, has since been replaced with a black and white photograph. When John Major's photograph was hung in 1998, every other portrait was shuffled down one position, and the same dance will take place when Blair becomes a two-dimensional image rather than a three-dimensional flesh and blood presence at Number 10. In the staircase well is a large globe presented to Mrs Thatcher by President Mitterrand; embarrassingly, it gives the Falklands their Argentine title, the 'Islas Malvinas' – it was suspected that he was being deliberately mischievous.

Another large Ante Room, matching that outside the Cabinet Room, greets one at the top of the stairs. Off it leads Raymond Erith's formal staircase up to the private flat. To the west is the room called the Prime Minister's Study. Before the flat was installed, when the State Rooms were largely for private use by the Prime Minister and family, this room was the Prime Minister's bedroom and bathroom. Several post-war prime ministers have used it as their study, notably Attlee and Thatcher; others, like Major and Blair, have preferred to work downstairs.

The three State Drawing Rooms lead off the Ante Room. Until the 1940s, the White Room was kept by prime ministers and their wives for their private use. This room was Lady Churchill's favourite, and is where she posed in the window for the famous portrait by the society photographer, Cecil Beaton (see page 143). Norma Major sits in the same window for possibly the most successful portrait painted of John Major (by John Wonnacott) at Number 10 (see page 165). The Quinlan Terry designs have changed the appearance of this room irrevocably, converting it from domestic to grand or state status.

▲ White Drawing Room, showing the ornate moulding above the door.

▼ White Drawing Room – fireplace detail.

▲ A mirror in the White Drawing Room.

▶ The White Drawing Room, from west to east. Through the open door can be seen the Green Drawing Room. Note Terry's unadulterated use of space.

The antique Waterford glass chandelier, matching the chandelier in the middle Green Drawing Room, originally bore candles but was converted to electricity with the rest of the house in 1894. Traditionally, this room has been used when prime ministers are interviewed on television. When the Green Drawing Room, with its double doors at each end connecting it to the White and Pillared Rooms, is not in use as a reception room, it is an audience room, used, like the White Room, for smaller meetings between Number 10 staff and visitors.

▲ A mirror in the Green Drawing Room (**above left**).

▲ Door from the Ante Room to the Green Drawing Room.

▶ The Green Drawing Room, displaying Terry's lavish ceiling and ornamental designs. The White Drawing Room and St James's Park lie beyond.

◀ Green Drawing Room – fireplace detail.

The Pillared Room at the opposite end is the largest of the three rooms; it measures over 11m/37ft x 8.3m/28ft; the two smaller Drawing Rooms are each approximately 9m/30ft by 5.6m/20ft. Visitors tend to gravitate into the Pillared Room. The room is also used for signing official international agreements, and for entertaining high-powered visitors such as the Italian Fascist leader, Benito Mussolini, who visited in 1922. A few years later, the inventor John Logie Baird had also used the room to demonstrate one of the new television sets to Prime Minister Ramsay MacDonald and his children.

The Pillared Room has a reputation for being haunted, but since no photographic evidence of such apparitions has been recorded, readers must let their imagination do the work as they gaze at the photographs of this elegant

◀ Pillared Room — fireplace detail.

◀ The Pillared Drawing Room as it looks today. In constant use for receptions, the room is largely devoid of furniture.

▶ Chippendale Mirror in the Pillared Drawing Room.

room. Jane Parsons, who became head of the 'garden room' secretaries in 1968 and who worked at the house for many years, recalls one particular spectral story: 'In my early years at Number 10,' she remembers, 'I was often told of a tall man wearing a top hat who would walk down the corridor and out through the (closed) front door!'

The tour of the official house is completed with the two Soane dining rooms. The Small Dining or Breakfast Room leads off the Pillared Drawing Room. It was in this room that prime ministers and their families used to have their domestic meals, until the flat upstairs became better appointed, soon after the Second World War.

◀ The Small Dining or Breakfast Room, looking through to the State Dining Room. The Small Dining Room is suitable for meals of up to twelve, and was a favourite room of Lloyd George. Ornaments from the Silver Trust adorn the tables.

▶ Silverware in the State Dining Room. This item was on loan from a private donor, and has now been removed. It symbolises Number 10's desire to constantly renew itself.

Double doors lead through to the larger State Dining Room; Soane himself was a guest at the first formal dinner there on 4 April 1826. At 12.6m/42ft x 7.8m/26ft, or 98sq m/1,092sq ft, it is the largest room in Number 10, albeit much larger than the Pillared Room.

The room has seen many of the most celebrated events to have been held in the building, including Churchill's retirement dinner, and the dinner hosted by Mrs Thatcher in 1985, to celebrate the 250th anniversary of the house, to which the Queen and six surviving prime ministers came. This magnificent room makes a fitting end to our historical and geographical tour of the building.

◀ Detail of Soane's vaulted roof design for the State Dining Room.

◀ The State Dining Room. The table can seat up to forty, but if a horseshoe table is used, up to sixty-five. Soane's near-perfect design gives an air of intimacy rather than grandeur.

A House in the Headlines

Ever since Walpole took possession of Number 10 in 1735, the house has been at the heart of many of the country's key moments in history: the Jacobite rising of 1745; the Seven Years' War and the War of American Independence in the eighteenth century; the Napoleonic and Crimean Wars and the Indian Mutiny in the nineteenth century; the Boer War at the turn of the century; the First and Second World Wars, the Cold War, the Suez Crisis, and the Falklands and Gulf Wars in the twentieth century. Within its walls, key decisions have been taken, many pivotal to the rise and fall of the British Empire.

▶ Neville Chamberlain, facing right, on the Number 10 steps, on his return from the famous meeting with Hitler in Germany, the year before the Second World War broke out.

◀ Churchill in his famous 'siren suit', during one of his wartime broadcasts from Number 10.

THE WORLD LOOKS AT No. 10

Crises bring crowds of onlookers to Downing Street. It isn't just that they want to see the Premier. Their instinct draws them to be near the heart of things

IN times of excitement crowds always gather outside No. 10 Downing Street, official residence of the British Prime Minister. Their first impression of the house is nearly always one of disappointment. It is a perfectly ordinary private house of the 17th century, built of red brick, and its most interesting features—such as they are—are not immediately noticeable.

Have you ever noticed, for example, the lamp which hangs over the entrance—and indicates, by being lit or unlit, whether the premier is officially "at home" or not?

There was a night when deputies of miners

came to Baldwin to plead their cause. Would he be "at home" or not? On the signal of the lamp hung a £3,000,000 government subsidy to assist their wages. Crises and conferences have depended on the switching on or off of that lamp. Early morning on the day of the general strike, it burned until 1.30 a.m. Then the door opened and a policeman announced to the excited crowd waiting outside—"the light is out, nothing doing. . . ."

Then there is the peculiar door-knocker. In 1924 a new phase of crowd psychology began. One member of the impatient crowd was suddenly

inspired to step out and touch the door-knocker on No. 10. Immediately about 1,056 other people followed suit, and a queue was formed to touch the knocker. Said veteran door-keeper: "They never actually knock on the door, but when I asked them why they did it, I found they wanted to be able to say they had touched the Prime Minister's door-knocker. Now it is the custom !"

In spite of its dingy appearance, no other building can claim to be so interwoven with history, so associated with world-shattering crises and decisions, as No. 10.

Before No. 10 became the home of Prime

Ministers it was lived in by Cromwell's aunt—Elizabeth Hampden. Then the Scout-Master General of Cromwell's army in Scotland—Sir George Downing—bought it, and after a nice little bit of housing speculation founded the whole of Downing Street—"a pretty open place where are four or five very large houses fit for persons of honour and quality."

The Duke of Buckingham lived there for a while, and then, in 1720, it was first secured by the Crown for the official residence of the First Lord of His Majesty's Treasury, although surprisingly enough, up to 1806 only one First Lord of Treasury lived

" So when you're grown-up, you'll remember. . . . "

" Perhaps it'll all blow over."

" Well, it's no good pulling a long face."

" . . . And we have to do the fighting."

THE DOOR THAT THOUSANDS GAZE AT AND FEW PASS THROUGH.

" Twenty years ago we thought we'd

" To-day talk—to-morrow . . . ? "

" Surely it's not too late to do something."

" . . . if they'd made a stand about Abyssinia."

" Well, but what does he look like, anyway ? "

" Wasn't one lesson enough ? "

Over the years, Number 10 has witnessed debates of great domestic import: decisions over the extension of the franchise in the great Reform Acts of the nineteenth century; the emancipation of slaves; the protracted Irish question; trade union militancy, which reached high points in the 1920s, with the General Strike, and in the 1970s, when on three occasions trade unions played a significant part in bringing down the government of the day. It has also been the nerve centre for decisions taken during great financial crises, including harvest failures and trade policy in the eighteenth and nineteenth centuries, the economic crisis in 1931 after the Wall Street Crash and worldwide depression, and the occasion in 1976 when the government had to go, cap in hand, to the International Monetary Fund to ask for money to bail out Britain's economy. The house has witnessed riots in the streets, prime ministers being jostled and struck by flying objects, and the deaths of several prime ministers or their wives. It has been bombed by the Germans and by the IRA, and is on constant twenty-four hour alert against terrorist attack. Throughout its history, Number 10 has been neither a quiet nor a safe place. In the passages that follow, I hope to give a flavour of the role it has played during some of the more dramatic phases in British history.

▲ Number 10 is always the focus of the public's attention, especially at times of national crisis.

THE GORDON RIOTS: 1780

In 1780, Number 10 came under siege during the Gordon Riots. The War of Independence (1775–83) had been going badly for the British in North America, and Lord North (1770-82) had come under mounting political pressure. Closer to home, he had to contend with a dissatisfied Protestant faction which bitterly resented concessions that he had made to long-oppressed Roman Catholics. The leader of these excitable Protestants was Lord George Gordon, president of the recently formed Protestant Association. In January 1780, Gordon went to Number 10 to see North and demand the withdrawal of concessions to the Catholics. North stood his ground, which incensed Gordon and his fellow Protestants. As the summer of 1780 approached, their anger spilled over, and by early June riots had broken out across London.

On June 7th, North was entertaining friends to dinner at Number 10, presumably in the Dining Room, which is on the Whitehall side of the building. At that time, with the cul-de-sac still in place, Whitehall was the sole entry point for the thronging crowds. An eye-witness account was penned by one of North's guests, Sir John Macpherson, later Governor General of India: 'We sat down at table, and dinner had scarcely been removed, when Downing Square, through which there is no outlet, become thronged with people, who manifested a disposition, or rather a determination, to proceed to acts of outrage.'

Lord North was told that there were 20 or more grenadier guards standing by, armed and ready to fire on the mob. Anxious at all costs to avoid bloodshed, which would only inflame volatile passions still further, he ordered envoys to be dispatched to the crowd outside, to tell them about the grenadiers and what

◀ The Gordon Riots of 1780, with the grenadier guards inspecting the protesting mob. They did not engage each other.

awaited them if they did not desist. The Prime Minister clearly showed some sang-froid; Macpherson records how 'we then sat down again quietly at the table and finished the wine'. But the assembled company were not through with the evening yet, as Macpherson records: 'Night was coming on, and the capital presenting a scene of tumult or conflagration in many quarters. Lord North, accompanied by us all, mounted to the top of the house, where we beheld London blazing in seven places, and could hear the platoons firing regularly in various directions.'

> 'The populace continued to fill the little Square, and became very noisy, but they never attempted to force the front door . . . By degrees, as the evening advanced, the people . . . began to cool and afterwards gradually to disperse without further effort.'
>
> SIR JOHN MACPHERSON

THE FIRST WORLD WAR: 1914-18

Number 10 had seen some prolonged wars, including the Seven Years' and the Napoleonic Wars, but had never before witnessed 'total' war, where not just London, and Number 10, were in the front line, but the whole nation's labour force and economy were swept up in the whirlwind.

Unrest in Europe had been mounting in the late nineteenth and early twentieth centuries, with the nation states dividing themselves into two rival camps: on the one side, Britain, France and Russia; on the other, Germany and Austria Hungary. Yet the Cabinet of Prime Minister Henry Asquith did not focus on the imminent prospect of war, even after the assassination in Sarajevo of Archduke Franz Ferdinand, Crown Prince of Austria Hungary on 28 June 1914. On July 24th, Foreign Secretary Sir Edward Grey read Austria Hungary's ultimatum to Serbia to the Cabinet. Britain, he said, would not be involved if war came, and he packed his bags for his summer holiday fishing in Hampshire.

Other Cabinet ministers, too, left London in search of sun, game or mountains. Winston Churchill, then First Lord of the Admiralty in Asquith's Cabinet, alone remained in London, believing that Britain would enter the war and anxious that his navy should be ready. A week later, with friends and foes on the Continent beginning to mobilise, ministers scurried back to London, and Cabinet sat at Number 10 in almost continuous session. A map was passed around the table as ministers grappled with names and places new to them, places where the relentless groan of heavily laden trucks and carts indicated that war was indeed on its way.

The Bank Holiday weekend coincided with an escalation of the crisis. On Sunday, August 2nd, crowds swept into Downing Street, as they always did at times of crisis. Inside the Cabinet Room, the balance of opinion among ministers shifted towards taking a tough line with Germany. David Lloyd George, Chancellor of the Exchequer, recorded how 'We could hear the hum of the surging mass from the Cabinet chamber.'

By Monday, August 3rd, the crowds in Downing Street were so thick that Cabinet ministers had to be helped through to reach the front door of Number 10. On Tuesday, August 4th, Britain dispatched an ultimatum to Germany, demanding that it respect Belgian neutrality, or face the prospect of war. By midnight, no response from Berlin had been received.

The war that people expected to be 'over by Christmas' dragged on for four and a quarter years, and resulted in the deaths of 1,200,000 British and Empire servicemen. The fear among Londoners remaining in the capital was from bombs dropped by Zeppelin airships; searchlights and guns were set up on Admiralty Arch, in Hyde Park and on other open spaces in central London. For the first nine months, Asquith ran the war with his Liberal Cabinet, holding regular meetings in the Cabinet Room. In May 1915, after failures to break through the German lines, now consolidated in a series of fortified trenches on the 450-mile Western front from the English Channel to Switzerland, and with reports of serious shell shortages in the British army, a change of government was demanded. Asquith was forced to set up a coalition government, bringing into the Cabinet a number of Conservatives, including Andrew Bonar Law, Austen Chamberlain and former Prime Minister Arthur Balfour, as well as Arthur Henderson from the Labour Party. Lloyd George became Minister of Munitions, to improve supplies to the troops;

▲ Henry Asquith, Prime Minister at the time of the First World War.

although he ceased to be Chancellor of the Exchequer, he continued to live at Number 11. When Lord Kitchener (of the popular 'Your Country Needs You' recruiting poster) drowned at sea when HMS Hampshire was sunk by a mine off the Orkneys en route to Russia, Lloyd George took on his portfolio of Secretary of State for War.

Asquith found life more difficult with the changes in his government. A bitter Cabinet dispute preceded conscription, or universal call-up, in January 1916, while in France the smaller scale (but still devastating) loss of life in 1915 at the battles of Loos, Vimy Ridge and Neuve Chapelle, were

> 'I looked at the children asleep after dinner before joining Henry [her husband] in the Cabinet Room. Lord Crewe [Lord Privy Seal] and Sir Edward Grey were already there and sat smoking cigarettes in silence; some went out, others came in; nothing was said. The clock on the mantelpiece hammered out the hour and when the beat of midnight struck it was as silent as dawn. We were at War. I left to go to bed, and, as I was pausing at the foot of the staircase, I saw Winston Churchill with a happy face striding towards the double doors of the Cabinet Room.'
>
> Diary of Margot Asquith, entry for 4 August 1914

followed in 1916 by the utter disaster of the major battle of the Somme (July 1st-November 18th). At the cost of over 100,000 British lives, an advance was made of, at best, seven miles. At the end of four and a half months of fighting, the preliminary objective, the German-held town of Bapaume, had yet to be reached.

For Asquith, there were brief interludes of happiness: in 1915, his daughter Violet married his secretary, Maurice Bonham Carter, and he still managed occasional games of chess and bridge at Number 10. But moments of respite dwindled as the long lists of casualties came into Number 10 day after day, and he began to drink more heavily. On 15 September 1916, his beloved and brilliant son, Raymond, was killed on the Somme. The writer John Buchan said of his friend, 'Our roll of honour is long, but it holds no nobler figure . . . Debonair and brilliant and brave, he is now part of that immortal England which knows not age or weariness or defeat.' Raymond Asquith is buried in a cemetery with over 2,000 white gravestones, just to the west of Mametz, where fellow officer Siegfried Sassoon, the poet, fought. The year could not possibly have gone worse for the Asquiths. Margot lamented in her diary: 'It is only a question of time when we shall have to leave Downing Street.'

In December 1916, her prediction came true, and Lloyd George became Prime Minister, forcing Asquith from office and moving sideways from Number 11 to Number 10, at the head of a new coalition government. Margot records how 'we had to leave Downing Street without a roof over our heads'.

Lloyd George was single-minded in his focus. As he said, 'One man cannot possibly run Parliament and run the War,' so he left the former to Bonar Law, who became Leader of the Commons (and subsequently, 1922-3, Conservative Prime Minister), while Lloyd George was left relatively free to concentrate on the conduct of the war. Number 10 became the nerve centre; top military commanders and politicians would file in and out daily. Through that door, in the late spring of 1917, walked Field Marshal Haig, Commander-in-Chief of the British Armed Forces. His task was to persuade the politicians that a major offensive, on the scale of the Somme, had to be launched that summer. Haig spread out his maps on the rectangular Cabinet table. He outlined the plan, pointing in excited manner to the troops' planned progress on the map as he did so.

The place for the break-out was to be the Belgian town of Ypres; the objective, the towns of Zeebrugge and Ostend, from which ports German U-boats were creating havoc with allied shipping. A combined naval and army operation was envisaged, with the Royal Navy pounding the ports from the sea, while the troops were to advance on the ports from the relatively unprotected land side. Haig's battle, however, got bogged down on a sloping hill below a small village outside Ypres. For four months, the British army slogged their way up, often disappearing into the quagmire of mud churned up by shells in an unusually wet summer. The battle was officially known as the Third Battle of Ypres, but is more commonly known by the name of that village, Passchendaele. Guns from the opening British bombardment could be heard in Downing Street. The advancing British armies did not reach even one tenth of the way to Ostend and Zeebrugge.

LLOYD GEORGE AT NUMBER 10

Cabinet had been reduced in size by Lloyd George to a core 'War Cabinet' of between five and seven ministers. A 'Cabinet Secretariat' was created to ensure that Cabinet's discussions and action points were fully circulated. Hitherto, incredibly, no records of Cabinet discussions had been made, although the Prime Minister did write a letter to the sovereign, summarising them. A far more orderly and bureaucratic approach was now called for. The secretariat was partly based at Disraeli's former home in

Lloyd George on the Western Front

After the stalemate on the Western Front during 1917, the tide of war turned the following year. The failure of the German spring offensive to sustain its advance, and the arrival of fresh and well-equipped troops from the United States, which had joined the war the year before, tipped the scales. By the summer, the Germans were in full flight and it seemed likely that a cease-fire would be agreed before the end of the year.

In the early hours of 11 November 1918, a messenger hurried up to the bedroom on the first floor of Number 10, in which Lloyd George and Margaret were sleeping. Lloyd George was told that an armistice would be signed at 11 am that day.

*Lloyd George acknowledges cheers from British troops as he emerges from a captured German dug-out at Fricourt on the Somme. (**above**). Lloyd George examines the scene on one of his frequent visits to the Western Front (**left**).*

nearby Whitehall Gardens, but also worked out of Number 10. Under Lloyd George's stewardship, Downing Street expanded into a pulsating office complex, with huts erected all over the gardens to house secretaries and others involved in the war effort; it became known as the 'garden suburb'. The Prime Minister's own secretariat was also housed in this expanded temporary accommodation.

Lloyd George stayed overnight in Number 10 for much of the duration of the war, but when he could, drove out to his Surrey home at Walton Heath, where the air was fresher. He had a dread of high explosives. He was alone one night in Number 10 with his daughter Olwen when they heard a crash of bombs landing on Piccadilly. They went out into the street in their night clothes, only to be asked by a policeman: 'Don't you think you ought to go in now, sir?'

Lloyd George would rise early, and hold working breakfasts in the small Soane Dining Room. He would often only at the last minute tell his wife, Margaret, that extra guests would be arriving, and ask if they could be fed. Margaret and the daughters, Olwen and Megan, would join the assembled Cabinet ministers and official guests, as would the Lloyd Georges' sons, Richard and Gwilym, when back on rare visits from the war (a fifth child, Mair, died of appendicitis aged seventeen, in 1907). The girls would listen to the conversation, and absorb more than the adults probably realised. On one occasion, Megan saw an evening newspaper with a news story repeating in some detail what she had heard spoken that morning at breakfast. She went to her father and protested her innocence. He put his arms around her and consoled her: 'I would trust you with my life and, what is much more important, I would trust you with the future of our country.' Megan, aged fourteen when her father became Prime Minister, sought out Kitty Bonar Law, whose father had moved into Number 11 when they vacated it. The friends would climb to the top of the stairs and scramble across the roof between the two houses to see each other, to avoid using the very public interconnecting door.

Lloyd George's new broom in Number 10 extended to the domestic staff, who he ensured came from Wales, including the maids and cooks. 'Good God! What am I to do with all that?' was Cook's reaction when she saw the enormous vaulted kitchen with its rows of pans and pots. Like many expletives uttered during the Lloyd George premiership, the language was free, and Welsh. A similar mood of anarchy prevailed when Lloyd George was charged with looking after his granddaughters. His personal secretary, A J Sylvester, recalls how Lloyd George would stand with his back to the Cabinet Room fireplace and roar with laughter as he encouraged the tiny girls to run around atop the Cabinet table.

When the armistice finally came on 11 November 1918, crowds soon began to throng into the streets outside, and to their chanting of 'LG', he appeared at one of the first-floor windows overlooking Downing Street. That night, a dinner of celebration took place in Soane's State Dining Room.

> '*I loved living at Number 10. Famous people came and went, and Number 10 seemed to be the hub of the universe.*'
>
> OLWEN LLOYD GEORGE

THE IRISH TROUBLES COME TO DOWNING STREET

Before the First World War was over, the Irish troubles, which had dominated the immediate pre-war years, erupted again. The 1916 Easter uprising in Dublin had resulted in British troops being diverted from the war to quell the republicans who were pressing for an independent Ireland. Wooden barricades, 3m/10ft high, were erected at the end of Downing Street to prevent protestors for Irish independence from attacking the Prime Minister. For Lloyd George it was also a personal inconvenience; he enjoyed his walks in St James's Park, and he was warned that, while there were threats from Irish protesters, such perambulatory pleasure would be foolhardy. After the Irish Free State was established in 1922, disturbances died away, and prime ministers were once again free to walk in the park – until security ruled it out in the 1960s. Downing Street itself was again opened to the public – until 1989, when fear of terrorist attacks resulted in it being permanently sealed off by high metal gates.

▲ Barricades being erected to shut off the east end of Downing Street against Irish demonstrators during the First World War. The Foreign Office is visible in the background. Policemen stood on guard in front of the gates.

The General Strike

The most severe single episode of industrial unrest in the twentieth century was the 1926 General Strike. Number 10 was again at the centre of the government's response. The coal industry, which employed over a million workers, had been in trouble for some years because of cheaper foreign imports, the uneconomic scale of many individual mines, outdated technology and, since the 1925 return to the gold standard, an overvalued pound. In 1925, coal owners (the industry was then in private hands) decided they could no longer maintain wage levels for their workers. A crisis loomed. The Prime Minister, Stanley Baldwin, intervened, and at a special Cabinet meeting at 6.30 pm on 30 July 1925, ministers agreed to a nine-month subsidy to allow miners' wages to be maintained at current levels until a royal commission, set up to investigate the coal industry, reported.

Baldwin stands firm

When it reported, in March 1926, its findings were rejected by the miners. On April 30th, the Council of the Trade Union Congress (TUC) decided to call a general strike of all union workers, although it gave reassurances that food would be distributed to avoid panic and famine. Cabinet had called a state of emergency four days earlier. Ministers and union leaders met on the evening of Saturday, May 1st, and continued until 1.15 am on Sunday morning. Baldwin, a conciliator, called for an extension of the subsidy for three months to buy time. Cabinet met at noon that Sunday, May 2nd, and decided that an extension would be seen as a surrender to union militancy. Still Baldwin held out, and at 9.30 pm Cabinet met again, this time at Number 11, because Baldwin was holding separate discussions at Number 10. At 11.30 pm he joined his ministers and said that the TUC would withdraw their strike notice if negotiations were resumed. At this point a message arrived at Number 10, announcing that print workers at the *Daily Mail* had refused to print a leading article on the crisis. This was viewed as trade union interference with the free press. Baldwin handed waiting TUC officials a note, telling them to repudiate the printers' action. If they did not, then the dialogue was over. He then retired to bed.

The die was cast, and a general strike became inevitable. Beginning in the early hours of Tuesday, May 4th, it lasted eight days, before the TUC General Council called it off, after further talks at Number 10. In a broadcast to the nation from the Cabinet Room, Baldwin appealed for calm, and asked that there should be no recrimination or blame. The miners' union alone held out, until driven back to work by hunger and lack of money the following year.

Baldwin on the steps of Number 10 during the General Strike (opposite). A food convoy, with military escort, passing through the London Docks on its way to Hyde Park (right). Sir Douglas Hogg arrives for the Sunday, May 2nd Cabinet meeting (below).

THE 1931 FINANCIAL CRISIS

Few domestic crises in Number 10 were ever conducted with such acrimony and enduring bitterness as the 1931 financial crisis. Its importance in history was that, unlike the financial crises of 1949 (devaluation), 1967 (devaluation), 1976 (IMF loan) and 1992 ('Black Wednesday'), it also became a political crisis of enduring proportions. The Wall Street Crash in 1929 had precipitated a general world economic crisis, and unemployment rose steeply in Britain in 1930 and 1931. Labour had been in power under Ramsay MacDonald since 1929: how should they react to the depression? Government revenue from taxation inevitably fell, while demands on expenditure, not least to look after the unemployed, rose. Something had to give.

The government coped until the closure of the great Kreditanstalt Austrian Bank in May 1931. Foreign investors began to withdraw money from London banks, while the Bank of England could only secure further credits to keep the country afloat if the government balanced its budget. To achieve this, cuts in government spending would be required. Meanwhile, the run on the pound continued. After a message from Philip Snowden, Chancellor of the Exchequer, MacDonald returned to Number 10 from Scotland on Tuesday, August 11th, to co-ordinate the government's response, and for the following two days the Cabinet Economy Committee met at Number 10. No solution was found, so it reconvened on August 17th and 18th, although no records of its deliberations survive. Very reluctantly, the committee agreed to recommend that cuts, including a cut in unemployment benefit, would have to be made. Their conclusions were discussed by Cabinet on Wednesday, August 19th, a meeting that began at 11 am and continued until 10.30 pm that evening. As this was a full Cabinet, minutes were taken. They record how MacDonald and other members of the Economy Committee 'explained the grave character of the financial position, the reasons for immediate action and the various measures designed to secure budgetary equilibrium, which in the view of the Committee must be taken forthwith if public confidence at home and abroad is to be re-established'.

The majority, including the left-wingers, were adamant that unemployment benefit cuts were unacceptable, and the TUC General Council expressed the same view to MacDonald the next day, its leaders insisting that there should be neither cuts in unemployment benefit, nor wage cuts for essential workers such as teachers and policemen. Cabinet was again in deadlock. Cuts in expenditure were necessary to secure foreign loans, but there was no agreement on how the money was to be saved. On Friday, August 21st, King George V, who had left Sandringham in Norfolk for Balmoral in Scotland that day, was told he would be required back in London. He took the overnight sleeper, arriving back at Buckingham Palace on the morning of Sunday, August 23rd.

It was a fateful day. The King became convinced that the only solution to the grave crisis, given the impossibility of securing agreement within the Labour

▲ Ramsay MacDonald leaving Number 10 in 1929. On the left, hat in hand, stands Oswald Mosley, who left MacDonald's government in 1930 and later formed the British Union of Fascists.

movement, was a national government that would include both Conservatives and Liberals. Later that Sunday, he saw Conservative leader Stanley Baldwin, who had cut short his traditional long holiday at Aix-les-Bains, and Liberal leader Herbert Samuel, separately, to discuss how to resolve the impasse. He also saw MacDonald, and discussed with him the idea of setting up a national or coalition government.

Throughout the day, MacDonald had been awaiting a response to his request for credits from George Harrison, President of the US Federal Reserve Bank. Cabinet met at 7 pm on the evening of Sunday, August 23rd, and MacDonald announced that the telegram from New York had still not come; at 7.45 pm the meeting was adjourned until 9.10 pm, while Cabinet Ministers strolled around the gardens of Number 10 in the late evening light. When the meeting reconvened, MacDonald slowly read out the telegram, which had finally arrived from Mr Harrison; it was full of provisos before any credits would be given, and offered the Cabinet little succour. Effectively, it put Cabinet at the mercy of the bankers.

The Cabinet minutes record the following: 'The Prime Minister informed the Cabinet that a situation had now been faced of a peculiarly difficult character because, if the Labour Party was not prepared to join with the Conservatives and Liberal Parties in accepting the proposals as a whole, the conditions mentioned in Mr Harrison's message regarding a national agreement, would not be fulfilled . . . The country was suffering from a lack of confidence abroad. There was, as yet, no panic at home, but the Prime Minister warned the Cabinet of the calamitous nature of the consequences which would immediately and inevitably follow from a financial panic and flight from the pound. No one could be blind to the very great political difficulties involved in giving effect to the proposals as a whole. But, when the immediate crisis was over and before Parliament met, it would be possible to give the Labour Party a full explanation of the circumstances which had rendered it necessary for the government to formulate such a drastic scheme.'

Despite MacDonald's pleas, it was clear he would win insufficient support for the ten per cent cut in unemployment benefit, and that a majority of ministers remained adamantly against cuts. MacDonald secured the agreement of Cabinet to advise King George V to hold a conference of the three party leaders. He told Cabinet he would see the King, and the entire Cabinet agreed to place their resignation in the Prime Minister's hands. MacDonald left Downing Street for the palace at 10.10 pm on the Sunday evening, and arrived, looking 'scared and unbalanced', according to the King's private secretary, to tender his and his government's resignation. He returned to Number 10 at 10.40 pm and informed his colleagues that he would meet the King the next morning with Baldwin and Samuel. It seems likely that, on the Sunday evening, MacDonald was himself intending to resign.

A NATIONAL GOVERNMENT

At the Monday meeting, the King persuaded MacDonald to remain as Prime Minister, at the head of a government of individual ministers, and Baldwin and Samuel agreed to serve under him. At noon, the Labour Cabinet met for the last time. MacDonald told his colleagues that he would form a national government and that he would invite selected Labour ministers to join it. Sankey (one of three, with the Chancellor of the Exchequer Philip Snowden and the Dominions Secretary J H Thomas, to be invited) recorded Cabinet's 'warm appreciation of the great kindness, consideration and courtesy invariably shown by the Prime Minister when presiding at their meetings'.

No hint was given by that bald statement of the submerged feelings. Philip Snowden remained Chancellor of the Exchequer in the new national government. Britain left the gold standard, which had overvalued the pound and resulted in so many of the country's economic problems because of over-priced exports. The hotly disputed economies, including unemployment benefit, were imposed, along with other cuts. In time, the economy began to recover, and foreign capital began to flood back into the country. The damage to the Labour party was not so easily healed. Fourteen years were to pass before Labour returned to government, in 1945, under Clement Attlee. MacDonald was viewed as a pariah by many, and not just those on Labour's left, for splitting the party. He remained as Prime Minister until 1935 at the head of the national government, an increasingly ineffective and isolated figure. It was a sad end for a man who had done so much to build up Labour as a major force in British politics.

THE SECOND WORLD WAR

The image of Prime Minister Neville Chamberlain (1937-40) returning from his meeting with Hitler in Munich in September 1938, to greet the cheering crowds outside Number 10 with a declaration of 'peace in our time', is one of the enduring images of twentieth-century Britain. Chamberlain had earlier landed at London's Heston airport with an agreement, signed by 'Herr Hitler' and himself, to maintain peaceful relations between both countries in the future. BBC television saw his return, and filmed him walking down the aeroplane steps – the only appearance on television of a prime minister before the Second World War.

> *'Immediately after Chamberlain's return to Downing Street a full meeting of the Cabinet was held. Within half an hour the Cabinet had approved everything the Premier had done. After the meeting, Mr Chamberlain dined quietly at home and, following the advice he had given to his admirers, went early to bed – to sleep in peace.'*
>
> THE 'TIMES', 1 OCTOBER 1938

The crowds bore in on Number 10. Chamberlain leant out of a first-floor window and recalled Disraeli's return from the Congress of Berlin in 1878: 'My good friends, this is the second time in our history that there has come back from Germany to Downing Street peace with honour.'

But had Neville Chamberlain's handling of the Czechoslovakian crisis been an act of statesmanship, or weakness? Historians are divided on the matter. By 'appeasing' Hitler, did he embolden the German leader to even greater acts of daring, or did he buy vital time to allow Britain to re-arm and prepare for war? Peace did not come in September 1938. Within six months, Hitler had taken over the whole of Czechoslovakia, and it was made clear to him that the invasion of other countries, such as Poland, would not be tolerated. News of the Nazi–Soviet pact of August 22nd caused grave apprehension in London; this most unlikely alliance of Nazi Germany with communist Russia was seen as Hitler's way of securing Germany's eastern border with Russia, while he turned his attention elsewhere.

Ministers scurried back from their summer holidays, much as they had done during the crises of 1914 and 1931, and met for a Cabinet meeting on

► Neville Chamberlain
on 3 September 1939,
the day Britain entered
the Second World War.
Behind him stands
Lord Dunglass, his
Parliamentary Private
Secretary, who himself
became Prime Minister
as Alec Douglas-Home
twenty-four years later.

Wednesday, August 23rd. Parliament was summoned to return from its summer recess and met on August 24th, passing an Emergency Powers Bill. On August 25th, Sir Nevile Henderson, British Ambassador in Germany, flew back from Berlin and was driven straight to Number 10 to brief Chamberlain on the latest developments. Cabinet met twice on both Saturday and Sunday, August 26th and 27th. It determined not to yield to Hitler, and instructions were given that women, children and invalids should be evacuated from London.

German forces went into Poland on the night of August 31st-September 1st. An ultimatum was sent to Hitler to halt his advance into Poland by 11 am on September 3rd. Just as on 4 August 1914, no German withdrawal took place, and no reply was received. At 11.15 am, from his seat in the Cabinet Room, Chamberlain addressed the nation: 'You can imagine what a bitter blow it is to me that all my long struggle to win peace has failed.' The country, he said, was now at war with Germany.

Chamberlain immediately set up a small War Cabinet. It met each morning at Number 10 until the Central War Rooms in the secure basement underneath the Office of Works were ready in October 1939.

Churchill had been in the political wilderness during the 1930s, preaching the need to do more to re-arm. Now he was brought into the War Cabinet as First

Lord of the Admiralty, the post he had held on the outbreak of the First World War. The Board of the Admiralty signalled at once to all ships in the royal navy, 'Winston is back'. Churchill was the most outspoken minister in the War Cabinet, and meetings were often tense.

The Chamberlains continued to live at Number 10 during the 'phoney war', from September 1939 to May 1940. The 200,000 casualties from German bombs that the War Cabinet had been told to expect in the first week did not transpire. There were none of the big battles of the opening days of the First World War, such as those at Mons, the Marne and Ypres. Instead, there was an uneasy lull. It was rudely broken when Hitler, with Poland securely under his control, turned his attention westwards. On 9 April 1940, he invaded Norway. British attempts

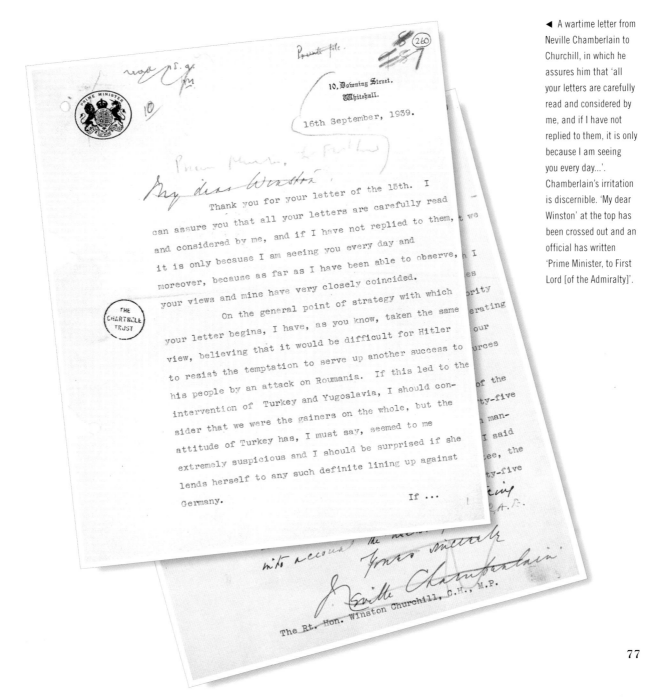

◀ A wartime letter from Neville Chamberlain to Churchill, in which he assures him that 'all your letters are carefully read and considered by me, and if I have not replied to them, it is only because I am seeing you every day...'. Chamberlain's irritation is discernible. 'My dear Winston' at the top has been crossed out and an official has written 'Prime Minister, to First Lord [of the Admiralty]'.

to provide support at Narvik and Trondheim proved abortive. Chamberlain, like Asquith before him, saw his conduct of the war increasingly under fire. Angry exchanges in the House of Commons over Norway on May 7th and 8th brought Chamberlain under great personal pressure.

As in 1915 and 1931, the Prime Minister decided to form a national government to broaden support. Labour, now indisputably the second party, was reluctant to join a coalition under him. It seemed likely Chamberlain would have to resign. Churchill was summoned to Number 10 on the afternoon of May 9th, and sat on a seat in the garden talking to Lord Halifax, the other main contender for the premiership, while Chamberlain spoke inside to the Labour leader, Clement Attlee. Halifax, being a peer, thought he would be marginalised; not since Lord Salisbury, thirty-eight years before, had a premier sat in the Lords. On May 10th, the international crisis heightened immeasurably when, in the early hours of the morning, Hitler's forces invaded Holland, Belgium and France. Cabinet met throughout the day as dismal reports of the German advance flooded in. The possibility of German paratroopers landing in Britain was even aired. During the day's third Cabinet, at 4.30 pm, Chamberlain was handed a message from the Labour party confirming they would not join a government under him. Churchill promptly went to Buckingham Palace to tender his resignation, and, that evening, he was summoned by the King. 'I suppose you don't know why I have sent for you?' George VI asked him. 'Sir, I simply couldn't imagine why,' Churchill replied. The King went on in this light-hearted way to invite Churchill to become Prime Minister. That night, Churchill formed his own small War Cabinet, which included Chamberlain, Attlee and Halifax.

▲ Churchill's bedroom at the Cabinet War Office.

The Churchills did not move into Number 10 until June, in order to give the displaced Chamberlains time to make alternative arrangements. Chamberlain had not much longer to live, and died of cancer on November 9th. Churchill was delighted to enter the historical house. He kept his office there that summer and he and his wife, Clementine, settled into the second-floor flat. Churchill used the bedroom on the left as you enter the Prime Minister's flat. Only their youngest daughter, Mary, moved in with them; their son, Randolph, was in uniform, and their two older daughters, Diana and Sarah, were married.

John Colville, a career diplomat who had been Chamberlain's Private Secretary, found the change of allegiance initially difficult, but soon developed a benevolent fondness for his new boss, as shown in the diary extract opposite.

Churchill would dictate to Mrs Hill and other secretaries until 3 am, or even later. Mrs Hill and her two assistants slept at Number 10 so that one of them could be constantly on call. Churchill would wake at about 8 am, and after breakfast and the morning papers, he would be ready, propped up in bed, mandatory cigar in hand, to begin dictating letters, memos and speeches. Tears would sometimes well into his eyes, with the emotion of the words, as he composed his speeches. Drafts were typed on heavy manual typewriters, corrected by Churchill in red squiggles, and left on the bed for secretaries to collect and type out in final draft form for him – with just four or five words to the line – to read in the House of Commons that afternoon. Mrs Hill recalls him dictating his 'Battle of Britain' speech, delivered on 20 August 1940, from his bed in this way. The drafting over,

> '*Went up to the PM's bedroom at about 10.00. He was lying in bed, in a red dressing gown, smoking a cigar and dictating to Mrs Hill, who sat with a typewriter at the foot of the bed. His box, half full of papers, stood open on his bed and by his side was a vast chromium-plated cuspidor. His black cat Nelson, which has quite replaced our old Number 10 black cat, sprawled at the foot of the bed and every now and again Winston would gaze at it affectionately and say "Cat, darling".'*
>
> DIARY OF JOHN COLVILLE, 27 JUNE 1940

Churchill went for a bath in the adjoining room, emerging with a towel around his ample girth, to be handed the complete script, the pages joined together with a Treasury tag. The finished text gave no inkling of the chaotic, last-minute preparation that has characterised Number 10 speechwriting over the years.

◀ The War Cabinet Room. In front of Churchill's seat is the red box which, full of state papers, always accompanied him. The room's red girders were there to support the ceiling if the building above collapsed. The coloured lights over the door showed whether or not an air raid was in progress.

▲ The room used by Churchill as his study during the war.

The Battle of Britain speech's most famous passage 'Never in the field of human conflict has so much been owed by so many to so few', had in fact been composed by Churchill not from his bed but in the car, four days earlier. On August 16th, he had been visiting RAF Fighter Command in west London, and watched while almost all Britain's fighter squadrons took to the air. When being driven away, he said, 'Don't speak to me; I have never been so moved.' When she read the text of his Commons speech, Asquith's daughter Violet wrote to him to say that the words would 'live as long as words are spoken and remembered'.

Churchill remained a night worker until the end of the war. If he sensed there would be a lot of work, he would say, 'I think I'll need two ladies tonight,' with a mischievous grin spread across his broad face.

The blitz on London, long dreaded, began in the late summer of 1940. John Colville recorded on August 26th, 'I stood in the garden, heard midnight strike on Big Ben, watched the searchlight display and wondered at the unaccustomed stillness of London. Not a sound, and scarcely a breath of air. Then suddenly the noise of an engine and the flash of a distant gun. The PM . . . came down in his particularly magnificent golden-dragon dressing gown and, tin hat in hand, retired to sleep in the shelter.'

Several near misses to Number 10 fell that September. But it was not until mid-October that the serious threat came. On October 14th, Churchill was dining at Number 10 in the reinforced temporary dining room in the Garden Rooms, below the Cabinet Room. In his book *Finest Hour*, he wrote: 'We were dining . . . when the usual night raid began . . . The steel shutters had been closed. Several loud explosions occurred around us at no great distance, and presently a bomb fell, perhaps a hundred yards away, on the Horse Guards Parade, making a great deal of noise. Suddenly, I had a providential impulse. The kitchen at Number 10 Downing Street is lofty and spacious, and looks out through a large plate-glass window about twenty-five feet high. The butler and parlourmaid continued to serve the dinner with complete detachment, but I became acutely aware of this big window, behind which Mrs Landermare, the cook, and the kitchen maid, never turning a hair, were at work. I got up abruptly, went into the kitchen, told the butler to put the dinner on the hot plates in the dining room, and ordered the cook and the kitchen maid into the shelter . . . I had been seated again at table (in the Garden Room) only about three minutes when a really loud crash, close at hand, and a violent shock showed that the house had been struck. My detective came into the room and said much damage had been done . . .'

▲ Churchill, in his wartime siren suit, delivering a BBC radio broadcast from the Cabinet Room.

The bomb had missed the house and the Treasury but fell on Treasury Green, about 18m/20yds to the east of Number 10, causing extensive damage to the Number 10 kitchens and slighter damage to the Soane Dining Rooms and to the State Drawing Rooms. Parts of some ceilings gave way and collapsed into the middle of the rooms, and most windows on the north and east side of the building were blown in. Five days later, Churchill and his secretaries were woken up in Number 10 to be told that a German mine had landed in St James's Park and that

▲ The Pillared Drawing Room takes a battering under the bombing **(above left)**.

The picture of Churchill with President Roosevelt escaped undamaged, but the ceilings, windows and chandeliers did not. Taken looking from the middle into the White Drawing Room. These photographs were restricted during the war for fear of damaging morale **(above right)**.

it could blow 'to pieces' all buildings within 400 yards. The mine was defused, but Churchill refused to leave Number 10 while the bomb disposal crew were at work and appeared chiefly worried about the fate of 'those poor little birds' on the St James's Park lake.

The proximity of these bombs finally convinced Churchill, however, that he had to move out of Number 10 into the Number 10 Annexe, prepared on the ground floor of the Ministry of Works, immediately above the Central War Rooms. The long process of moving out of Number 10 began on October 20th. In the main part of the house, only the Cabinet Room and the Private Secretaries' Room next door remained furnished; all the other rooms were stripped bare. The reinforced Garden Rooms did continue to be used, as the photographs reveal, providing a small dining room, a meeting area and a bedroom, which Churchill was accustomed to use. Colville lamented the move, confiding in his diary: 'It is sad to leave the old building, especially as I fear it will not survive the Battle of London [i.e. the blitz].'

Colville's fears were not borne out. Number 10 did survive the blitz, although it suffered more close misses. Repairs to the damage after the October 14th bomb cost £1,000, and a shelter 'of citadel standard' was constructed under Number 10, to hold up to six people, sufficient for the small numbers still using that building. It was into this shelter that Churchill would be encouraged to go by the Downing Street air-raid warden (often a Number 10 official) when the air-raid sirens sounded. Churchill would grumble endlessly as the muffled sound of bombs exploding in the distance could be heard overhead. Even George VI twice sought shelter here. A plaque in the Garden Rooms reads: 'In this room during the Second World War His Majesty the King was graciously pleased to dine on fourteen occasions with the Prime Minister, Mr Churchill . . . on two of these occasions the company was forced to withdraw into the neighbouring shelter by the air bombardment of the enemy.'

On the night of 20 February 1944, three bombs fell close by: on Horse Guards Parade, on the corner of Downing Street, and on the nearby Guards' memorial. Damage was caused to Number 10's windows, roof lights and internal walls and repairs were necessary in almost every room. Several doors had to be replaced – at a total cost of £2,000. Within months, flying bombs, first the V1s (or doodlebugs) and then the more powerful V2 rockets, began to land on the capital. Much misery and havoc was caused before, in the spring of 1945, the danger passed. Colville records on April 3rd, 'The PM spent the day at Number 10 – V bombs are apparently finished – for the first time since Christmas. It is a great deal pleasanter to work there than at the musty [Number 10] Annexe.'

By the end of May 1945, with war in Europe over, the transfer back from the Number 10 Annexe was almost complete. Colville wrote approvingly, 'Number 10 is being refurbished and made ready for constant use and we may soon be able to leave the dismal Number 10 Annexe for good.' In the intervening four and a half years, the Churchills did their best to make their bedroom, dining and

▼ A bomb crater on Horse Guards Parade, with Number 10 in the background **(below left)**.

Workmen scale the ladders to repair war-damaged windows **(below right)**.

T. 355/4

No. 586

PRIME MINISTER TO PRESIDENT ROOSEVELT   21 February, 1944.
Personal and Most Secret

Your No. 467 of 15 February.

1. Sir Samuel Hoare had already been instructed to give his fullest support to your Ambassador and I have now seen reports of the further representations made by our Ambassadors at Madrid.

These show that a settlement which I should myself regard as eminently satisfactory can now be reached on all points, if we act quickly. This settlement would include the complete cessation of Spanish wolfram exports to Germany for six months. If all goes as we hope, I do not think we need anticipate much difficulty in maintaining this position when the six months have elapsed.

The Foreign Secretary is telegraphing in greater detail to the State Department. I hope you will agree that we should immediately clinch matters on the above basis, which I am sure would represent a major political victory over the enemy.

2. We have just had a stick of bombs around 10, Downing Street and there are no more windows. Clemmie and I were at Chequers and luckily all the servants were in the shelter. Four persons killed outside.

THE CHARTWELL TRUST

Distribution:

The King
Foreign Secretary
Minister of Economic
    Warfare
Sir E. Bridges
General Ismay

For information:

War Cabinet
Lord Privy Seal.
Secretary of State for
    the Dominions
Minister of Aircraft
    Production
Service Ministers.

◄ A message from Prime Minister Churchill to US President Roosevelt, date 21 February 1944. The text refers to confidential war business, including war damage to Downing Street. The distribution list includes King George VI.

drawing rooms on the end of the Number 10 Annexe as cheerful as possible. When the National Labour politician and diarist Harold Nicolson visited in 1942, he wrote: 'They have made it very pretty with chintz and flowers and good furniture and excellent French pictures – not only the modernists, but Ingres and David.' In the Central War Rooms below, the progress of the war was plotted on large maps. This was where Churchill met the War Cabinet and senior military figures and planners. On being shown the underground Cabinet Room in May 1940, he had declared, 'this is the room from which I'll direct the war'. Even though the room never acquired that degree of centrality, he did use it extensively, yet remained essentially a peripatetic figure, who would work from several different locations: the Central War Rooms, the Number 10 Annexe, Number 10 itself, and at weekends at Chequers, the Prime Minister's country retreat, or – on weekends closest to the full moon when Chequers was most visible from the air and thus vulnerable to enemy bombs – at Ditchley Park in Oxfordshire.

Clementine Churchill spent much of the war parted from her husband; on 14 January 1943, she wrote to him (see left) in melancholy vein. Churchill hated being apart from her, but work kept his mind occupied. As he sped away for weekends or back to London on Monday mornings, or travelled around the country, he would take a secretary with him in his official Humber car. Secretaries recall the compartment at the back being heavy with cigar smoke as they wrestled to keep their hands steady to record the Prime Minister's words. Secretaries would also accompany him on his often perilous journeys abroad, to Washington, Tehran, Marrakesh and Yalta. Always there would be dictation: at any hour, in any situation, the girls had to be ready.

> 'My darling, The Annexe and Number 10 are dead and empty – Smoky [the Number 10 Annexe cat] wanders about disconsolate – I invite him into my room and he relieves his feelings by clawing my brocade bed cover and when gently rebuked, biting my toe through it.'
>
> CLEMENTINE CHURCHILL TO HER HUSBAND

Even Churchill's VE-Day broadcast, delivered from the Cabinet Room at 3 pm on Tuesday 8 May 1945, was dictated at the last minute, from his bed. He was in buoyant mood. At one point during the morning, he slipped out of bed to deliver champagne personally to officers in the War Rooms. The writing over, and fortified by lunch at the Palace with the King, he delivered his speech into the BBC microphone: 'The German war is at an end.' Ten weeks later, on 26 July 1945, after the general election yielded a Labour victory, he resigned. He left Number 10 at once, and moved into a suite of rooms at Claridge's Hotel.

EDEN AND SUEZ: 1956

If 1931 was a domestic financial crisis which became a political one, then 1956 was an international political crisis which sparked a domestic political one. Churchill retired, finally, in April 1955. As he sat up in bed – predictably – in the Number 10 flat on April 4th, his last night as Prime Minister, he said of his successor, 'I don't believe Anthony [Eden] can do it.'

Eden had considerable experience in foreign affairs, but did not enjoy an easy time in his first year as Prime Minister, with searching questions being asked about the quality of his leadership, particularly on the domestic front, where he had far less experience. Ironically, the issue which eventually undid him was a foreign one, and the fact that it came within his area of greatest experience made it all the more painful for him (see pages 86-7).

After the failure of his Suez operation, the Edens went to Jamaica for a three-week rest on 23 November 1956. Lady Eden was responsible for one of the better-known quotations about Number 10, when she said she felt the Suez Canal was flowing through her Drawing Room at Number 10. At the height of the crisis, on November 4th, when Downing Street was closed because of threats from angry

Eden and Suez 1956

The 'Suez Crisis', as it became known, in one sense began and ended for the Edens at Number 10. On 26 July 1956, while they were entertaining the King and the Prime Minister of Iraq in Soane's State Dining Room, a telegram was handed to Eden. The Suez Canal, a joint Anglo-French concession since 1888, had been seized by the Egyptian leader, President Abdul Nasser. Britain's authority was being blatantly challenged. How should he react?

He convened a meeting at Number 10 at 11 pm. His Press Secretary recorded, 'Eden made it absolutely clear that military action would have to be taken and that Nasser would have to go.' Over the next few weeks, key meetings were held in the Cabinet Room and in Eden's study. To do nothing was unthinkable: recollections of the 1930s appeasement came to mind. But what precise 'military' action could be taken, when the United Nations did not favour a military solution? In Number 10, unminuted discussions took place of a French plan, first aired at Chequers, for a 'secret' agreement with Israel: by prior understanding Israel was to invade Egypt, and Britain and France would then engage militarily in the role of 'peace-keepers' to separate the warring factions. Eden indicated to his Cabinet that he had some knowledge of the impending Israeli attack, but his words fell a long way short of revealing in full to the Cabinet the extent of British collusion in the scheme.

Eden appeals for support

On October 29th, Israeli radio announced that their army was advancing across the desert beyond the Egyptian frontier and the Suez Canal. An Anglo-French ultimatum to both countries to stop fighting and withdraw to within ten miles of the Canal was complied with by Israel, but not by Egypt. On October 31st, at

first light, British and French bombers began to attack Egyptian targets. The action was immediately criticised not just by the US President, Eisenhower, but by the Labour Leader Hugh Gaitskell, who moved a vote of censure in the House of Commons. The next morning, Cabinet debated whether to send in troops. On the evening of November 3rd, Eden spoke to the nation on BBC television, the first live television broadcast ever made from Number 10. He strove desperately to gain support for his government's actions, claiming that Britain only sought to separate the two armies, describing himself, in pained tones, as 'a man of peace, a League of Nations man, a United Nations man'. On November 5th at dawn, British and French troops were parachuted into Egypt near Port Said. But on November 6th, bereft of the support of the United States, and with much world, and domestic, opinion against him, and with a run on sterling, Eden called off the British action.

Anthony Eden and
Selwyn Lloyd during
the Suez crisis
(**left**). Anti-Suez
demonstration in
Whitehall (**right**).
Crowds keep a
watchful eye on
Downing Street
during the crisis
(**below**).

mobs, she wandered incognito up to Trafalgar Square to witness the anti-government rally. She was mortified to hear Labour's Aneurin Bevan proclaim, 'Either Mr Eden is lying or he is too stupid to be Prime Minster.' The Prime Minister, whose health had not been strong since a failed operation in 1953, was under great physical and psychological strain. When he returned to Number 10 in December, it was clear he lacked the stamina and health to continue and, on 9 January 1957, he went to Buckingham Palace to hand in his resignation. Harold Macmillan, his successor, recalls being summoned to Downing Street to be told of Eden's news. Rarely has the house seen so much concentrated unhappiness as that experienced by Anthony and Clarissa Eden in those months from July 1956 to January 1957.

> 'I could hardly believe that this was to be the end of the public life of a man so comparatively young, and with so much still to give. We sat for some little time together. We spoke few words about the First War, in which we had both served and suffered, and of how we had entered Parliament together at the same time . . . I can see him now on that sad winter afternoon, still looking so youthful, so gay, so debonair – the representation of all that was best of the youth that had served in the 1914-18 war.'
>
> HAROLD MACMILLAN ON ANTHONY EDEN'S RESIGNATION

THE IMF CRISIS: 1976

Number 10 became the focal point for another late autumn crisis exactly twenty years later, focusing again around a new Prime Minister who had also, only a short time before, been Foreign Secretary. This was an example of an economic crisis that threatened to but did not become a political crisis.

James Callaghan, who succeeded Wilson in April 1976, was told by Chancellor Denis Healey, after his first week at Number 10, that the need for a huge international loan, probably from the International Monetary Fund (IMF), might become inevitable. Rising inflation, unemployment, balance of payments difficulties, sterling problems and a large government deficit were all responsible. But Callaghan went into the summer break of 1976 feeling some relief. Between 6 and 21 July, he had worn down Cabinet opposition to cuts in government expenditure, thereby hoping to avoid recourse to foreign creditors; time was bought with a six-month £5.3bn standby credit, agreed in June with a consortium of banks, including the US Federal Reserve. On August 5th, the Callaghans left for their beloved farmhouse at Ringmer, Sussex, believing the cuts would satisfy the markets and that the threat of an economic crisis would disappear.

From June to August, the standby credit allowed the pound to be held at $1.77. But, in September, the pound slipped to a record low of $1.70, and reserves continued to flow out of London. The markets increasingly felt that the July cuts in expenditure were insufficient, and that further action was required. On September 9th, Callaghan and Healey told the Bank to stop supporting the pound once the standby credit was exhausted. With talk of the pound falling to $1.50 by the end of the month, it was decided to seek an IMF loan of £3.9bn, the largest sum ever sought from it. Callaghan delivered a combative speech at the Blackpool party conference, in which he spoke the seminal words for a Labour politician: 'We used to think that you could just spend your way out of a recession and increase employment by cutting taxes and boosting government spending. I tell you in all candour that that option no longer exists.' The speech went down badly with the Labour left, who held out against cuts in public spending.

In November, the IMF negotiating team came up with an initial proposal of a £3.9bn loan, provided cuts were made in the Public Sector Borrowing Requirement (PSBR). Callaghan used all his international contacts, including with US President Ford and Helmut Schmidt of Germany, as he tried desperately to find an alternative to the IMF loan and the stringent cuts in government deficit

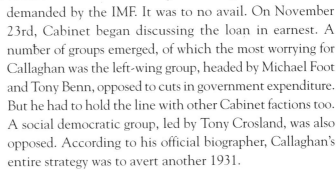

demanded by the IMF. It was to no avail. On November 23rd, Cabinet began discussing the loan in earnest. A number of groups emerged, of which the most worrying for Callaghan was the left-wing group, headed by Michael Foot and Tony Benn, opposed to cuts in government expenditure. But he had to hold the line with other Cabinet factions too. A social democratic group, led by Tony Crosland, was also opposed. According to his official biographer, Callaghan's entire strategy was to avert another 1931.

Callaghan worked night and day to bring the factions into agreement. On December 2nd, after a series of Cabinet discussions, Denis Healey told fellow Cabinet ministers with utter frankness that unless cuts were made in the government deficit, the IMF would not lend Britain the money, and that there was no hope of other borrowing abroad. Cabinet eventually agreed to cuts of £1bn, and a further £500m from the sale of BP shares. Further hard bargaining with the IMF to spread the cuts brought agreement, and Callaghan skilfully managed to bring Foot and Crosland into line. On December 15th, Healey announced to the House of Commons the terms of the IMF loan of £3.9bn; tension simmered below the surface, with Benn denouncing the statement that Cabinet had been united as a 'bloody lie'.

▲ James Callaghan's negotiation skills were tested to the extreme during the 1976 IMF crisis.

A crisis had been averted. The government remained united, and threatened resignations failed to transpire. The economy began to improve, and the government's standing to rise. But even though Callaghan had prevented a Labour split, a split did occur two years after Labour's election defeat in 1979, with the breakaway Social Democratic Party. Old Labour, Callaghan-style, was never to rule again. Indeed, Callaghan was to be the last old-style, trade union Labourite Prime Minister to occupy Number 10 in the twentieth century.

FIVE FORMER PMs AND A CURRENT ONE: 1985

Most Prime Ministers develop a deep affection for Number 10. Mrs Thatcher was no exception, and it was a real delight for her when she discovered that she would be in office on the 250th anniversary of Robert Walpole's move into Number 10, to establish it as the official First Lord's residence.

She conceived a great dinner in celebration, to which she invited not only the Queen and the Duke of Edinburgh, but all surviving Prime Ministers: Harold Macmillan (1957-63), Lord Home (1963-64), Harold Wilson (1964-70, 1974–76), Ted Heath (1970-74) and James Callaghan (1976-79). Also invited were the senior family members of all twentieth-century Prime Ministers since Asquith. Guests included Olwen Carey Evans, daughter of Lloyd George, Lady Lorna Howard, daughter of Stanley Baldwin, and Clarissa Avon (Eden). To Geoffrey Howe, then Foreign Secretary, it was a 'sparkling dinner occasion', while daughter Carol Thatcher, also a guest, described it as 'a magical evening'.

▲ Queen Elizabeth II with six Prime Ministers in the White Drawing Room, on 4 December 1985. From left to right are Callaghan, Home, Thatcher, Macmillan, Wilson and Heath. The official deputised to look after the Prime Ministers until the Queen's delayed arrival described the atmosphere as a little tense, as several of the Premiers were barely on speaking terms.

Dinner for the fifty guests was in the Soane State Dining Room. The special horseshoe-table was set up, and decorated with eight candelabra, as well as carnations and orchids. The Queen gave a speech in which she quipped that by this stage in her father's, George VI's, career, he had been to Number 10 far more often: 'I was beginning to wonder what I'd done wrong!' She continued: 'You may or may not be surprised to hear that as Queen of eighteen realms, and following the swearing-in the other day of a new Prime Minister in Papua New Guinea, I have now had ninety Prime Ministers.'

Rarely have there been six British Prime Ministers alive at any one time; never before in history had so many been present at Number 10 at the same time.

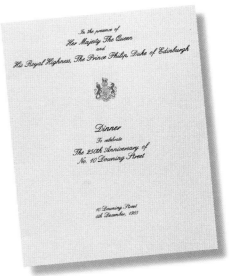

▲ An invitation to the 250th anniversary dinner.

Mortar Attack: 1991

Only once since the Second World War has Number 10 come under fire. Following their failure to kill Mrs Thatcher in 1984, in the attack at the Grand Hotel, Brighton, the IRA planned a further attempt. No matter that Mrs Thatcher was no longer Prime Minister. John Major, who succeeded her in November 1990, would be as good a victim in their strike at the heart of the British state. Such operations took months to plan, and the evidence suggests that the IRA conceived this attack as early as the mid-1980s.

On Thursday, 7 February 1991, at 10 am, a white Ford Transit van, bought in south London six months previously, was driven into and parked in Whitehall, close to Banqueting Hall. The van's roof had been removed and a platform built inside, on which rested three mortar tubes; temporary flimsy roofing had then been put back over on top. The driver parked the van at a carefully pre-arranged angle, and ran off to climb on the back of a waiting motor bike. The mortars were fired and the van burst into a ball of fire.

Only one mortar exploded, in the back garden of Downing Street, 12m/40ft from where Major was chairing a War Cabinet meeting to discuss the imminent Gulf War. After the explosion there was a moment's pause, and Charles Powell, a Private Secretary sitting on Major's right, grabbed Major by the shoulder and shoved him to the ground. When it became clear that no more mortars would explode, Major calmly announced, 'I think we'd better start again somewhere else.'

A crater 1.2m/4ft wide had been formed in the Number 10 gardens and a cherry tree had been blasted out of the ground; the bang could be heard twelve miles away. Number 10 in fact escaped the worst of the blast, while windows in Number 11 were blown in and offices in Number 12 were badly damaged. The two other mortars flew right over the top of the Downing Street houses and landed on a patch of grass in Horse Guards Parade, by the Foreign Office. The unexploded bombs emitted pungent black and brown smoke, and could have caused mayhem had they detonated. As it was, only four people were slightly hurt. Before continuing the meeting, Major was anxious to check that no one had been injured, especially the telephone operators at the top of Number 10, and some ministers phoned their wives to reassure them lest they heard the news first on radio or television. Discussions resumed in the underground Cabinet Office Briefing Room (known as COBRA). A meeting of the full Cabinet followed, not in Number 10 but in the Cabinet Office, the security services having by then ensured that all the nearby streets were safe. Long discussions took place on South Africa and cold weather payments. David Hunt recorded in his private diary, 'It's probably only in the United Kingdom that you get the Cabinet, an hour after a mortar bomb, discussing severe weather conditions in East Anglia and the South East of England!' Snow lay on the ground in central London, too; bitterly cold wind was sucked in through the shattered windows of Downing Street.

▲ A workman erects barbed wire to the rear wall of Number 10, following the IRA mortar attack.

The IRA had failed in their bid. One result was the further strengthening of Number 10, already a concrete stronghold following the rebuilding of the early 1960s. John Major, typically, bore no malice, and within a year was working hard to bring about a lasting peace in Northern Ireland, work which was to bear further fruit under Tony Blair after May 1997.

GARDEN TAKES CENTRE STAGE: 1995

The garden at Number 10 had never seen anything quite like it. At 4.30 pm on 22 June 1995, the country's senior media reporters waited in the garden, having been summoned to a press conference. No one knew why. Michael Brunson of ITN said, 'As we stood around waiting, one or two asked, " He couldn't possibly be going, could he?" The rest of us almost laughed them out of court, and said, "Good God, no, he wouldn't go that far. . ." What he said was a genuine bombshell.'

The bombshell was that, in a move unprecedented in history, a prime minister was to stand down as leader of his party and submit himself for re-election by his MPs. If he lost, one of the other contenders would become Prime Minister.

Major's move was prompted by his wish to bring support from Conservative MPs into the open, and put an end to the in-fighting that had dominated the party since 'Black Wednesday', when Britain came out of the Exchange Rate

Mechanism in September 1992. The press, too, including traditionally Tory newspapers, had been scathing about his leadership and were busy suggesting replacements. Flying back from a G7 summit in Halifax, Nova Scotia, on the night of 17-18 June 1995, Major finally decided he had had enough. He would put a gun to Tory MPs: they had, in his own words, either to 'back him or sack him'.

During party political periods, such as general election campaigns, Number 10 itself takes a low profile. The Number 10 officials are there to serve the Prime Minister in his capacity as head of government, not as head of his or her party. Alex Allan, the Principal Private Secretary at Number 10, liaised closely with Robert Fellowes, the Queen's Private Secretary, over the possible outcomes. Constitutionally, Major's move had created all kinds of uncertainties.

The headquarters of Major's re-election campaign thus became not Number 10, but a nearby private house in Cowley Street. The election was set for Tuesday, July 4th. Major was edgy that morning. His campaign team gave him their revised range of expectations: a vote for him of 205-215 would be a sufficient, if not overwhelming, margin for victory. He scarcely responded, his mind elsewhere. Major's spirits were not high when he was driven that afternoon from Number 10 to the Commons for Prime Minister's Questions. Being stuck behind a van in Whitehall and arriving late heightened the tension. Tony Blair attacked him over top people's salaries (a good subject to drive a wedge between Major and his right wing), and over the release of Private Clegg, a British soldier in prison for killing a Belfast joyrider. Major performed adequately, but did not sparkle, and he knew it.

Throughout the day, a fear that Major might quit even if he won the election began to spread among Tory MPs. He was lobbied hard throughout Tuesday

▶ John Major in the Number 10 garden, addressing the press at the famous news conference of 22 June 1995. ITN's Michael Brunson is second from left on the front row.

▶ John Major in the Number 10 garden with Cabinet Ministers on 6 July 1995. From left to right are John Gummer, Michael Heseltine, Gillian Shephard and Michael Portillo.

afternoon, by backbenchers, and by ministers, including his closest allies Lord Cranborne (his campaign manager) and Patrick Mayhew. Even Norma encouraged him to stay. Many MPs left notes on his desk in the Prime Minister's office in the House, imploring him not to abandon ship, whatever the margin of victory. At 4.30 pm, 30 minutes before the poll closed, Major cast his own vote in the Commons, where the party officials running the election oversaw the ballot papers, and he returned to Downing Street, deep in thought. A select group was invited to Number 10 to be with him when the news arrived. Cranborne had invited Mayhew, Douglas Hurd and Ian Lang – the 'tall men', as he called them – to join him to exert pressure lest Major had a last-minute change of heart when the results were announced, and decided to quit.

They assembled in the Cabinet Ante Room minutes before the 5 pm announcement. Major appeared, and Cranborne asked if he would prefer to hear the result in the upstairs flat alone with Norma. 'No, come on up,' he called from the Grand Staircase. Up they trooped to the second-floor flat, where Major fussed around the small sitting room, ensuring that everyone had a chair and a drink, while the tension continued to mount.

It was planned that when the party officials in the Commons had counted all the votes, Number 10 would be phoned so Major could prepare himself before any announcement was made to the media. Just after 5.10 pm, one of Major's Downing Street aides took the phone call from the Commons and wrote the numbers down slowly on a piece of paper; wordlessly, he showed them to Major. Major studied them for about ten seconds – it seemed an age to the campaign team who were waiting to hear – and then read them out: Major 218, Redwood 89, abstentions 20.

Jonathan Hill, Major's former Political Secretary, was studying his master: 'He didn't react at once. He didn't say, "That's it, we've exceeded my hurdle, I've won, fantastic." He didn't in fact show any positive pleasure at all. He was very quiet and thoughtful as he composed himself, and simply hugged Norma.'

Yet frantic activity was taking place among his supporters elsewhere when, at 5.20 pm, Marcus Fox, Chairman of the 1922 Committee of Tory backbenchers, announced the result in front of the cameras. 'It was clear it was not going to be the most overwhelming of victories, seeing he was an incumbent Prime Minister,' recalled Cranborne. 'So it was important we got people out there to say that it was convincing.' (The folklore about the November 1990 contest was that Mrs Thatcher lost the contest in the hours after the first ballot was declared, because insufficient positive 'spin' had been offered.)

Ian Lang had been busy during the day, preparing a table of numbers and victory margins, and how each could be spun. He also nominated people to approach the two big political editors, Robin Oakley (BBC) and Michael Brunson (ITN). 'It had to be a line that was plausible, that they would be willing to accept. We got a big roll of ministers and trusties out onto College Green [opposite Parliament] to approach other key media people too. It was bedlam but it worked.'

> 'Some days ago I called a leadership election and I did so in the knowledge that it would very likely be an election that was contested . . . We have now seen the verdict of the parliamentary party. It is a very clear-cut decision . . . I believe that has put to rest any question or any speculation about the leadership of the Conservative party up to and beyond the next election . . . the election is now over. The message that I would give to every Conservative . . . is that the time for division is over.'
>
> John Major, 4 July 1995

Norma Major thinks winning the leadership election probably gave her husband as much satisfaction as any single event during his premiership, though she added that he still had reservations: 'I don't know that he ever really is fully content.' Major was disappointed – he had hoped for 220 votes or more – but he had no intention of resigning. Within weeks, however, even the ultra-Tory *Daily Telegraph* had turned on Major. So, too, had his Tory MPs. As one of them said, 'The referee blew the whistle for the end of the "let's get Major" game, but the players just carried on playing.' Major survived another 22 months in Number 10, under fire from all sides. He had not been sacked, but neither was he now being backed. The garden press conference, which heralded the leadership election, had in fact settled little or nothing.

WALPOLE TO BALFOUR 1735-1902

We have looked so far at the history of the Number 10 building, and at some of the major events that have taken place within it. In the next three chapters, we explore how different First Lords have used the building, and discover what some of them thought of it. We begin with the house's first official incumbent, Robert Walpole.

► Prime Minister Arthur Balfour leaving Number 10 for a drive. Balfour had a passion for wheels, and was the first Premier to bring a car to Downing Street.

ROBERT WALPOLE: 1735-42

Walpole was almost sixty, and had been First Lord since 1721, when he entered Number 10 in 1735. A man of wealth, and a bon viveur, he enjoyed living in London's fashionable St James's Square, spending weekends at his hunting lodge at Richmond, and holidays at his estate in Houghton in Norfolk.

Walpole had many passions, one of which was redesigning his homes. He liked what William Kent, the celebrated architect of his day, had done for him at Houghton, and when George II offered him the house in Downing Street, he again called on Kent to advise on improvements. Perhaps he thought it too humble as it stood; we do not know.

The largest ground-floor room, on the north-west side of the house, was to be Walpole's study. Kent gave it long windows, looking out onto the garden and Horse Guards Parade beyond; French windows on the west side looked out over St James's Park. This room later became the Cabinet Room. The rooms adjoining his study on the west side he used as a dressing room and parlour. The two rooms next to his study on the north side were used as a deputation room and parlour. Upstairs, the Walpoles lived in the rooms facing north onto Horse Guards Parade. Lady Walpole's bedroom was on the east (Whitehall) corner, the dining room was in the middle, and the room on the opposite corner, overlooking St James's Park (now the White Drawing Room) became Lady Walpole's drawing room. The walls were covered in brocade, as they were at Houghton.

Within a week of their arrival, they were busy entertaining illustrious guests: Queen Caroline, wife of George II and a close friend of Walpole, the princesses and leading courtiers breakfasted with the Walpoles and their three children – Lord Walpole, Edward and Horace. On offer were sweetmeats, choice fruits, wines, tea and chocolate. The Queen seems to have enjoyed the fare and she left 'a handsome sum to be distributed among the servants'.

Walpole was a lavish entertainer, and during his seven-year tenure a steady stream of politicians, writers and soldiers came through the house and up Kent's elegant staircase to the drawing room on the first floor. His youngest son, Horace, also enjoyed bringing friends to the house, including the poet Thomas Gray. After Eton and King's College, Cambridge, Horace went on to become a distinguished writer.

Little is known about Walpole's working day, but when tension became too much in meetings, he would rise abruptly from the table and declare, 'nobody was fit for business once they had lost control!' Nor do we know in which room

The said Emanuel Boltz has besides the Loss of his All, suffer'd very much by the blind Zeal of the Roman Clergy, in using him very barbarously, so that his Health is very much impair'd, and putting him into Prison afterwards, out of which he made his Escape.

Yesterday the Right Hon. Sir Robert Walpole, with his Lady and Family removed from their House in St. James's Square, to his new House adjoining to the Treasury in St. James's Park.

Last Sunday the Duke of Somerset set out for his Seat at Petworth in Sussex, with a numerous Retinue.

We hear, that a Treaty of Marriage is on foot, and will soon be concluded between the Right Hon. the Lord Gray, Son and Heir Apparent to the Right Hon. Harry Earl of

▲ The *London Daily Post* announces the Walpoles' arrival at Number 10 on 23 September 1735.

◄ Robert Walpole addressing his ministers, by Joseph Goupy. The location is uncertain, but appears to be inside Number 10.

he slept, but it is known that he became estranged from his wife and took a succession of lovers. One, Maria Skerett, would come openly to Number 10. Within a year of Lady Walpole dying in 1737, Walpole had married Maria. Sadly, she died of a miscarriage three months later, but further mistresses soon followed.

Walpole's blood pressure must have risen in 1741 when, aged sixty-five, he had to fight off a censure motion attacking his leadership. Horace noted the change that came over his father's sleeping habits: 'He who was asleep as soon as his head touched the pillow, for I have frequently known him snore ere they had drawn his curtains, now never sleeps above an hour without waking.' Walpole resigned in February 1742 after further turbulence in the House of Commons, and moved out of Number 10 later that year. In March 1745, his long and flamboyant life came to an end, a stone having lacerated his bladder.

GEORGE GRENVILLE: 1763-65
LORD NORTH: 1767-1782

Walpole's wish that subsequent First Lords live at Number 10 was not at first followed. Prime Ministers Henry Pelham (1743-54) and the Duke of Newcastle (1754-56 and 1757-62) lived in their own residences elsewhere. Not until April 1763, when George Grenville became Prime Minister, was the house again occupied by a premier. A single-minded figure, according to Edmund Burke, 'He took public business not as a duty he was to fulfil but as a pleasure he was to enjoy.' Perhaps he sought distraction from his large young family, the oldest only thirteen when he moved into Number 10. But the children scarcely had time to find their bearings in the rambling house before George III dismissed their father in July 1765. The King blamed him for insensitive handling of the North American colonists, and for the imposition on them of the unpopular Stamp Duty.

Lord North lived at Number 10 for three years as Chancellor of the Exchequer (1767-70) and a further twelve years as First Lord (1770-82). He

▲ Furniture made especially for Clive of India, one of Lord North's regular guests, is located in the first-floor Ante Room.

became extremely fond of the house, especially the large north-west corner study where he held his meetings, and his first-floor bedroom immediately above it. A home-loving figure, he often spent evenings alone in the first-floor drawing room, reading or playing chess with his wife, on whom he doted. He was neither a gambler nor a womaniser. When whist was played, the stakes, history recalls, were always 'very small'. He seems to have left little mark on the fabric of the house.

The writer Samuel Johnson was one of the celebrated visitors to North's Number 10. Not that the servants were always pleased to see him; he would growl and grunt as he walked in, 'always dressed in untidy, filthy garments, his shoes caked with mud and looking like a scarecrow'. Clive of India was another frequent visitor, but a civilised one: furniture made for him (see above) is found today in the first-floor Ante and Green Drawing Rooms. Mr Hansard was another of North's friends. In 1774, while North was Premier, Hansard began to publish his journal of the House of Commons, and in 1803 his printed Parliamentary Debates began to appear on a regular basis.

Lord North's premiership was dominated by the problem of the disaffected North American colonies. After several years of rising discontent, culminating in the first shots being fired at Lexington in 1775, the colonies signed the Declaration of Independence in 1776. The surrender of the British forces, under Burgoyne at Saratoga, in 1777, resulted in criticism of North's leadership reaching new heights, and during the war's duration (1775-83), he became an increasingly isolated and ineffectual figure. The hapless North confessed that he found taking decisions in the Cabinet Room very difficult and spent much of the war alone at Number 10 with his wife, neglecting affairs of state, caught up in a pool of self pity. As the war dragged on and American markets were lost, crowds converged on Downing Street, booing him on his rare appearances. The Gordon riots of June 1780, in protest over concessions to Catholics, further undermined his position. In October 1781, Lord Cornwallis's troops finally surrendered to the Americans at Yorktown, bringing to an end all hope of retaining the American colonies as part of the British Empire. The news of the loss arrived at Falmouth in Cornwall, from where it was rapidly transmitted to London. It was brought to North in late November. According to a contemporary account, he received the news 'as he would have taken a bullet in the breast'. He 'opened his arms, exclaiming wildly, as he paced up and down the apartment during a few minutes. "Oh God! It is all over," he said over and over again.'

North's fate was sealed. George III, who had encouraged him to stay in office for too long, eventually accepted his resignation in March 1782. North saw the King, announced the news to the House of Commons the same day, then, according to the records, drove off to Number 10 through the snow for dinner with some friends, at which he seemed 'calm' and 'cheerful'.

WILLIAM PITT: 1782-1806

Shortly after Lord North resigned, William Pitt ('the Younger') wrote to his mother: 'Lord North will, I hope, in a very little time make room for me in Downing Street, which is the best summer town home possible.' But North was reluctant to leave the house in which he had lived for 15 years. Pitt wrote again to his mother two weeks later (opposite).

> 'I expect to be comfortably settled in the course of this week, in a part of my vast, awkward house.'
>
> WILLIAM PITT

Pitt was the son of Lord Chatham ('Pitt the Elder', Prime Minister in the 1760s), and had been elected to Parliament in 1780, at the age of twenty-one. Two years later, he was appointed Chancellor of the Exchequer, and was anxious to move into his official abode in Downing Street. It is unclear how much of Number 10 Pitt lived in as Chancellor in 1782–83, but for a few months in 1783 the house was occupied by the Duke of Portland, a brief but important premiership, before Pitt succeeded him that December. At the age of twenty-four, Pitt became Britain's youngest ever Prime Minister.

The condition of Number 10 had been causing increasing concern during North's tenure. The foundations were the major problem; they were only

1.2-1.8m/4-6ft deep, built on wooden slabs which had become rotten as water drained across into the River Thames. Repairs and shoring up work had been in progress since 1766 and in 1782, the Board of Works (the government department responsible for looking after Number 10) were faced with a bill of £11,078, ten times the estimate for repairs in 1766.

Not all of this amount was for repairs: at this time, the architect Robert Taylor extended both the study (now the Cabinet Room) and the north-east drawing room (now the Pillared Room), and built the great vaulted kitchen and several comfortable 'lodging rooms'. Pitt now had a dwelling to be proud of, and one which was well on its way to becoming, in terms of cost per square metre, the most expensive house in London. The press were not amused by the cost – a leitmotif throughout the years, whenever repairs have been undertaken at Number 10.

Pitt was to live in his grand home, now no doubt less 'awkward', for 24 years. He was to make it more his home than any other Prime Minister after him, according to one commentator. In Pitt's time, the cul-de-sac stretched around the west end of Downing Street, and Number 10 was the only official house in a road otherwise occupied by private dwellings.

How Pitt used the rooms in Number 10 is not fully known, though he appears to have met with his ministers in the ground-floor Cabinet Room of today, and to have lived and slept in rooms at the back of the house. Here, he planned some of his great projects, including Parliamentary reform, free trade and the improvement of national finances, and worked on the administration of India, Canada and Australia, which, unlike the United States, all became embryonic parts of the British Empire. More is known of his lifestyle. He had 27 servants, whose wages amounted to £321 a year. A keen entertainer and a heavy imbiber of port, he ran up huge bills. Pitt's visitors to Number 10 included William Wilberforce, who was working on the abolition of slavery, and George Canning, the future Foreign Secretary and Prime Minister. Aged only 21, Canning had asked Pitt if he could come and meet him; writing of their encounter in August 1792 to a friend at Oxford, he described 'being ushered into that study [almost certainly the current Cabinet Room] in which so many great statesmen and great scoundrels have at different times planned their country's ruin and the advancement of their own futures'. At Number 10, in September 1786, Pitt underwent an operation for the removal of a facial cyst. According to his biographer, John Ehrman, 'Pitt showed a sang froid equal to the standards of a pre-anaesthetic age. He would not allow [the surgeon] to tie his hands as was normally done, assured him that he would not move, and asked how long [it] would take.' The operation over, Pitt chastised the surgeon for exceeding his allotted time of six minutes by thirty seconds. The same month, his devoted sister Harriot, who had worked so hard to keep the house in order, died at Number 10, following childbirth.

> *'So much has this extraordinary edifice cost the country – for one moiety [fraction] of which sum a much better dwelling might have been purchased.'*
>
> THE 'MORNING HERALD'

▶ George Romney's portrait of Pitt the Younger, c. 1783, which has hung in the Pillared Drawing Room.

On 27 May 1798, Pitt put his own life at risk in a duel with a man whom he had offended. He made his will, left it in Number 10, and went out early in the afternoon to St James's Park from where he took a chaise to Putney Heath. Two shots were fired; both missed, and Pitt returned to central London and his dinner. He displayed a similar indifference to danger when Number 10 was besieged and several windows were broken by crowds protesting at the high cost of food. Pitt wrote to his mother to allay her fears which had been raised by lurid press stories: 'A mob is magnified by report; but that which visited my window with a single pebble was really so young and little versed in its business, that it hardly merited the notice of a newspaper.' Pitt resigned in February 1801, after falling out with George III over Catholic emancipation, but was back in Number 10 as Prime Minister in May 1804, at a time when Napoleon was threatening to invade Britain.

During his latter years in Number 10, he was joined by his lively niece, Lady Hester Stanhope, who brought back the cheer to the house that his sister, Harriot, had provided during her brief sojourn. Hester was a free-living character; sitting opposite Pitt at table, playing the hostess from the outset, she could be intolerant, opinionated and rude to guests, including even the Prince of Wales. Hester brought crowds to Number 10, but also drama, ridicule and debts.

Pitt's official life fared little better in his last two years at Number 10. Never as comfortable with foreign affairs as with domestic policy, he tried and failed to build an international coalition against Napoleon. Victory at the battle of Trafalgar in 1805 brought some relief, but he was deeply upset to learn of the death of Nelson during the sea battle, and spent a sleepless night pacing his bedroom at Number 10. His consumption of port increased to four bottles a day. Illness, no doubt related to alcohol abuse, took him to Bath for the waters, but the shattering news of Napoleon's victory at Austerlitz necessitated a quick return to London. He was taken ill on the outskirts of the city and managed to get only as far as his home in Putney, where he died, aged forty-six, on 23 January 1806. Hester records how, 'the carriages had been waiting at the door, ready for a long time,' to take him back to Downing Street. On his death, Hester's brother James took Pitt's Number 10 keys (in those days, Prime Ministers had their own) and went to Downing Street where he 'sealed up everything' and locked the front door.

LORD GRENVILLE: 1806-7

Pitt's 20-year tenure was followed by a Prime Minister who was his cousin, and much saddened by his death. Lord Grenville lived in the house for just a year, after insisting that it be refurbished after Pitt's rather slummy domestic arrangements. We know that he held audiences between 11 am and 3 pm, and responded in the evenings to his mail bag of 60 letters a week. Otherwise, little is known of his use of Number 10. His character was oblique: in 1807, Lord Liverpool wrote of him that 'he has no feelings for anyone,' yet Grenville lost his reserve with close family: he began letters to his wife, 'My dearest Angel'. Even two hundred years ago, incumbents of Number 10 had to mask their inner feelings.

SPENCER PERCEVAL: 1807-1812

Lord Grenville's successor, Spencer Perceval, came to Number 10 in a hurry and left in a coffin, the only one of 50 prime ministers to be assassinated. An admirer of his patron, Pitt, he first entered Number 10 in 1807 as Chancellor of the Exchequer. Perceval was a man of high moral principle and an active Anglican, who lent his support to Wilberforce and the anti-slavery campaign. A devoted husband and father, he neither gambled nor drank. Appointed Prime Minister in October 1809, he coupled his job as Premier with that of Chancellor of the Exchequer. It was a precarious prime ministership. The Napoleonic Wars

continued to be a heavy drain on the Exchequer, while the difficulty of forming a stable administration at Westminster created continuing problems. But Perceval successfully oversaw the passing of the Regency Bill in February 1811, making the Prince of Wales Prince Regent on account of the growing mental instability of the king, George III, then in his fifty-second year on the throne. The accomplishment was all the greater as the Prince had to accept tighter restrictions on his powers as Regent than he would have liked.

Number 10 was once again a family home. With the Prime Minister's six daughters and six sons in residence, every spare room was occupied. The ground floor was used for Cabinet meetings and office space, while the first floor was devoted to official entertaining, and housed the Prime Minister's and his wife's bedrooms. The children seem to have been secreted away in nurseries and bedrooms on the second floor, while the cooks, chambermaids, governesses and other servants must have slept in the basement rooms. Perceval himself would rise early, eat his breakfast alone, and then begin the day's work. His evening

▲ The assassination of Spencer Perceval, 1812. His body was returned to Number 10, where it remained for five days.

meal consisted of a single course, after which he would return to work in his ground-floor study, continuing often until the early hours of the morning.

As father to so many young children, the events of 11 May 1812 were particularly tragic. Entering the lobby in the House of Commons at 5.15 pm to listen to a debate, he was approached by a man who, according to *The Times*, 'had a short time previously placed himself in the recess of the doorway within the Lobby. [He] drew out a small pistol and shot Mr Perceval in the lower part of the left breast.' Perceval staggered forward, and collapsed into the arms of fellow MPs, dying shortly afterwards. The assassin, John Bellingham, had been imprisoned for five years in Archangel, and had been obsessed with Perceval's failure to secure his release. Bellingham later said he had written to the Prime Minister, but, as he did not receive a satisfactory answer, had decided to shoot him – a grave warning to future prime ministers to be attentive to their postbags. Perceval's body was taken back to Number 10, where it remained for five days before being buried in the family vault in Charlton, Kent. Little is known of how his family received the news, but the government did ensure that they would be looked after regally: Perceval's widow received a grant of £50,000 and an annuity of £2,000.

SHADOWY PRESENCES: 1812-28

Within a month of Perceval's death, Lord Liverpool had become Prime Minister, a position he held for 15 years, until 1827. Liverpool chose not to live at Number 10, preferring instead his father's Whitehall dwelling, Fife House. Fife House was also used for government business, and Liverpool's secretaries worked there. Number 10 was instead assigned to his Chancellor, the obscure Robert Vansittart, who lived there until 1823 when 'Prosperity' Robinson took over the house – as Chancellor of the Exchequer. These years saw the Battle of Waterloo and the conclusion of the Napoleonic Wars in 1815, the death of George III in 1820, and, from 1825, Soane's construction of the two oak-panelled Dining Rooms.

On Lord Liverpool's resignation, George Canning became Prime Minister in April 1827. Aged fifty-seven, he was ill for all of his four months at Number 10. When he moved in, with his devoted wife Joan and their two youngest sons, he was already suffering from acute rheumatism, as well as a severe cold caught at the Duke of York's funeral. Canning was a man with a brilliant mind, thought by some to be too clever by half. He certainly had some highly creative friends: Walter Scott, the novelist, was particularly close, and they spent part of the summer of 1825 together in the Lake District, where they met the poets William Wordsworth and Richard Southey. The four rode together during the day and paddled in the lake by moonlight. In July, suffering from gout and his continuing cold, Canning decided to stay with the Duke of Devonshire in Chiswick, west London, where he died on August 8th. His body was taken back to Number 10, and from there to the funeral at Westminster Abbey. He was buried at the feet of his mentor, Pitt the Younger.

Robinson, who had become Lord Goderich, took over but remained for only four months. He did not enjoy the stress of the premiership, and in January 1828 went to see King George IV, to offer his resignation. He burst into tears and the King promptly offered him his handkerchief.

LORD WELLINGTON: 1828-30

Lord Wellington took over as Prime Minister, arriving at Number 10 on his horse, Copenhagen. He was, however, displeased by the cheering crowds, seeing their exuberance as an expression of mob feeling. Commander-in-Chief of the Allied Armies at the end of the Napoleonic War, and the victor of the Battle of Waterloo in June 1815, Wellington is unique in British history – a military hero who became national leader. Wellington was a man of immense wealth. He had bought Apsley House, a mansion in Hyde Park, from his brother with the money presented to him after Waterloo by 'a grateful nation'. Like others before and after him, he saw little need to abandon the splendour of his town house for the comparatively small Number 10. But Apsley House had to undergo repairs, so he had no option but to avail himself of his free residence.

Wellington's name was to be perpetuated in a variety of ways, including a style of boot, a dish of beef in a pastry crust, a great public school, Wellington College, 30 public houses in London alone, the capital city of New Zealand, a famous regiment, while his greatest military battle was chosen as the name of London's largest railway station, Waterloo. But Wellington was never wholly at ease in the combative world of party politics. He introduced the Catholic Emancipation Act in 1829, an overdue and significant achievement, but came up against economic unrest following the bad winter of 1829-30, and the widespread tension that followed the death in 1830 of George IV. He remained a highly principled, dedicated and hard-working, if not hugely bright, premier, attending to his large correspondence with almost excessive zeal, reading and answering each letter personally and working late into the night in his study. For light relief, he would organise races along the corridors of Number 10: ladies would sit on rugs, whips in hand, and be pulled by male guests with harnesses. When, in January 1830, the renovation of Apsley House was completed, he moved back, but continued to work in the Number 10 study, riding home each night. He lent Number 10's residential rooms upstairs to his old friend and colleague, Earl Bathurst. The tide of opinion turned against Wellington during 1830 and, on November 15, he was defeated on a vote in the Commons, causing the government to fall. Dining at Apsley House when the news came through, his recorded comment was: 'Do not tell the women.' He resigned the next day.

> 'Part of the furniture of the Duke of Wellington's residence in Piccadilly was begun to be removed to the house in Downing Street belonging to His Grace as First Lord of the Treasury, which His Grace, it is expected, will occupy during the time that Apsley House is undergoing repair.'
>
> 'THE TIMES' APRIL 1828

GREY, MELBOURNE, PEEL: 1830-46

Earl Grey, Leader of the Whigs, moved into Number 10 as Prime Minister almost immediately. His achievements were numerous: the passage of the Great Reform Act in 1832, which extended the franchise, ended 'rotten boroughs', and laid the foundation for 'modern' political parties; a Factory Act and a Poor Law Act and the final abolition of slavery, passed by Parliament just a month after Wilberforce's death.

Very tall, and said to be the most handsome man in Europe, Grey was sixty-six when he moved into Number 10 with three of his fourteen children. Grey's Number 10 was busy with frequent entertainment: Talleyrand, Napoleon's Foreign Secretary and then French Ambassador to London, was a visitor, as was Lord Palmerston, the great War and Foreign Minister. Soane's new Dining Rooms no doubt provided a splendid backdrop for the high living. When Parliament was not sitting, Grey took every opportunity to spend time at his house, Howick Hall in Northumberland, to which he was very attached.

A new round of urgent repair work forced the Greys out of Downing Street for three months in late 1832. The cost came to £1,247, a figure that did not include the new curtains and furniture Lady Grey was keen to install. The latter caught the eye of the Whig MP, diarist and letter-writer Thomas Creevey, who was impressed with the bright, new look (above).

Few premiers leave Number 10 at a time of their own choosing. Grey did. At the age of seventy, and with the Reform Act and other legislation passed, Grey resigned. The Whig Lord Melbourne succeeded Grey as Premier from 1834-41 (with a break for six months in the first year). Not a man with strong reforming zeal, his was an unremarkable premiership, best known perhaps for his seeing in the new monarch, Queen Victoria, following the death of William IV in 1837. Melbourne and the Queen formed a remarkable relationship: 'He alone inspires me with that feeling of great confidence and I may say security, for I feel so safe when he speaks to me and is with me,' the Queen confided in her journal.

Not all were as impressed. Lady Lyttelton, noting Melbourne's fondness for food and wine, wrote that nothing would remove him from the premiership, 'unless he

> *'I might as well say a word of the new furniture in Downing Street at Earl Grey's, everything therein being all spick and span new. The two principal Drawing Rooms opening into each other are papered with a pattern . . . a large gold rose or flower of some kind . . . The curtains are yellow silk . . . and gay and handsome as possible.'*
>
> THOMAS CREEVEY

▲ The Number 10 kitchen as it looked in 1827, when Melbourne was First Lord.

contrives to displace himself by dint of consommés, truffles, pears, ices and anchovies, which he does his best to revolutionise his stomach with every day'.

Although Melbourne clearly adored good food, he had an obsessive hatred of smoking: 'I always have a great row about it. If I smell tobacco, I swear perhaps for half an hour.' Melbourne showed no inclination to move into Downing Street, choosing to remain in his own more comfortable house in nearby South Street. Perhaps the cooking was better. Yet Cabinet meetings probably continued to be held at Number 10, and the adjacent rooms were used by two secretaries, who also had bedrooms upstairs. Melbourne would ride periodically to Number 10, and then onward to the House of Commons, which from 1840 met in the great medieval Westminster Hall, while the Houses of Parliament were rebuilt to a design by Charles Barry, following the fire of 1834. This massive undertaking took 20 years to complete. Melbourne was one of the first premiers to benefit from the great Victorian advance, the railway train, which shrunk the British Isles and made travel both much easier and quicker.

Tory Robert Peel succeeded Melbourne in August 1841. Like his predecessor, he preferred his own house at 4 Whitehall Gardens to Number 10, a quarter of a mile away and near the river. Peel's secretary, Edward Drummond, replaced Melbourne's secretaries at Number 10 from early 1842. Drummond's tenure was brief: walking along Whitehall en route to Number 10 he was shot dead by a half-crazed Irishman who mistook him for Peel. Had the assassin done his detection work better, the subsequent history of the Tory party might have been very different; for Peel was unable to unify his party over the repeal of the Corn Laws in 1846, and the party split, remaining out of office for a generation.

Peel seems to have had no special interest in Number 10, but there is some evidence that he used the building for work and for Cabinet meetings. On 25 June 1846, he wrote a letter to Queen Victoria from Downing Street, marked 'two o'clock' (in the morning). The day before had seen heated Cabinet discussions over the Corn Law divisions, and ministers decided that the government could not continue. On June 29th, Peel went to the Queen's country residence, Osborne House on the Isle of Wight, to tender his resignation in person.

RUSSELL, DERBY, ABERDEEN, PALMERSTON: 1846-1868

Peel's resignation in 1846 was followed, as far as we can tell, by a 30-year period when the residential rooms in Number 10 were unused. Lord John Russell was installed as Liberal Prime Minister with the help of Peel's supporters from the Tory party; his position was strengthened by the 1847 general election, but he continued to lack an overall majority and his government had the air of being reactive. The severe famine in Ireland of 1846-48 hit Russell's position hard, the failure of the potato harvest resulting in the deaths of a million people, and Russell was criticised for not securing sufficient funds to alleviate the disaster.

Russell held Cabinet meetings in the Cabinet Room, and the offices on either side were used by secretaries. One of these, Colonel Keppel, lived upstairs until 1847. Russell himself lived at Pembroke Lodge in Richmond, Surrey, a house offered to the Russells by Queen Victoria. The Cabinet Room saw angry scenes between Russell and his combative Foreign Secretary, Lord Palmerston, whose unilateral decision to approve of Napoleon's *coup d'état* in Paris led to his dismissal by Russell in December 1851. Palmerston had his revenge when he helped bring down Russell's government in February 1852.

The Earl of Derby, the new Prime Minister, chose to stay in his house in St James's Square and his successor, the Earl of Aberdeen, also lived at home, at 7 Argyll Street. The start of the Crimean War with Russia in March 1854 undid Aberdeen: he was criticised for failing to conduct the war efficiently, and in January 1855 was replaced by the domineering figure of Palmerston, now aged seventy-one.

Palmerston's first letter as Prime Minister was written to his brother: 'here I am writing to you from Downing Street as First Lord of the Treasury.' Palmerston continued the trend of using Number 10 as an office and for Cabinet meetings,

▼ The Derby Cabinet of 1867, with Disraeli fifth from left (standing). The fireplace is clearly visible in the background. The bookcases were removed later in the century, and now remain only at the east end of the room.

but living elsewhere. One of his biographers, however, writes puzzlingly that during his research he had analysed 25,000 letters and 'in all the documents I read there was no mention at all of 10 Downing Street'. During the week, when Parliament was sitting, Palmerston stayed at his palatial home in Piccadilly which he had bought from the Duke of Cambridge in 1850 (it later became the Naval and Military Club). He would walk (or ride) to Westminster or Whitehall across Green Park and St James's Park, probably unescorted. At weekends, he went to Broadlands in Hampshire (which later became the home of Lord Mountbatten of Burma). Palmerston was the commanding political figure of the mid-nineteenth century: his achievements included the successful conclusion of the Crimean War in 1856 and the foundation in 1859 of the modern Liberal party.

Like many premiers who used Number 10, he wanted to make 'improvements'. Having sat in the Cabinet under ten different prime ministers, he had ample personal experience supporting his request to have larger windows built in the Cabinet Room. This request involved him in a difference with the Office of Works. An internal memo of 3 September 1859 records how Palmerston's Private Secretary had complained 'that the alteration in the Cabinet Room' was 'being made with single windows'. He says that Lord Palmerston 'determined to have them double'.

Palmerston wrote from Broadlands on September 7th to the Office of Works to back up his suit. He had his way, and Parliament voted an extra £10 for the larger windows (a sum that contrasts with the £100,000 it had voted the month before for the massive new Foreign Office building facing Number 10). The ground floor of Number 10 seems to have been a busy, chaotic place even during the 1850s and 1860s; why the large rooms upstairs were not used as a spillover (it certainly appears they were not) remains a mystery. Ministers strode in through the Downing Street door, walked down the corridor and hung up their coats in the Ante Room before entering the Cabinet Room. The Prime Minister would work with his back to the fire, looking out on the garden – by now a less cluttered view, as stabling for the horses had moved from Horse Guards Parade to College Mews, near Westminster Abbey. Fireplaces in Number 10 were far more than decorative: they were the only source of heat, and remained so until later in the century.

> 'The Cabinet Room is dark and in winter cold: by opening two windows it will be made light, but unless the windows are double, the Room will be much colder.'
>
> LORD PALMERSTON

DISRAELI: 1868, 1874-80

Benjamin Disraeli was no stranger to Downing Street: as Chancellor of the Exchequer he had earlier worked from Number 11, writing at the end of each day to Queen Victoria about the events in Parliament, and thus beginning their long period of mutual admiration. When he first became Tory Prime Minister, from February to December 1868, he moved his office across from Number 11 to

Number 10. He was not overly enchanted by what he found, and described it as 'dingy and decaying'. Disraeli chose to live elsewhere, only moving, with reluctance, from 2 Whitehall Gardens into Number 10 in November 1877, in order to avoid 'my terribly steep Whitehall stairs which I cannot manage'. His health and lack of energy were by then giving problems: he was afflicted by gout, rheumatism and asthma, and he spent his last years (he died in 1881) almost perpetually unwell. By the time he was appointed Prime Minister for his second spell in February 1874, he was sixty-nine, and had lost the vigour of his earlier career, when he had earned a reputation for unrivalled brilliance and debating skill. Disillusionment rapidly set in with his lack of direction.

Disraeli grew to rely heavily on his Private Secretary, Montague Corry. One of his Cabinet Ministers wrote of Disraeli: 'He detests details . . . He does no work . . . Montague Corry is in fact the Prime Minister.' These disparaging comments were fairer of Disraeli's contribution to domestic than to foreign policy, where he pulled off several coups, notably the buying of shares in the Suez Canal from the bankrupt ruler of Egypt in 1875. His successful chairmanship of the Congress of Berlin in 1878, which ended the Russo-Turkish War, was another high point. He returned in triumph by train to Charing Cross from the channel ports; great banks of flowers greeted him at the station and Downing Street itself was hung with scarlet. Disraeli spoke of having achieved 'a peace, I hope, with honour'.

> 'From all his speeches I had quite expected that his mind was full of legislative schemes, but such did not prove to be the case; on the contrary he had to rely entirely on the suggestions of his colleagues.'
>
> RICHARD CROSS, HOME SECRETARY

▼ A bust of Disraeli, by J Adams Acton, which is located in the Cabinet Ante Room.

Disraeli's reluctant move into Number 10 in 1877 might have spared him the stairs of Whitehall Gardens, but the residential rooms were in a shocking state of repair after 30 years out of commission. He must have known what he was letting himself in for, since he had used the offices and Cabinet Room from the start of his premiership, though the print of Disraeli, with his back to the fire (opposite), chairing the Cabinet Council in January 1877, shows the Cabinet Room in a good state of repair. After a prolonged battle with the Treasury, it was agreed that the state should pay for renovation to the entrance halls, the staircase and the first-floor rooms used for public occasions, but that Disraeli himself must pay for the rooms that were for his private use. The Middle and Pillared Drawing Rooms received silk curtains and upholstery, new fine rugs and carpets, and a number of tables. No expense was spared: two large silk-covered sofas cost £106.10s.0d, while an Axminster Persian carpet set the state back £140. Disraeli's own first-floor bedroom and dressing room were improved, and a 'bath with hot and cold water in the First Lord's Dressing Room' was put in for £150. 3s. 6d. Yet the hot water, it would appear, did little to improve Disraeli's rheumatism, or his humour.

▶ Disraeli (back to fire, leaning forward) presides over an 1877 Cabinet meeting.

WILLIAM GLADSTONE 1868-74, 1880-85, 1886, 1892-94

Four times Liberal Premier, Gladstone chose to live at the grand 11 Carlton House Terrace during his first, longest and arguably most successful period of office, 1868-74. But, as was the custom, he used Number 10 for work and for Cabinet. His first Private Secretary, Algernon West, would work from the 'little room, looking to the west' (i.e. one of the rooms to the left of the Cabinet Ante Room). Here, West would have breakfast brought to him, 'and by eleven o'clock had succeeded in analysing the correspondence'. On becoming Prime Minister for the second time, in April 1880, Gladstone occupied both Numbers 10 and 11 (he combined the premiership with being Chancellor of the Exchequer for the first two years). In his diary, Gladstone notes that he moved back into Number 10 before midnight on 12 May 1880, finding it 'a wilderness and a chaos'. His biographers offer little explanation for his decision to live in Downing Street, though Roy Jenkins (see left) suggests an economic motive.

Gladstone clearly missed the splendour of the former dwelling, and thought little of Disraeli's taste in furnishing; within weeks of arriving he was pressing for new furniture. He had his way, at an extraordinary cost of £1,555.5s.0d.

'In the mid 1870s, he decided he had become poor, sold Carlton House Terrace and acquired 73 Harley Street, which he did not like nearly as much; for his last three governments he therefore occupied Number 10.'

ROY JENKINS

▶ Gladstone (middle right, leaning forward) chairs a Cabinet council. Most premiers have preferred to chair meetings from the other side of the table, in front of the fire.

During his second administration, 1880-85, we know from his Private Secretary, Edward Hamilton, that Gladstone rarely slept beyond 9 am and would spend the time until 11 am reading; he was a great consumer of literature. Meetings and paperwork would take up the time until lunch, and afternoons and early evenings were spent in the House of Commons.

Gladstone's first administration had seen much reform, including the disestablishment of the Irish Church and the 1870 Education Act, which introduced public elementary education, but his second government was dogged by misfortune. On 6 May 1882, the Irish Secretary Lord Frederick Cavendish and the senior Irish Office civil servant were stabbed to death by terrorists in Phoenix Park, Dublin. Cavendish was Gladstone's nephew by marriage. Mrs Gladstone was told the news on returning to Number 10 from a dinner. She was still standing in the Inner Hall trying to take it in when Gladstone arrived back from a night-time walk. Gladstone was stunned, seized his wife's hand and knelt with her as he uttered prayers. Worse news was to follow from the Sudan when Khartoum fell and General Gordon and all his British soldiers were massacred in January 1885, just two days before a relief force arrived. Queen Victoria, who disliked Gladstone, and had earlier said, 'He speaks to me as if I was a public meeting,' exploded with rage on hearing the news, and sent Gladstone an unciphered telegram at Number 10, blaming him for the tragedy: 'all this might have been prevented and many precious lives saved by earlier action.'

Gladstone's night-time prowlings aroused suspicion among his colleagues. Detractors noted that he spent a disproportionate amount of time trying to save more attractive prostitutes in better districts, and that his 'conversion' rate of the prostitutes was not notably high. One commentator noted: 'It was not uncommon for members of the Cabinet, calling late at Number 10 on some important issue, to find the Drawing Room still filled with cheap scent, or even to pass a prostitute in the hallway as she was being shown out by the butler.'

We must assume Gladstone used the ground floor for Cabinet and offices, the Middle Drawing Room and Pillared Room for entertaining, and the first-floor rooms on the west side for sleeping and private use. However, in October 1892, his Private Secretary wrote that Cabinet met 'in his own room – the corner room on the first floor [over the old Cabinet Room].' We do not know if Gladstone brought with him a telephone on his return to Number 10 in 1880, but he had shown considerable interest in the telephone's introduction to London, and seems to have had one in his Welsh home, Hawarden. He proclaimed the device 'most unearthly'.

Gladstone's final ministry (1892-94) was not his happiest. He moved back into Number 10 with all his furniture and his piano, and promptly demanded an extra £1,780 be spent on renovations and new furniture. When appointing him this final time, Queen Victoria complained he had 'a weird look in his eyes, a feeble expression about the mouth'. He thought little better of her: their conversation, he later recalled, had been of the kind that Marie Antoinette might have had with her executioners. Gladstone failed to pass his Irish Home Rule Bill (granting self-government to all Ireland) through the Lords. Blocked at every turn, and isolated in Cabinet, he decided at the age of eighty-four that he had had enough. On 1 March 1894, he assembled his ministers for the last Cabinet of the 556 he had chaired. Known as the 'blubbering Cabinet', it was an event which had been eagerly awaited since at least 1880 by many of his Liberal colleagues. Several present, however, wept with the emotion of the occasion. Gladstone uttered 'God bless you all,' and then, in the words of one present, 'went slowly out of one door, while we with downcast looks and oppressed hearts, filed out by the other; much as men walk away from the graveside'. Gladstone walked down the long corridor and out into the fresh air of Downing Street to go to the Commons for the last time as Premier.

▼ William Gladstone photographed with his wife and granddaughter, Dorothy Drew.

FIN DE SIECLE

The last years of the nineteenth century saw a succession of inhabitants at Number 10. The Marquess of Salisbury, the last premier to serve as a member of the House of Lords, had succeeded Gladstone in June 1885 but was far too grand to live at Number 10, offering the house instead to Stafford Northcote, who was the First Lord. On arrival, Northcote met Gladstone, who was leaving, on the grand staircase. The old man was 'very civil' to him, and gave him three books

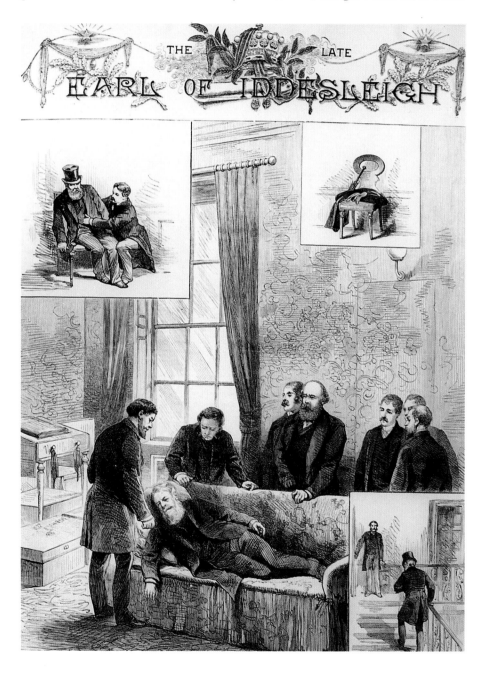

◄ The death of Lord Iddesleigh on 11 January 1887. The bottom inset picture shows him staggering up the grand staircase; the top left inset picture shows him being attended to. The room is clearly recognisable as the White Drawing Room. Salisbury (centre, main picture) later wrote 'as I looked at the dead body stretched before me . . . I felt that politics was a cursed profession!'

on Homer. When the Tories returned to power in July 1886, Salisbury again became First Lord, and used Number 10 as an office. Northcote (now Lord Iddesleigh) came to see him to remonstrate about his job. In January 1887, Iddesleigh staggered at the top of the grand staircase and was carried into the corner room (now the White Drawing Room), where he died.

Lord Rosebery became Prime Minister on 3 March 1894 and held his first Cabinet in the Foreign Office. He told Gladstone's secretary, Edward Hamilton, that 'he will eventually sit at Number 10, when Mr Gladstone is cleared out; but this will not be for some days'. Rosebery had a bedroom in Number 10, but seems not to have used it, preferring to live at his home in Berkeley Square. His biographer, Robert Rhodes James, confirms, 'Rosebery certainly did not live [at Number 10] and his dislike of his premiership was such that he could hardly bring himself ever to enter its portal again.' His was a joyless and an unsuccessful premiership, alleviated by his twice winning the Derby, with Ladas in 1894 and Sir Visto in 1895.

Salisbury became Premier again in June 1895 and ruled for seven years. His nephew, Arthur Balfour, moved into Number 10 as First Lord. Salisbury's first name, Robert, and his penchant for promoting his family, gave birth to the popular expression, 'Bob's your uncle'. Salisbury himself never liked Number 10. He found the Cabinet Room a 'cramped, close room', especially when Randolph Churchill, his Chancellor of the Exchequer, smoked. Salisbury duly switched Cabinet meetings to the larger and much grander Cabinet Room in the Foreign Office (he was Foreign Secretary until 1900). Balfour was left to inhabit Number 10 largely in peace, a peace shattered periodically by noise from his new toy: he was the first inhabitant of Number 10 to bring a motor car to Downing Street.

▼ Arthur Balfour, nephew of Lord Salisbury, continues the family line.

BALFOUR TO HOME 1902-64

Arthur Balfour's decision to live at Number 10, which was followed by all his successors, meant that throughout the twentieth century the building has had three overlapping functions: as the office of the head of the British government; as a house for official entertaining, at times on a lavish scale; and, finally, as the dwelling place of the Prime Minister and his family.

▶ Mr and Mrs Baldwin leaving Number 10 for the country in May 1928.

◀ Harold Macmillan with US President John F Kennedy.

ARTHUR BALFOUR: 1902-5

Balfour, a Scot from an ancient family, philosopher and statesman, lived continuously at Number 10 from 1895, when his uncle, Lord Salisbury, appointed him First Lord following the Tories' general election victory. Balfour wrote A *Defence of Philosophic Doubt*, published in 1879, hardly the manifesto for an activist Premier, while his Clifford Lectures, given in 1915, were on theism and Humanism. Balfour was also a member of the aristocratic clique called the 'Souls', so-named because they spent much time talking about their eternal beings. He disliked the press, commenting to his sister, Lady Rayleigh, in 1893, that he had not looked at a paper for weeks, though he knew he ought to read them. Books, on the other hand, he devoured, having a particular liking for Walter Scott, Jane Austen and R L Stevenson. He shared one preference with the century's last Prime Minister, Tony Blair: '[Balfour] must be the first Prime Minister who in accordance with modern ways is called by his Christian name by the bulk of his colleagues,' recalled one senior civil servant.

Balfour's car, a De Dion Voiturette, moved slowly – it broke down about every three miles when he used it in the summer of 1900. It was not the only aspect of Balfour's life to move at a leisurely pace; his official life was punctuated by similar misfortunes. During the worst week of the Boer War of 1899-1902, when the Boers defeated the British at Colenso, Balfour would leave Number 10 each night between 11 pm and midnight and walk to the War Office in Whitehall where he climbed the stairs – there were no lifts at that time – and went through the late night telegrams. 'There never was any news except defeats,' he recorded.

Balfour's government saw the end of the South African war in 1902, and the Education Act the same year, but the Tory Party was falling apart on the issue of 'tariff reform'. This proved the most serious split in the party since the Corn Laws 60 years before, and in December 1905 Balfour resigned as Prime Minister, with his government in disarray. He retained the leadership of the House until he resigned from it in 1911 but he continued in politics, responsible, as Foreign Secretary, for the Balfour Declaration of 1917, promising Zionists a national home in Palestine. In July 1928, Parliament presented him with an object that he loved – a Rolls Royce motor car. He died two years later.

HENRY CAMPBELL-BANNERMAN: 1905-8

Aged sixty-nine when be became Prime Minister, the Liberal Campbell-Bannerman had had to wait long for the prize which ill-health decreed was to be his only briefly. He doted on his wife, Charlotte, but she had long been unwell and had suffered a paralytic stroke in 1902. She agreed to move from their comfortable house in Belgrave Square only so that her husband could live above his work. But she found Number 10 unpleasant: 'It is a house of doom,' she said when they moved in, with some prescience. A lift was installed in the inner well, to make life easier for her. At the start of her husband's premiership, she hosted a large party at Number 10, directing guests while propped up in a chair and fighting to control her pain. It was an unequal struggle, and in August 1906 she died while on holiday in Marienbad. Her body was brought back to Number 10 before being taken to Scotland for burial.

Charlotte Campbell-Bannerman's death took away much of her husband's pleasure in his job. Despite an overwhelming majority for the Liberal party at the 1906 general election, he was frequently under pressure. In November 1907, he suffered a serious heart attack after standing for an hour at the Guildhall because the guest of honour, Kaiser Wilhelm II of Germany, arrived late. In January 1908, suffragettes demanding the vote chained themselves to the railings outside Number 10. Hacksaws fetched from nearby Scotland Yard soon freed the vociferous ladies, but the issue they were campaigning for would not go away as easily. On February 12th, Campbell-Bannerman returned to Number 10 after a busy day in the House of Commons, and retired to his bed. He was not to leave the house again alive. Edward VII, who had succeeded his mother Queen Victoria in 1901, was less than pleased to learn of his Prime Minister's incapacity, as he was anxious to leave for Biarritz in southern France for a six-week holiday. On March 4th, the King visited Campbell-Bannerman at Number 10, making it clear that a change of prime minister should be avoided while he was away. But the Prime Minister was failing fast, and on April 4th the King summoned H H Asquith to Biarritz, to invite him to take over as Premier. At one stage, the King even considered inviting the entire Cabinet to Paris to collect their seals of office from him at the exclusive Hôtel Crillon, so as not to upset his holiday too much.

▲ Henry Campbell-Bannerman. He was sixty-nine when he took up his prime ministerial post. He described Number 10 as 'his rotten old barrack of a house'.

Asquith arrived back from Biarritz on the evening of April 5th, his train steaming into Charing Cross just before 6 pm, and went to see Campbell-Bannerman in bed. Asquith's wife Margot waited in the car in the road outside. She recorded the melancholy scene: 'The street was empty, and but for the footfall of a few policemen there was not a sound to be heard. I looked at the dingy exterior of Number 10 and wondered how we would live there. Leaning back, I watched the evening sky reflected in the diamond panes of the Foreign Office windows, and caught a glimpse of green trees. The [Number 10] door opened and the Archbishop came out. The final scene in a drama of life was being performed in that quiet by-street. The doctor going in and the priest coming out; and as I reflected on the dying Prime Minister I could only hope that no sound had reached him of the crowd that had cheered his successor.' Two weeks later, in the first-floor room overlooking St James's Park and Horse Guards Parade, Campbell-Bannerman died.

H H ASQUITH: 1908-16

On Wednesday 20 May 1908, *The Times* announced: 'Mr and Mrs Asquith formally entered into occupation of 10 Downing Street, yesterday afternoon.' Margot Asquith found the inside of her new abode no less dingy than the outside. 'It is an inconvenient house with three poor staircases,' she later wrote, 'and after living there a few weeks I made up my mind that owing to the impossibility of circulation I could only entertain my Liberal friends at dinner or at garden parties.' The building to her was 'liver-coloured and squalid', and she complained that the address was so unfamiliar to taxi drivers that they would take her to the wrong destination. '10 Downing Street ought to be as well known in London as Marble Arch or the Albert Memorial,' she complained, 'but it is not'.

The Asquiths arrived with a brood of children in tow. By his first wife, Helen Melland, who had died of typhoid in 1891, Asquith had five children; two, Raymond and Herbert, were married but Arthur (aged twenty-five), Violet (aged twenty-one) and Cyril (aged eighteen) were not. By Margot, he also had Elizabeth (aged eleven) and Anthony, called 'Puffin' (aged five). The corridors echoed with the bustle and chatter of children. Number 10 staff found themselves banished into the basement or attics as every available space was used for children's rooms or nannies. On one occasion, Anthony got lost with Megan Lloyd George, who lived next door in Number 11 with her three brothers and sisters. The police were called for fear of kidnap by the suffragettes, Irish protestors or anarchists. The children were found asleep in the lift, which was stuck on the servants' top floor, its door wide open. Anthony was fascinated by the development of flight (the Wright brothers had just flown), and his mother complained of retrieving his home-made planes from the shrubs in the garden.

Margot was a flamboyant entertainer and filled her diary with bizarrely assorted lunch and dinner parties. But even she periodically tired of the social round, complaining that the house could be about 'as exclusive as Epsom on Derby day!'. Asquith's own feelings about entertaining fluctuated. At one point he was writing excitedly on the subject (opposite), yet after a similar occasion, in December 1913, he wrote, 'The guests have slowly disappeared from a regular Downing Street dinner. Thank God, they are all now in their taxis and I am alone.'

> '*Are you coming to lunch tomorrow? You must. We have at any rate three poets – Yeats, De La Mare and 'A E' [Russell].'*
>
> ———————————
>
> H H ASQUITH, LETTER

Roy Jenkins, Asquith's biographer, writes that, 'during the eight and a half years for which the Asquiths were tenants of Number 10, they identified themselves more closely with the house and gave it a more distinct social character than had been the case with any prime ministerial family for several decades past'. The Asquiths used the Cabinet Room and private offices downstairs much as they had been used in the nineteenth century. On the first floor, the State Dining Room and Middle and Pillared Drawing Rooms were used for official entertaining. The

north-west corner room was the Asquiths' bedroom. Next to it, on the west side facing St James's Park, was the Prime Minister's sitting room, which had been partitioned off to provide a separate bathroom, almost the only one in the house. On the first floor in the front, overlooking Downing Street, Violet Asquith had her room. Violet would often return there in the early hours, having spent the evening dancing, and would glance across at the Foreign Office, into the rooms of the young diplomats who had entertained her. Telephones, now well established, were situated at various points around the house, handy for her use.

Asquith's most creative work was done as Liberal Home Secretary under Gladstone and Rosebery (1892-95), as Chancellor of the Exchequer (1905-8), and in his first three years as Prime Minister, when he oversaw the legislation which introduced an embryonic welfare state into Britain. But a succession of crises – over Ireland, the House of Lords and the budget – militant trade unionism and women's suffrage all took their toll. He found increasing solace in

▲ Suffragettes appeal to Mr Asquith outside Number 10 in 1909.

the company of Venetia Stanley, a beautiful and intelligent young woman, an exact contemporary and friend of his daughter Violet. In 1912, Venetia, then aged twenty-five, accompanied the Asquiths on a holiday to Sicily. Asquith began to write to her, and this soon became a daily missive; he even jotted notes to her during the Wednesday Cabinet meetings. On most Friday afternoons he would find time to go with Venetia to the country – he was an enthusiastic motorist – driven by his chauffeur in his recently acquired Napier.

It was a hopeless relationship of a man of status in love with a girl more than thirty years his junior. Pain was bound to come. War was declared in August 1914, and with little sign of success, his need for solace grew. Yet in April 1915 he sensed that Venetia's feelings were cooling. News of the death of the poet Rupert Brooke in the Aegean, en route to the Dardanelles, came at the same time, causing him more pain than any previous loss in the war. In desperation, he wrote the impassioned letter above from Number 10 on 10 May 1915.

> 'Shall I try to tell you what you have been and are to me? First, outwardly and physically, unapproachable and unique. Then in temperament and character, often baffling and elusive, but always more interesting and attractive and compelling than any woman I have ever seen or known. Above all, and beyond all, in the intimacy of perfect confidence and understanding for two years past, the pole-star and lode-star of my life.'
>
> H H ASQUITH TO VENETIA STANLEY, 10 MAY 1915

Two days later, Venetia wrote to Asquith to tell him she had decided to marry Edwin Montague, his former secretary and now one of his Cabinet Ministers. Five days after receiving the news, Asquith, broken in spirit and politically outmanoeuvred, agreed to form a coalition government with the Conservatives. The following year saw both the disaster of the Battle of the Somme and the death, in the battle on September 15th, of his beloved and brilliant son, Raymond. On September 17th, the news was conveyed by telephone to Margot Asquith. She told her husband, who 'put his hands over his face and we walked into an empty room and sat down in silence.' He lamented, 'Whatever pride I had in the past and whatever hope I had for the future – by much the largest part I had of both was invested in him. Now all that is gone.'

DAVID LLOYD GEORGE: 1916-22

In December 1916 David Lloyd George became Prime Minister of the coalition government. Lloyd George's premiership brought an immediate expansion of Number 10, with offices bursting out into the garden and Horse Guards Parade, creating the 'garden suburb'. His 'presidential style' as Premier, and the size of the Prime Minister's offices under him, aroused suspicion and resentment among other politicians, but it set the pattern for future premiers to follow, especially with the development of the media directing ever greater personal focus on the incumbent of Number 10.

On 11 November 1918, Lloyd George was woken in the Prime Minister's first-floor bedroom with news of the armistice that brought the First World War to an end. On 28 December, President Wilson of the United States, en route for Paris, where peace treaty negotiations were to be held, was entertained by Lloyd George's War Cabinet. Lloyd George spent the early part of 1919 at the peace talks at the Palace of Versailles. Becoming aware that his telephone conversations with Number 10 were being tapped, and told that no sure means of confidentiality could be devised, he fell back on speaking in Welsh. Any eavesdroppers were apparently baffled.

In contrast to the well-oiled bureaucratic machine that Lloyd George established in Downing Street to help win the war, the domestic side was anarchic, and remained so after the war finished. Lloyd George had lived in Number 11 with his family since 1908, and on becoming Premier had moved sideways with his wife Margaret and their children, the youngest of whom, Megan, was only fourteen when her father became Prime Minister. Grandchildren would also have the freedom of the house. They were not the tidiest family, and Lloyd George himself was absent-minded, forgetting on one occasion to tell the kitchens that the Prince of Wales (the future Edward VIII) was coming to lunch. Lord Riddell, dining with the Lloyd George family, noted that it looked as if a small suburban household were picnicking in Downing Street – the same simple food, the same little domestic servant, the same mixture of tea and dinner. Field Marshal Haig was equally struck. The Prime Minister's house, he wrote in February 1918, reminded him of 'summer lodgings at the seaside, where a sort of maid-of-all-work opened the door'. Riddell was even more disparaging when on Christmas Day, 1920, he dined with Lloyd George, describing it as 'the sort of Christmas a shopkeeper spends when he eats his Christmas dinner on the counter surrounded by his goods'.

▲ Lloyd George was known for his haphazard approach to domestic matters.

► William Orpen's painting of Lloyd George, 1927, which has hung in the ground-floor Lobby.

The state of Lloyd George's bedroom can be imagined from the diary of Tom Jones (below), a senior official in the new Cabinet Secretariat set up by Lloyd George in December 1916.

Lloyd George's emotional life followed a similarly unconventional pattern. His biographer, Kenneth Morgan, believes that he shared a bedroom with his wife Margaret, but also into Number 10 came his mistress and secretary, Frances Stevenson. The lovers were discreet and did what they could to avoid gossip; they did not travel together and tried to minimise their public appearances together. Frances supplied Lloyd George with the love, excitement and admiration he felt he lacked from Margaret. For her part,

> '*About 10 am went to Number 10 and was sent upstairs. PM in bed in dressing gown. His head looked bigger than ever. A large room with huge pieces of mahogany furniture and a hotch potch of feeble pictures higgledy-piggledy on the walls.*'
>
> TOM JONES, 1916, DIARY

Margaret tried her best to ignore Frances, but no wife can possibly inhabit the same house as a mistress without succumbing to powerful feelings. As Margaret's daughter Olwen said: 'Mother certainly never mentioned her, but she quickly realised what was going on.' Frances, for her part, felt she cared more for, and had a better understanding of, the man they shared, as shown by her words on the right.

Lloyd George's departure from Number 10 had been long heralded, with disillusion growing among Conservative backbenchers of the Coalition Government he headed. Tory MPs had been antagonised by the Irish Treaty in 1921, which conceded independence to southern Ireland, and were disturbed by Lloyd George's style, and by a sale of honours scandal in June 1922. In October 1922, a majority of Tory MPs voted at the Carlton Club to end the Coalition, and a general election was called a week later. Lloyd George resigned. The last Liberal Prime Minister of the century called his staff into the Cabinet Room to bid them farewell. For them it was a highly emotional occasion, but Lloyd George seemed oddly playful.

> *'He and Mrs Lloyd George were not on speaking terms. She had closed the bedroom windows on the quiet, thinking that the room was cold, but knowing that he always gets a headache when he sleeps with windows closed. She does not study him in the least.'*
>
> FRANCES STEVENSON, 1917

After Lloyd George lost office in 1922, his relationship with Frances fluctuated, but a daughter (said at the time to be adopted by her) was born in 1929. Margaret died in 1941 and Lloyd George married Frances in 1943 at Guildford Registry Office. He died within eighteen months.

BONAR LAW: 1922-23

Lloyd George's successor had been Unionist leader in the Commons since 1911. His was to be the briefest premiership of the century – just seven months, from October 1922 to May 1923, when ill-health caused him to retire. Bonar Law held his first Cabinet, on the day he succeeded, at his home in Onslow Gardens; thereafter he reverted to holding Cabinets at Number 10, and to adopting a less autocratic style of leadership than his predecessor, a change dictated not least by his failing health.

In November 1922, a ticker tape machine was installed for the general election just outside the Cabinet Room, at the end of the (then) red-carpeted long corridor; it hammered out the results in the constituencies to eager bystanders (this machine was state-of-the-art technology then; the BBC did not start radio broadcasts until 1923). The Conservatives won the election with an overall majority of 77. Bonar Law was 64 when he moved into Number 10 after the election. His wife had died in 1909 and he still mourned her loss. Two of his four sons had been killed in the war, both in 1917. He moved in with his sister, Mary Law, and his younger children. His elder daughter, Isabel, acted as hostess for her father at official dinners and receptions. The most celebrated, if infamous, visitor

▲ Bonar Law with Italian Premier Benito Mussolini, French Prime Minister Raymond Poincaré and Belgian Prime Minister Georges Theunis, in the Pillared Room for the Conference of European Prime Ministers, which took place in London during December 1922.

during Bonar Law's premiership was the Italian dictator, Benito Musssolini, who came to London in December 1922 for a conference of European prime ministers, held in Number 10's State Drawing Room.

In May 1923, Bonar Law was ordered by doctors to go abroad for a rest; for the previous few weeks he had barely been able to speak in the Commons because of with the pain in his throat. At Aix-les-Bains in France he took a turn for the worse. Tom Jones records in his diary how the Prime Minister contacted his close friend, the newspaper magnate Lord Beaverbrook: 'From Aix, B.L. sent a de profundis letter to B. [eaverbrook] begging him to come out or he would throw himself under a train. When B. got there he found B.L. taking about ten doses of anti-carnia daily, to keep down the pain he was suffering.' Beaverbrook met his friend at the Hôtel Crillon in Paris, where Bonar Law's doctor, who had also come over, diagnosed cancer of the throat. As was then the custom, the two men decided not to tell the sufferer the grave nature of his affliction, but they advised him that it would be best to retire from politics immediately. Beaverbrook recalled that Bonar Law was almost lighthearted in his relief at the idea of laying down a burden which had been crushing his failing vitality.

STANLEY BALDWIN: 1923–24, 1924-29, 1935-37

Baldwin was the only Premier this century to have had three separate spells at Number 10. He moved in first in May 1923, a comparative unknown, aged fifty-six with five children. A steady, pipe-smoking figure, more than any other political leader he was to reassure the nation during the tense and economically unsettled inter-war years.

The house was crowded during the Baldwins' first two periods at Number 10 (1923-24, 1924-29). The three younger children moved in with them, two older children having already married. The ground floor continued to be used for Cabinet meetings and Private Secretaries as before, with the Garden Room secretaries in the basement below. The first-floor state rooms continued to be used for receptions, while the north-west corner drawing room seems to have been used as the Baldwins' private sitting room. Next to it, on the west side, was Mrs Baldwin's bedroom, with the bathroom leading off it. The Prime Minister slept in the Ante Room outside, which was curtained off, not least because Baldwin was anxious to avoid the caretaker seeing him indulge his passion for reading cheap detective stories while in bed. His bedroom was described by Mrs Charlton, who became Neville Chamberlain's secretary, as 'a kind of passage room without windows or direct ventilation'.

▶ Baldwin being filmed for newsreels outside Number 10 in 1929. He was the first Prime Minister to exploit successfully the new arts of radio and film.

Baldwin decided to call an election in late 1923, to secure a mandate for the Tories' favoured policy of imposing protective tariffs on foreign imports to preserve British jobs. The election did not go as planned; although not the overall victors, Labour were called upon in January 1924 to form their first-ever government. But within a year the Tories were back in office, and Baldwin moved back to Number 10 with his wife, his youngest daughter, Betty, and younger son, Windham. It was to be the calmest of the three spells at Number 10, and the Baldwins settled into a routine that was to last for four and a half years. Breakfast was often a working affair, with officials or fellow ministers, after which Baldwin seems to have settled down in the Cabinet Room for the morning, to work and read the papers (*The Times*, *The Daily Telegraph* and *The Morning Post*), summoning his Private Secretaries from their adjacent rooms as he needed them. Robert Vansittart, who became his senior official, recalls: 'My table backed on to the Cabinet Room, and raised voices came through the double doors in chorus or duet.' Baldwin would have lunch at Number 10 or at a club (The Travellers' was a favourite) before going on to the Commons, which, in common with most premiers then, he led. Afternoon meetings would be held either in the Prime Minister's room in the Commons, or back at Number 10, with tea at 4 pm. Mrs Baldwin, meanwhile, held quite simple 'At Homes' on Thursdays at Number 10. Evenings were spent in the house, or entertaining, or reading in his library.

Baldwin certainly relished sloping off into the library, which seems to have been at the front of the house, with high shelves specially put in to accommodate his large collection of books. He would retreat here to escape the entertaining – his son, Windham, recalled his misery when penned in by small talk, or 'events' organised by his wife, such as the visit by the White Russian Cossack choir, who used the Cabinet Room as their dressing room, or the wives of South Wales miners, with their display of traditional quilting work. But Windham Baldwin dispels an image of his father being a mere bookworm: Baldwin was also an athlete and cricketer (as was his wife), and his son recalls how he would spring over sofas and armchairs, out of low windows and up flights of stairs.

The success of the years 1924-27, which included the Locarno Treaty in 1925 and the resolution of the General Strike in 1926, gave way to a difficult final two years, and defeat at the hands of Labour in the general election of 1929.

The Baldwins returned for a final two years between June 1935 and May 1937, years that saw growing anxiety about the rise of the dictators, Hitler and Mussolini, the Abyssinian Crisis, the remilitarisation of the Rhineland, the outbreak of Civil War in Spain and the abdication crisis of 1936 – and a collapse of the Prime Minister's health from nervous exhaustion. Yet Baldwin left on a high note: Edward VIII had abdicated

'Everyone was rather uncomfortable, uneasy about the results and as the evening wore on the gloom deepened and the experts from Central Office had to confess that their worst expectations were exceeded by the losses ticking away on the tape in the passage outside the room of the Private Secretaries.'

TOM JONES ON ELECTION NIGHT, 1929

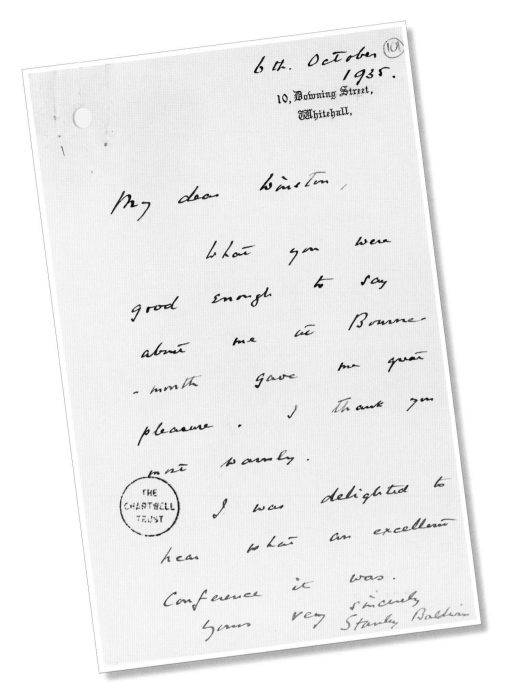

in favour of his younger brother, Albert, who became George VI; the economy was improving, and his policy of not confronting the dictators appeared successful. Just before the Baldwins left Number 10, George VI and Queen Elizabeth came to dinner – only the second time in the century that the monarch and his consort had dined at Number 10 (the first was in 1911). Appointed an earl on his retirement from the premiership, Baldwin vowed to withdraw from politics. Into Number 10 moved fellow Tory, Neville Chamberlain.

MacDonald in Number 10

Ramsay MacDonald was Britain's first Labour Prime Minister. He was called to the Palace to be offered the premiership by George V in January 1924, after Baldwin's Tories suffered a 'No Confidence' defeat in the Commons.

The day before the King offered the premiership to her father, Ishbel MacDonald, who moved into Number 10 with him, received a telephone call from Mrs Baldwin, asking if she would like to see the house. Ishbel went immediately to Downing Street, accompanied by the housekeeper from their motherless North London home. She later recalled being appalled by the rambling passages and by the sheer number of rooms – over forty, excluding the basement and ground-floor offices. Worse, they were required to supply some of the furniture, and all the linen, crockery and cutlery. The Asquiths, Lloyd Georges and Baldwins had all brought

their furniture with them, and taken it away. MacDonald lived in a modest house in Hampstead, and neither possessed nor could afford good quality sofas and tables, so the state agreed to purchase furniture, but not other items. MacDonald's sister went to the January sales and bought bedsheets, table linen, cutlery and crockery, while Ishbel used £50, given to her by an aunt, to buy some green Venetian glass vases for the State Drawing Rooms. Uncertainty about the length of their stay, with no parliamentary majority, contributed to the profound unease MacDonald felt about the expenditure.

MacDonald took over the first-floor room on the north-west

corner as his study, with his bedroom next to it, facing the park, and his bathroom alongside. Ishbel slept in the room above the front door, from where each night she would hear two bangs on the ceiling as the caretaker dropped his boots on the floor in the second-floor flat above. MacDonald's two younger daughters, Joan and Sheila, slept nearby; aged thirteen and fifteen in 1924, they took the bus each day to school in Camden Town.

Sheila would amuse herself hitting golf balls down the long corridor leading to the Cabinet Room. The building now had three bathrooms, and the noisy urinal off the Ante Room makes one of its first recorded appearances in the annals of Number 10's history; it was so noisy that MacDonald's personal secretary, Rose Rosenberg, was forced to move from her poky room next to it to the larger west-facing room close to the Cabinet Room.

MacDonald was a man who appreciated fine art, and he managed to persuade the National Gallery to loan some paintings, including some Turners and a de Wint. He wanted Number 10 to recover some of the grandeur of the days of Walpole and Pitt. A proper library, containing more than the Hansard parliamentary reports that filled the Cabinet Room's bookcases, was seen by him as a pre-requisite. So he started the Prime Minister's Library, housed originally in the Cabinet Room, with shelves being added on the wall facing the fireplace. A bookplate was designed, and the custom grew of the Prime Minister and others donating books to the library; Churchill presented biographies of his father, Randolph, and his ancestor, Marlborough.

*MacDonald buys a poppy (**opposite, left**). A letter from MacDonald to Churchill in which he states 'I wish we didn't disagree so much'. (**opposite, right**). MacDonald with his daughter Ishbel, who took on the role of lady of the house in Downing Street (**above**). Indian leader Mahatma Gandhi visiting MacDonald in September 1931 (**left**).*

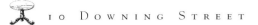

RAMSAY MACDONALD: 1924, 1929-35

Like Gladstone and Disraeli in the nineteenth century, Baldwin and MacDonald boxed and coxed in their holding of the premiership. MacDonald was fifty-seven when he became Prime Minister. He had been brought up in the Scottish fishing village of Lossiemouth and suffered poverty in his early life. Further hardships came when, after fifteen years of marriage, his wife Margaret died in 1911, leaving him with three daughters and two sons. Ishbel, aged twenty when they moved into Downing Street, was a constant source of support.

The King was not displeased with his new First Minister, writing in 1924: 'I had an hour's talk with him – he impressed me very much: he wishes to do the right thing. Today twenty-three years ago dear Grandmamma [Queen Victoria] died. I wonder what she would have thought of a Labour Government.'

MacDonald worked in the Cabinet Room, chairing meetings from the Prime Minister's chair in front of the fireplace. At the first Cabinet meeting, on January 23rd, Lord Haldane gave ministers a lesson in etiquette: MacDonald was always to be addressed as 'Prime Minister', and other ministers by their surnames or titles of their jobs; while MacDonald asked ministers to make every effort to be punctual. They then proceeded to business, discussing measures to reduce unemployment.

> 'Without fuss, the firing of guns, the flying of new flags, the Labour Government had come in. At 4 we held our first Cabinet. A wonderful country. Now for burdens and worries.'
>
> RAMSAY MACDONALD, 1924

The lack of a parliamentary majority meant that despite some notable achievements in housing and foreign affairs, the government was destined not to last long, and by the end of the year had been ousted in a general election. MacDonald had not found it easy to carry the supreme burden with no wife at his side. Of Ishbel, he wrote on her twenty-first birthday, 'Daily she grows more like her mother. How happy I am with her.' But the joy she brought him could not fill the vacuum left by her mother's death. After opening a baby clinic in 1924, set up as a memorial to his wife, he lamented, 'It is an odd thing to have a dead man as a Premier to look after a living world.'

MacDonald returned to Number 10 in 1929. Labour's foundations in government were more secure than in 1924, but Number 10's were visibly crumbling: after a concert by the Glasgow Orpheus choir in the Pillared Room, the ceiling in the Private Secretaries' Room below began to crack. The ingenious solution was for the cracks to be papered over, literally, with stamp paper.

Ishbel returned in 1929 to act as her father's hostess, and immediately insisted that new chairs be purchased for the State Drawing Rooms and Soane Dining Rooms. The National Gallery was again raided for paintings, including a portrait of Gladstone to be hung in the State Dining Room. The house was now emptier: of his younger daughters, Joan was a medical student in London and Sheila was at Oxford. His son Malcolm, by that time a Labour MP, moved into the room that Baldwin had used as his retreat, overlooking Downing Street. Malcolm boarded up Baldwin's bookshelves, and hung Japanese prints over them. Ishbel recalled: 'For us, Number 10 was just a colony of bed-sitting rooms with a large communal dining room where we met for breakfast at eight o'clock. The place was always so very quiet at night save for the clatter of dustbins which woke one up very early in the morning.'

MacDonald was eventually ostracised by the Labour Party and became an increasingly isolated and ineffectual figure as Prime Minister at the head of the National Government. Tired and demoralised, and having had an operation for glaucoma in each eye, in the summer of 1935 he exchanged offices with Baldwin, who became Prime Minister for the third time.

NEVILLE CHAMBERLAIN: 1937-40

Number 10 had for quite some years been recognised as being in a rather dilapidated state. The departure of the Baldwins in 1937 provided the opportunity for serious structural work to be undertaken. Many of the floors sagged, while one of the first-floor internal walls was found to be 10cm/4in out of line. The builders moved in and the Chamberlains remained in Number 11 for ten months while the repairs were done. According to Mrs Charlton, the personal secretary who later supervised the Chamberlains' move back to Number 11 in 1940, Mrs Chamberlain was in frequent touch with the Office of Works, and with Sir Philip Sassoon, its minister: she wanted to give Number 10 the feel of the original 'House in the Park'. Sassoon, an art connoisseur, was sympathetic.

Mrs Chamberlain chose country chintz curtains for the new bedroom facing the park, and Sassoon altered the first and second floors, making them much closer to what we see today. The first-floor bedroom/ boudoir on the north-west corner became an extra drawing room, creating the line of three inter-linked drawing rooms that we see today. Mrs Chamberlain also used the corner room as a personal study/drawing room, which was decorated in yellow. The next room, known as the Red Drawing Room, with pink walls and the red upholstered furniture that had belonged to Clive of India, was in the middle. The large State

▲ Chamberlain makes a quick dash towards that famous door.

or Pillared Drawing Room on the opposite north-east corner was painted white, and was supplied with new furniture, including some eighteenth-century and Regency sofas. Many new paintings were acquired, including a large landscape by Claude Lorraine. The grand staircase walls were painted yellow, and a deep red stair carpet was laid. The first-floor bedroom facing the park became the Prime Minister's upstairs study, and Baldwin's airless corridor-bedroom next to it was restored to a passageway, though a new formal staircase was built out of it from the first to the second floor. The second-floor attic rooms were converted into a flat for the Chamberlains, and the staff moved elsewhere. New bedrooms and bathrooms were created, and larger windows provided more light. A comfortable bedroom was created for Chamberlain on the north-west corner, with a smaller one opposite for Mrs Chamberlain. At the same time, the kitchens were modernised, and a service lift installed in the inner well. The total cost of the renovations was £25,000. By Easter 1938, the work complete, the Chamberlains were ready to move in.

Neville Chamberlain was a tireless worker, surviving on just five and a half hour's sleep a night. He would come down for a 'good cooked breakfast' at 8.30 each morning in the smaller Dining Room, see his secretaries to plan the day and discuss constituency matters, take a regular morning walk with his wife to the bridge in St James's Park and, on his return, work in the Cabinet Room until lunch, meeting with the Chief Whip at 11 am. Afternoons were spent in the Commons when the House was sitting, and on his return he would work steadily on his red boxes in the upstairs study, staying up until 2 am when occasion demanded.

Where possible, Chamberlain avoided the social occasions at which his wife excelled. Apart from lunch and sherry parties, Mrs Chamberlain also held regular evening parties on consecutive days, an arrangement designed to optimise the fresh flower displays and the hiring of cutlery.

> 'There was a frenzy of excitement. People were dancing in the street, on the car. It was a very emotional time, very emotional. People did not want war. He came up to the first floor, to Marjorie Leaf's [his secretary's] room over the front door looking out over Downing Street. But the window shelf was quite high up. So we had to fetch him a small stool, on which he stood to address and wave to the crowd.'
>
> MRS CHARLTON, 30 SEPTEMBER 1938

MPs and their wives were invited in rotation, to mix with other guests, who included senior military, ecclesiastical and diplomatic figures (Joseph Kennedy, the US Ambassador and a keen advocate of appeasement, was among the regular guests). Personal aides were placed at the interconnecting doors of the three State Drawing Rooms to encourage circulation, partly in order to avoid too great a concentration of people for the weak floor to bear. David Dilks, Chamberlain's biographer, described Mrs Chamberlain as 'a celebrated, conscientious and thoughtful hostess who went to endless trouble to entertain

▶ Chamberlain returning from Munich in September 1938, carrying the famous 'Peace in our Time', document, recently signed by Hitler, which declared that any future disputes between Britain and Germany would be settled amicably by negotiation.

▼ Victoria Cole, with the Prime Minister, Mrs Anne Chamberlain and Diana Chamberlain in the Inner Hall, preparing to leave for Court in March 1939. The distinctive Entrance Hall lantern can be seen over the Chamberlains' shoulders.

visitors from all over the world, especially from the Dominions and the colonies'. The Chamberlains' occupancy of Number 10 will be remembered more, however, for the Prime Minister's words of appeasement after flying back from a meeting with Hitler in Munich on 29 September 1938. Mrs Charlton recalled the mood when the Prime Minister's chauffeur-driven car appeared in Downing Street following a stopover at the Palace, where he had been to report to the King (opposite).

Chamberlain's declaration, which echoed Disraeli's words sixty years earlier of 'peace in our time', were to haunt him for the rest of his life. Within a year, Britain was at war with Germany and, on 10 May 1940, Chamberlain resigned as Prime Minister. Churchill, his successor, wanted him to remain close at hand for consultation, so the Chamberlains moved back into Number 11. But Chamberlain's health was failing fast, and six months later he died.

▶ Attlee at midnight on 14 August 1945, announcing the Japanese surrender. On his right is Ernest Bevin, the Foreign Secretary. The photograph is taken in the Cabinet Room, with Attlee sitting in the Prime Minister's seat.

CLEMENT ATTLEE: 1945-51

Churchill, as we have seen, spent the greater part of his premiership from 1940-45 living in the Number 10 Annexe. Clement Attlee, the intriguing Haileybury and Oxford-educated Labour MP, became the Labour party's second Prime Minister, after winning the landslide general election in the summer of 1945.

A greater contrast in working style, personality and interests could scarcely be imagined than that between Attlee and Churchill. The new Prime Minister was no master wordsmith; his words had, not wings, but leaden weights: 'We settled into 10 Downing Street,' he writes in his autobiography, 'and found it very comfortable.' 'Actually I saw more of my family during the period of my premiership than ever before.' Attlee, his wife Vi, and for part of the time their four children, lived in the flat throughout the six years of his premiership. The Attlees did not, however, move in immediately. Following the advice of Mrs Churchill, they had the second-floor rooms, which had already been altered for the Chamberlains, converted into a self-contained flat, with a front door, a kitchen, drawing room and further bedrooms. The conversion took three months, during which time the Attlees lived in the Number 10 Annexe overlooking St James's Park. The flat, however, had its problems: it made the

Prime Minister seem less accessible. The disjuncture was highlighted by Attlee's own monosyllabic conversation and his dislike of small talk.

Attlee loved the house, its sense of history, the stillness of the adjacent park at night and listening to the birdsong in the early morning. Mrs Attlee, however, was never happy at Number 10, and was jealous of the time others spent with her husband. She found it overwhelming, and her need for her husband was great. The tension rarely exploded in public, and Attlee did his best to spend as much time as he could with her, and to disguise her obvious lack of ease and resentment at her lot, but her illnesses seemed to his secretaries as much mental as physical. He would breakfast with Vi in the flat, and spend time with her afterwards, skimming the newspapers, principally for sports news; a Private Secretary, Geoffrey Cass, recalls him not caring much what the political comments were; he was more interested in reading the latest cricket scores from the 'ticker tape' machine. He would also try to fit in a morning walk in the park with his wife, followed at a discreet distance, as were the Chamberlains before, by a detective.

At 9.30 am, Attlee would come down to work in the Cabinet Room, to chair meetings (at which he was crisp and authoritative), talk with visitors or read official papers. He did not waste words on these papers, either penning 'No', or initialling 'CRA' (which meant 'Yes'), or writing 'Agreed – CRA' (which meant he was in warm agreement with whatever course of action was proposed).

Lunch was either a formal affair in the Soane Dining Room or a light meal upstairs with Mrs Attlee in the flat. In the afternoons he liked to spend an hour or two in the Commons, listening to a debate. If he had no formal dinner to

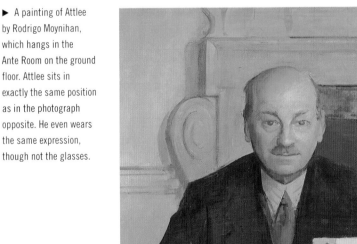

▶ A painting of Attlee by Rodrigo Moynihan, which hangs in the Ante Room on the ground floor. Attlee sits in exactly the same position as in the photograph opposite. He even wears the same expression, though not the glasses.

► Attlee, Labour Prime Minister, keeps Churchill, Conservative Opposition leader, informed in confidence about developments in NATO and European defence. From Churchill's period in office onwards, less important Number 10 letters would be stamped with the Prime Minister's signature, giving the appearance that they had been signed personally. The letter is written on the Prime Minister's stationery, which can be seen in the foreground of the painting on the previous page.

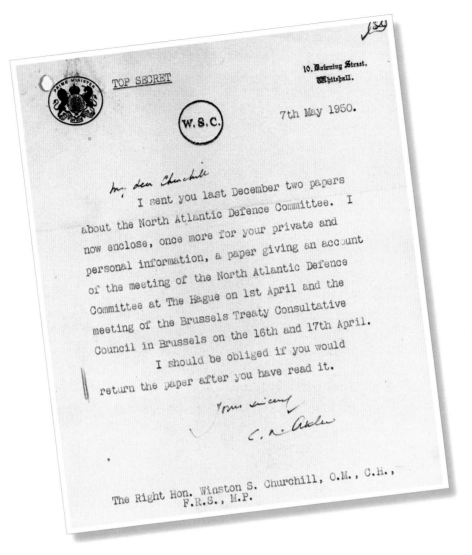

TOP SECRET

10, Downing Street, Whitehall.

W.S.C.

7th May 1950.

My dear Churchill

I sent you last December two papers about the North Atlantic Defence Committee. I now enclose, once more for your private and personal information, a paper giving an account of the meeting of the North Atlantic Defence Committee at The Hague on 1st April and the meeting of the Brussels Treaty Consultative Council in Brussels on the 16th and 17th April. I should be obliged if you would return the paper after you have read it.

Yours sincerely

C. R. Attlee

The Right Hon. Winston S. Churchill, O.M., C.H., F.R.S., M.P.

attend, he would go upstairs to eat with Vi in the flat, and would then come down to the Cabinet Room to work on boxes until the work was finished, which might be midnight or even 1.30 am.

The quality of work from the Number 10 office was exceptionally high; Attlee knew how to get the best out of his staff. Entertaining was cut back considerably compared with that of the Chamberlains; the Attlees had little aptitude for it, though Mrs Attlee managed charity fêtes and other similar occasions with some aplomb, and they both enjoyed hosting a dinner for the future Queen Elizabeth II just before her marriage to Philip in 1948.

Attlee's premiership may have been prosaic but it was effective, and laid the foundation of post-war British economic, social and foreign policy. Douglas Jay, an old friend and Labour colleague, caught the spirit of Attlee's Downing Street: 'The atmosphere in Number 10 was moral. You felt his policy was not just about what was good judgement and bad judgement, but about what was right and what was wrong.'

WINSTON CHURCHILL: 1951-55

Churchill returned to Number 10 in 1951 and quickly got back into his routine. He would wake at 7.30 or 8 am and ring for his valet who would bring him breakfast, usually just coffee and toast. His 'man' (in reality there were a succession, as they never stayed for long) would then help him wash; Churchill had never been without a valet and was unused to doing anything for himself. He then got back into bed, wearing one of his favourite brocade-patterned dressing gowns, while the valet puffed up the pillows behind his back. The Prime Minister's boxes were placed on a table to his right, leaving plenty of room to spread the papers all over the double bed. While working in bed, he would sip a glass of malt whisky and soda and puff on his cigar. He always had a gold Parker fountain pen given to him by his son, Randolph. Jane Portal, one of his secretaries, had to ensure that the pen was filled; Churchill's temper would flare if it ran empty. Churchill's two personal secretaries, Jane Portal and Elizabeth Gilliat, had the room next to his, and visitors would wait here before going through to see Churchill.

After midday, Churchill dressed and, if he had no visitors, lunched in the small Soane Dining Room with Clementine, invariably getting through half a bottle of Pol Roger 1934, which was sent to him regularly by Odette Pol Roger. On Wednesday mornings, Churchill chaired the Cabinet meeting in the Cabinet Room. On Tuesdays and Thursdays he would be joined in his bedroom by the Chief Whip, by his son-in-law, Christopher Soames (who became his Parliamentary Private Secretary) and by his Private Secretary and close aide, Jock Colville. They would prepare the old man for the twice-weekly Parliamentary Questions in the House.

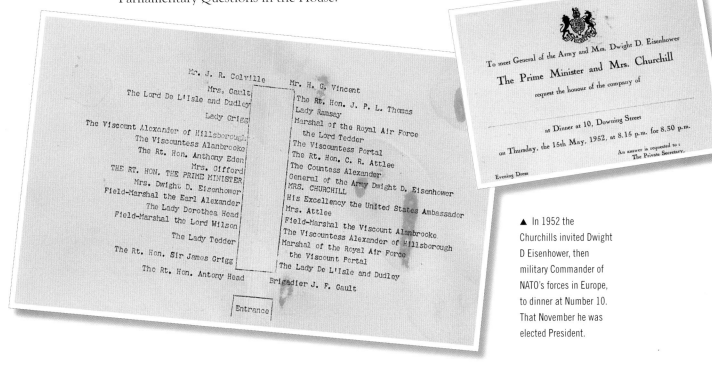

▲ In 1952 the Churchills invited Dwight D Eisenhower, then military Commander of NATO's forces in Europe, to dinner at Number 10. That November he was elected President.

The Churchills in Number 10

Winston and Clementine Churchill were delighted to be back in Downing Street in October 1951, after a gap of just over six years. In spite of her advice to the Attlees to have the second-floor flat completed, Lady Churchill moved back to the first floor: the Drawing Room became her private study and the room next to it, facing out over St James's Park, became her bedroom. Churchill's bedroom was upstairs in the second-floor flat immediately above it, and was reached by the lift from the ground-floor corridor. Its window faced out onto both St James's Park and Horse Guards Parade.

Churchill at Number 10 was certainly a contrast to the previous inhabitant; civil servants outside Downing Street, and some inside, contrasted his haphazard work methods unfavourably with the metronome style of Attlee. Churchill was similarly disenchanted, growling when presented with material in his Prime Minister's box arranged neatly in subject folders, 'Is this how Mr Attlee liked his papers?' He demanded instead that all important material be put 'top of the box' in a special folder. It was sometimes hard to make him concentrate; if a subject held little interest for him (which included much domestic policy), he would be reluctant to read anything or take decisions. This tendency increased considerably after his stroke

The Punch *cartoon of Churchill which read, 'Man goeth forth unto his work and to his labour until the evening' caused Churchill much hurt* (below). *Cecil Beaton's portrait of Lady Churchill in the White Drawing Room* (right). *With grandchildren Emma and Nicholas Soames, leaving for Buckingham Palace in 1953* (far right).

in June 1953 when, after a dinner for the Italian Prime Minister, de Gasperi, he was seen to slump. Guests were rapidly ushered away and news of his incapacity was kept from the media until he recovered his health in the early autumn. Jock Colville recorded in his diary that, 'at the end of the dinner Winston made a little speech in his best and most sparkling form, mainly about the Roman Conquest of Britain. After dinner he had a stroke, while he was in the Pillared Room among guests. He sat down and was almost unable to move.'

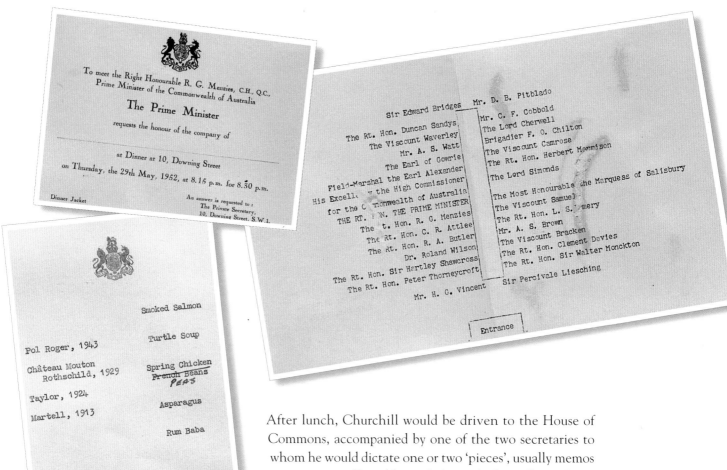

To meet the Right Honourable R. G. Menzies, C.H., Q.C.,
Prime Minister of the Commonwealth of Australia

The Prime Minister

requests the honour of the company of

at Dinner at 10, Downing Street
on Thursday, the 29th May, 1952, at 8.15 p.m. for 8.30 p.m.

Dinner Jacket
An answer is requested to :
The Private Secretary,
10, Downing Street. S.W.1.

Pol Roger, 1943

Château Mouton
Rothschild, 1929

Taylor, 1924

Martell, 1913

Smoked Salmon

Turtle Soup

Spring Chicken
French Beans
PEAS

Asparagus

Rum Baba

10, Downing Street,
15th May, 1952.

Sir Edward Bridges   Mr. D. B. Pitblado

The Rt. Hon. Duncan Sandys   Mr. C. F. Cobbold

The Viscount Waverley   The Lord Cherwell

Mr. A. S. Watt   Brigadier F. O. Chilton

The Earl of Gowrie   The Viscount Camrose

Field-Marshal the Earl Alexander   The Rt. Hon. Herbert Morrison

His Excell. y the High Commissioner   The Lord Simonds

for the C mmonwealth of Australia

THE RT. ON. THE PRIME MINISTER   The Most Honourable the Marquess of Salisbury

The t. Hon. R. G. Menzies   The Viscount Samuel

The Rt. Hon. C. R. Attlee   The Rt. Hon. L. S. mery

The Rt. Hon. R. A. Butler   Mr. A. S. Brown

Dr. Roland Wilson   The Viscount Bracken

The Rt. Hon. Sir Hartley Shawcross   The Rt. Hon. Clement Davies

The Rt. Hon. Peter Thorneycroft   The Rt. Hon. Sir Walter Monckton

Mr. H. C. Vincent   Sir Percivale Liesching

Entrance

▲ A dinner was held for Prime Minister Robert Menzies of Australia, in 1952. Menzies was an old friend of Churchill and had been a staunch ally during the Second World War. Churchill's favourite champagne, Pol Roger, was served.

After lunch, Churchill would be driven to the House of Commons, accompanied by one of the two secretaries to whom he would dictate one or two 'pieces', usually memos to ministers. He addressed the girls formally as 'Miss Portal' or 'Miss Gilliat', although the former would also be known as 'The Portal'. They addressed him as 'Prime Minister' or, in private, as 'the old man'.

If he found nothing to interest him in the House, he would return to Downing Street and check the ticker tape machine outside the Private Secretaries' room. He loved this piece of gadgetry, which kept him in touch with the outside world by hammering out the latest piece of national or world news. He might then work for a time in the Cabinet Room, buzzing for a Private Secretary if he required one. (The Private Office surreptitiously dampened the sound as he was prone to leave his finger on the buzzer and they found they were being deafened.) He would then go up to the flat, calling on his personal secretaries, and asking, 'Has anything come in?' He was always eager for some scintillating titbit. The girls would often draw his attention to things of interest to him; books, paintings, or the success of his racehorse, Colonist. He then slept for an hour or so, before being woken at 7 pm.

On the occasions when there was no dinner to go to, or reception at Number 10, he would don his one-piece 'siren suit'; if it was a formal occasion, he dressed meticulously in either black or white tie, with the right medals for the right occasion. Clementine continued to enjoy receptions and entertaining but Churchill had lost much of his taste for them. He was preoccupied with work, did not greatly enjoy small talk, and his hearing was not good; noisy receptions could be an ordeal. He would rarely be back after 10.30 pm and would work in the Cabinet Room until 1.30 or 2 am with a brandy, often dictating to one of the secretaries, who took it in turns to stay with him. The next day's newspapers would arrive before midnight, and he would spend an hour or so reading them carefully (even 'the dirties', as he called the tabloids). If he was irritated by a story, he would ring up the news editor to complain. When he felt he had done enough, he would go up to the flat where the secretary would help him undress and give him a bowl of jellied soup. It was a great relief to the girls when they heard the word 'soup' uttered, because they knew that he would almost be ready to fall asleep.

Churchill finally resigned on 5 April 1955. The night before, the Queen and Prince Philip came to a state dinner at Number 10. The Prime Minister was thrilled by the occasion and wore his Garter, Order of Merit and knee-breeches. Jock Colville, his ever-loyal Private Secretary captured the scene: 'On 4 April the Queen and Prince Philip dined at Number 10. It was a splendid occasion. The party consisted partly of the senior Cabinet Ministers, partly of grandees like the Norfolks and partly of officials and family friends – some 50 in all. Lady Churchill took special pains about the food and 10 Downing Street can seldom if ever have looked so gay or its floorboards [soon due to be demolished] have groaned under such a weight of jewels and decorations. There were incidents: the Edens, whose official precedence was low, tried to jump the queue, advancing to shake hands with the Queen, and the Duchess of Westminster put her foot through Clarissa's [Lady Eden's] train ('That's torn it, in more than one sense,' said the Duke of Edinburgh); Randolph got drunk and insisted on pursuing Clarissa with a derogatory article about Anthony Eden he had written for *Punch*; Mrs Herbert Morrison became much elated and could scarcely be made to leave the Queen's side; and I had a blazing row at dinner with Patrick Buchan-Hepburn because I had persuaded Lady Churchill to ask Alec and Elizabeth Home (he being the Minister of State for Scotland) while James Stuart, the Secretary of State, had not been invited.'

ANTHONY EDEN: 1955-57

Rarely had a premiership been more eagerly awaited – Eden had been heir apparent since 1940 – or more disappointing in the event than that of Anthony Eden. The contrast was all the more poignant given the high hopes with which Anthony and Clarissa Eden themselves had come to Number 10.

Lady Eden's father, Major John Churchill (Winston's brother), had lived in Number 10 during the war, and Lady Eden had held her wedding reception there in 1952. She was determined to make her mark on the house, and wanted to restore the main reception rooms to the style of Kent. She went to Houghton in Norfolk to see for herself Kent's work on Walpole's country home, and was shown

▶ The Churchills pose with bride and groom Anthony Eden and Clarissa Churchill, Winston's niece, in the garden of Number 10 on 14 August 1952. Clarissa herself came to Number 10 as Prime Minister's wife in April 1955, full of the highest hopes.

▼ Eden returns from convalescence in 1953, after an absence of six months. He never fully recovered his health.

some of Kent's brocades and damasks. The Ministry of Works, however, normally anxious to accommodate the wishes of Number 10's incomers, balked at her plans. The economic squeeze of the emergency budget of October 1955 militated against 'excessive' expenditure and it seemed rash to spend money on decoration when fundamental alterations would soon be required. So less expensive changes were made. Lady Eden introduced some of her own furniture into the Pillared Room and retained Lady Churchill's Persian rug in the first-floor drawing room. Fresh paintings from the National Gallery cellars brightened the walls. Anthony Eden, meanwhile, replaced the three inverted bowls of lighting in the Cabinet Room with two large chandeliers and a smaller one by the pillars at the east end of the room. The panels of the Breakfast Room, which they preferred to Soane's dark State Dining Room, were painted cream.

Eden's personal routine followed the familiar pattern. He and Clarissa lived in the second-floor flat, from where he would come down to work in the Cabinet Room at about 9.30 am, summoning Private Secretaries with the buzzer as he needed them. Lunch was often taken with Lady Eden on the first floor, afternoons were spent in the

Commons, and evenings would see Eden going up to the flat to work on his boxes. Guy Millard, a Private Secretary, recalls the Edens using the first-floor Drawing Rooms for their own purposes, not just for entertaining.

'At 5 pm I held my last Cabinet. I told them of the medical opinion, for which most were entirely unprepared. I think we were all affected by the personal side of this event, which I tried to make as short as I could.'

ANTHONY EDEN, 9 JANUARY 1957

But for all their high hopes and plans, the Edens were never happy at Number 10. Eden had not fully recovered from his botched abdominal operation in 1953, and an air of stress permeated the building, especially after the Suez Crisis erupted in July 1956. Eden describes in his memoirs, *Full Circle*, how he told his Cabinet, on 9 January 1957, of his decision to retire. He went to the Palace that evening to tender his resignation and, after a few days at Chequers, left for New Zealand to recuperate. 'On January 18th we sailed from Tilbury. We dropped down the river on a cold, misty winter's afternoon. Ships called to us and wirelessed their greetings as we passed. A message from the Captain told us that cadets of the training ship *Worcester* had asked to be allowed to make ship and speed us on our way. We came up on deck to see them. Their cheers were the last sound I heard in England.'

HAROLD MACMILLAN: 1957-63

After Eton (Macmillan was one of 18 prime ministers – over a third – to have been educated at that school) Macmillan went to Oxford and into the Army. The last British Prime Minister to fight in the First World War, he was severely wounded in the Battle of the Somme on the same day, 15 September 1916, that Raymond Asquith was killed. Macmillan married Lady Dorothy Cavendish, daughter of the 9th Duke of Devonshire, in 1920, and had an illustrious career in publishing and politics before being appointed Chancellor of the Exchequer in December 1955. When Eden's health collapsed, R A Butler, who had presided over Cabinet in Eden's absences, was considered the frontrunner, but after consultations with senior voices in the Tory party and Cabinet, it was decided Macmillan would be better able to lead government and country. At sixty-three, he was appointed Prime Minister.

The Edens left Number 10 at once, and the Macmillans moved in. The new Prime Minister was summoned to the Palace on January 10th; while waiting, he sat in the downstairs sitting room at Number 11, reading Jane Austen's *Pride and Prejudice*, which he found very soothing. Immediately on his return, he went into the Cabinet Room, settled into the Prime Minister's chair, and began the urgent task of forming his government.

The Macmillans made few changes to Number 10, knowing, even before they moved in, that major structural work was needed. In 1957, Macmillan set up the Crawford Committee to report on the condition of the house, which led

The Macmillans in Number 10

The Macmillans were pleased to move into their new home. They decided to sleep and live in the flat on the second floor, but Lady Dorothy would also take over the first-floor room on the north-west corner, and Macmillan used the next room, facing the park, as a study. After a month he confided in his diary his first thoughts on Number 10:

> 'It is very comfortable. I have a good room as a study, next to Dorothy's 'boudoir'. (She has arranged a work sitting room upstairs.) The Lounge is rather large, but has great character and charm. It is very "liveable".'

Lady Dorothy filled the house with her own large personality. Although their four children were grown up, grandchildren were regular visitors. Her admiring husband wrote of his wife:

> 'She filled [Number 10] with children and all their paraphernalia; she also filled it with flowers. But above all she made it seem like a family gathering in a country house with guests continually coming and going, with a large number of children's parties and with a sense of friendliness among all the staff and servants.'

The pleasure Macmillan derived from his idiosyncratic partner glows through his writing. The halls and corridor were filled with bicycles, tricycles, scooters, model 'Corgi' cars and perambulators. Lady Macmillan drove frequently between London and their country home, Birch Grove, in Sussex. According to her husband, she 'always arrived in a Ford or Austin van filled with vast quantities of vegetables and flowers and packages of all kinds'. She was also a generous hostess: soon after moving in she began to give regular tea parties for Tory MPs and their wives, and other Tory supporters. Macmillan was mortified when he learned in 1929 that his beloved Dorothy had been having an affair with one of these Tory MPs, Bob Boothby, since before the war. She was still romantically attached to Boothby while she was at Number 10, but the responsibilities of office now eclipsed the errant love affair. Macmillan knew that their youngest daughter, Sarah (b. 1930), was Boothby's. Somehow, their marriage survived, and Lady Dorothy became a strong and loyal supporter to him as Prime Minister.

Macmillan and Lady Dorothy in the White Drawing Room.

to the decision to renovate Numbers 10 and 11 and rebuild 12. On 1 August 1960, the Prime Minister and Lady Dorothy moved to Admiralty House, where they preferred the private accommodation to the cramped conditions at Number 10.

Macmillan settled quickly into his own groove, working closely with a particularly able and loyal Private Office. His biographer, Alistair Horne, says Macmillan saw being Prime Minster as 'fun', and was determined that working for the Prime Minister should also be fun. It was a marked change to Eden's Number 10, and, as if to highlight this, Macmillan penned the now famous lines, 'Quiet, calm deliberation disentangles every knot', which he displayed as the 'Motto for Private Office and Cabinet Room'. John Wyndham (later 'Lord Egremont'), an unpaid Private Secretary, wrote: 'My chief impression of the Private Office at Number 10 was of absolute calm. The calmest element of all was Mr Macmillan.'

This apparently most calm of Prime Ministers would wake early in the flat and work on his boxes. He took a light breakfast – he never ate much – of tea and toast and, like Churchill, would stay in bed for part of the morning, drafting responses and giving instructions to his secretaries, whose submissions in the boxes the night before would have had his careful marginal comments. In mid-morning he would descend to the first-floor sitting room, where everything was always in perfect order, with not a paper or book out of place. Luncheon was often taken at Number 10; his favourite dish was cold roast beef. When the House was sitting, afternoons were spent in the Chamber or in the Prime Minister's room behind the Speaker's chair, and evenings at Number 10. If he needed a Private Secretary late at night, the unparalleled 'Switch' (the Number 10 switchboard) would track them down. The Private Secretaries all had 'scrambler' telephones in their homes so he could speak to them in relative security (this was the height of the Cold War). Most secure of all was the direct line to the White House. This had started life as 'SIGSALY', the code name given to the top secret communications system devised in 1943 by the Bell Telephone Company for linking Churchill and President Roosevelt. The original, and not invariably reliable, machine was housed in the transatlantic telephone room in the Cabinet War Rooms, but was so large that part of the machinery was kept in the basement of Selfridge's Department Store in Oxford

▲ Moving out for the 1960–3 renovation work. The whole of Number 10 was cleared out – lock, stock and mattress – for the rebuild.

▲ Macmillan receives French President Charles de Gaulle at his Sussex Home, Birch Grove, in November 1961.

Street. By Macmillan's time, the link had shrunk in size – the White House telephone was a red instrument, and was wheeled in when needed on a sort of tea trolley. When it was plugged in, Downing Street and the White House were almost immediately connected. When possible, the Macmillans spent weekends away from London. As Norma Major reminds us, Macmillan was 'indifferent to the charms of Chequers, and preferred spending weekends at their country home, Birch Grove'. Birch Grove provided a forum for important international visits. Charles de Gaulle's visit in November 1961 is remembered chiefly for his blood, with which the French President insisted on travelling, so that he could receive an immediate transfusion in the event of an assassination attempt. The evening before de Gaulle was due to arrive, Lady Macmillan received a telephone call from the Foreign Office, asking where the President's blood could be stored. Lady Dorothy went to her husband in a state of high anxiety: 'I have been rung up by a young man from the Foreign Office with a short black coat and fancy pants,' she expostulated. 'How on earth could you tell what he was wearing?' her husband protested. 'Oh,' she replied, 'he spoke like it.' Finding somewhere to store the blood caused great concern in the household. The family cook, Mrs Bell, adamantly protested that the refrigerator was so full of haddock there was no room for the blood, General's and President's or not. Finally, an extra refrigerator was set up in the outhouse, as the only way to avoid a major domestic incident.

Ironically, it was not de Gaulle who was assassinated, but another visitor. John F Kennedy had been on tour in Europe, delivering his famous 'Ich bin ein Berliner' speech, and had helicoptered down to Birch Grove in July 1963 to discuss the Test Ban Treaty with Macmillan. Jackie Kennedy had written to Macmillan ahead of the visit, informing him that her husband liked plain food and had a distressingly normal palate. The Macmillans were a little taken aback by some of Kennedy's explicit conversation, but it was a happy visit and Lady Dorothy was thrilled to receive a gold dressing-table set from the American President. It was to be Kennedy's last foreign visit. Four months later, he was dead.

Macmillan's political life, too, was drawing to a close. The Kennedy visit came at the height of the Profumo sex scandal. Christine Keeler, the call girl at the centre of the fuss, had made an unscheduled visit to Birch Grove with a younger member of the large Macmillan family. Her name is not to be found in the Visitors' Book. Neither is that of the young blood.

The Profumo affair dragged Macmillan down, but he had been in trouble for some time – de Gaulle's veto of Britain's membership of the EEC had shattered his strategic direction. Over the summer of 1963, he fought for his political survival. In early October, he gave a television interview about the Denning Report into the Profumo scandal. His Press Secretary, Harold Evans, wrote in his diary: 'The broadcast was the PM's last official act at Admiralty House. When he left late at night to drive to Chequers he was leaving Admiralty House for good, since this week the office is moving back into Number 10. Tomorrow morning I shall be installed in my new room at Number 10. It will be good to be back.'

ALEC DOUGLAS-HOME: 1963-64

Macmillan's health broke down in the autumn of 1963 after months of strain. Alec Douglas-Home was the compromise candidate for the succession, and became the first minister to disclaim his peerage so that he could be elected to the House of Commons after taking up the premiership. When he became Prime Minister in October 1963, a circle was completed – he had been Chamberlain's Parliamentary Private Secretary and was with him on his return from Munich in September 1938. Home was an exceptionally gentle and kind family man. Whether he had the steel to have made a good Premier is hard to say, given the brevity of his tenure.

▲ The solitude of men in power. Alec Douglas-Home alone in the Number 10 garden in June 1964.

Home arrived at Number 10 with his accomplished wife, Elizabeth, who became a popular figure with the staff, a steady support to her husband, and an excellent hostess. Oliver Wright, future Ambassador to West Germany and the USA, but then a Private Secretary, said: 'She was wonderful. She took over all his private life, their houses in Scotland and London, the family, so he could focus utterly on his public business and on his fishing and shooting when he was relaxing. Everyone in the house adored her. She would give the Garden Room girls chocolates and chat to them at coffee time.' After a turbulent century, and some fiery premiers and unconventional relationships, the year the Homes spent at Number 10 was happy and harmonious. It was to be castigated unfairly by the new Labour team after 1964 as being like a morgue. It was not; it was the quiet before the storm.

WILSON TO BLAIR 1964-

Harold Wilson was Labour's third Prime Minister.
His Labour predecessors, Ramsay MacDonald
and Clement Attlee, arrived with fanfares
but left with divided parties. Wilson stole
into Number 10 meekly in 1964 and left
unexpectedly twelve years later, of his own
volition and with Labour tolerably unified.

▶ 2 May 1997. Tony
Blair makes his
triumphant way up
Downing Street to enter
Number 10 for the first
time as Prime Minister.

◀ The young Harold
Wilson.

HAROLD WILSON: 1964-70

Wilson had criticised Alec Douglas-Home's Number 10 for being like a monastery. He wanted, he famously said, to turn it into a 'powerhouse'. Labour had been out of office for thirteen years, since 1951, and were bursting to be back in control. Wilson was only forty-eight, and spoke about modernising Britain and galvanising it with a scientific and technological revolution. These were exciting times. State-school educated and possessing the common touch, Wilson seemed far more in tune with the young England of the Beatles, mini-skirts and Hovercraft than the staid Etonians, Macmillan and Home. He embodied a similar energy and zeal to that of John F Kennedy in the USA.

Harold Wilson did not succeed in making Number 10 a powerhouse. His formidable personal assistant, Marcia Williams, blamed this failure on being outwitted by the 'Whitehall establishment'. The real reason was that Wilson's ambition was unrealistic: Number 10 was much too small, with only ten figures of any weight, ever to be a powerhouse. He also failed to attract into Downing Street people of real authority and influence, in part because Marcia Williams was jealous of any challenge to her position. A minuscule Commons majority until the spring 1966 general election, and recurrent economic and factional problems thereafter, also conspired to make Wilson's Number 10 seem more reactive than trend-setting.

▲ Harold Wilson, aged eight, poses before the door of Number 10.

Harold Wilson was elected Labour leader in February 1963 and became Prime Minister on 16 October 1964. It was some months before his wife Mary, their two children, Robin and Giles, the family cat, Nemo, and dog, Paddy, moved into Downing Street from their home in Hampstead Garden Suburb. Giles continued as a day pupil at the independent University College School in Hampstead. The second-floor flat was never much liked by the Wilsons. Mary brought in some modern Swedish furniture for her bedroom, but the rest of the flat remained as the Homes had left it; only one year after the major rebuild, the Wilsons did not feel they could ask for alterations. Mary had the largest of the five bedrooms, with the Prime Minister sleeping next door in what was uncharitably described as 'a sort of dressing room'. The family did its best to make the flat's communal rooms – a sitting room, dining room and music room – as homely and undisturbed as possible, but government business often intruded. The telephone was always ringing, messengers arrived bringing in and taking out red boxes, and aides would come up in search of 'the boss'.

Harold Wilson relished the activity. His first task in the morning was to pore over all that day's newspapers, including the final editions of the 'big three', the *Daily Telegraph*, the *Daily Mirror* and the *Sun*. He read them in bed over breakfast – usually bacon and eggs, or, while stocks lasted, a kipper, an annual gift from the Labour MP for Aberdeen North. After a bath, he dressed and went down to the Private Office at about 8.30 am, where he checked his arrangements for the day and caught up on any developments that had occurred during the night.

The day's appointments would begin at 9 am and run on all morning, apart from Thursdays, when Cabinet met from 10 am to 1 pm, or when he was chairing a Cabinet Committee. If there were no official engagements, he ate lunch in the flat with Mary and, if they were at home, the boys. Marcia Williams would often eat with them, too, talking shop with the Prime Minister.

In the afternoon, Wilson would be driven to the Commons. On Tuesdays and Thursdays, before Prime Minister's Questions, officials and political aides would gather in his room to rehearse questions, possible supplementaries and answers. He knew how much hung on his performance, and was acutely aware of the need to be fully briefed. Other afternoons were spent in the chamber or in his office, where Marcia carved out the afternoon from Mondays to Thursdays for political rather than government business.

▲ Ambition fulfilled. Wilson at the Cabinet table in October 1964, shortly after taking office as Prime Minister.One of the chairs had to have its legs clad to protect Cabinet Minister Barbara Castle's stockings.

On Tuesday evenings, Wilson was driven to Buckingham Palace for his weekly audience with the Queen, not unlike the chief executive of a company going for a weekly meeting with his non-executive chairman. Wilson hugely enjoyed seeing the monarch, as did many premiers. The meetings had a tinge of the confessional, or a visit to the therapist. Some premiers resented the intrusion into precious time, but nevertheless felt better for having gone.

Until 1966/67, Wilson would work alone in the Cabinet Room, as his hero, Attlee, had done. His solitude, however, was frequently disturbed by meetings

The Wilsons in Number 10

Wilson's Number 10 saw a marked shift in the approach to entertaining. Receptions and dinners for the 'great and good' from politics, the Civil Service, armed forces and business still took place, but new faces began to appear at them. Guests would include entertainers like David Frost, Eric Morecambe and Ernie Wise or the Beatles, and the Apollo astronauts, the first men to walk on the moon. Some questioned his judgement in inviting 'show-biz' people to Number 10, but Wilson saw more clearly than many prime ministers before him the PR value of such guests. He would be unconventional, too, in inviting dinner guests – businessmen and university vice-chancellors, for example – to go down to the Cabinet Room after the meal for a free-ranging discussion sitting around the hallowed table.

Mary Wilson did not enjoy social occasions – or most other aspects of life at Number 10. As one insider commented,

'Poor Mary: she thought she was marrying an Oxford don; she found herself being married to a Prime Minister.'

She had no social or political ambition, nor interests. Initially, like many prime ministers' wives, she was overawed. A senior hospitality official, trying to make the Wilsons

With US President Lyndon Johnson, 1964, following two days of high-level talks **(above)**. *Mary Wilson in the Number 10 flat* **(below)**.

feel at ease, said to her early on, 'Is there any particular food that the Prime Minister would prefer we did not serve at official functions, because we would like to serve food he enjoys?' She thought about it, before replying, 'He doesn't like mince.'

Mary Wilson, however, refused to be cowed. She persisted in dressing informally and going hatless on all but the most formal occasions. She became a character in her own right, earning a popular following, not unlike Denis Thatcher later on. Both were satirised in *Private Eye*: 'Mrs Wilson's Diary' was every bit as eagerly awaited as Denis Thatcher's 'Dear Bill' letters of the 1980s. Unselfconsciously, ignoring the ridicule of the scoffing literary intelligentsia, she wrote verse, which caught the admiring eye of the poet John Betjeman, who became a friend. She remained shy to the end, and even in their sixth and final year had developed no greater liking of Number 10. As Ben Pimlott, Wilson's biographer, wrote:

'She regarded her job, grimly, as a protective one: of her family – her children, her husband and herself – from the artificial and alien circumstances in which they found themselves. There was a sense of gritting her teeth, waiting for it to be over.'

with MPs, trade unionists and others. The custom developed of favoured officials and political aides dropping into the study for a good evening gossip, giving rise to press talk about a 'kitchen' Cabinet. No such formal grouping ever existed, but a number of close aides did have Wilson's ear.

By 1970, he had persuaded his Private Office to reduce his 'homework' from five or six to just two or three red boxes. He would sit in an armchair by the window, papers spread out, with pop music playing quietly on the radio – a schoolboy doing his prep. In this six-year first spell at Number 10, Wilson had tremendous zest for his work. His alcohol consumption was low and he would not go to bed until his work was completed, which was never before 12.30 am. Just before going to sleep, he would read the first editions of the three newspapers which the proprietors ensured were personally delivered to Number 10.

Mary Wilson's feelings about Marcia Williams are unrecorded, but she did not enjoy having the ubiquitous Marcia in their dining room, kitchen, on the phone, in their car. She banned Marcia from their holiday home on the Isles of Scilly, but Marcia side-stepped the diktat by buying her own home on the island. Whatever their relationship had been, Marcia retained a deep and unfathomable hold over Wilson. She possessed a brilliant mind and an unrivalled grasp of Labour party politics and was at the height of her powers during the 1960s. Wilson depended on her intellectually, politically and emotionally. Civil servants recall vying with her for the Prime Minister's attention when he worked at his Cabinet table chair. The Private Office lay through the double doors at one end of the Cabinet Room and Marcia was ensconced in an office through the single door at the west end. She had obtained the room, and her title 'Personal and Political Secretary', only after a battle with the Civil Service hierarchy. The room had belonged to the Appointments Secretary, who dealt principally with church patronage, and he had to be moved upstairs to what was termed 'The Museum'. 'Tell him he can have a stained glass in his new room,' Wilson said dismissively of this senior state official.

Under Wilson, Number 10 was more bureaucratic and businesslike but also a less happy place than it had been under Macmillan and Home, with Marcia the principal reason for the tension. She bullied those weaker than herself and tried to undermine those in more established positions. She believed senior Civil Service officials were engaged in a plot to bring the Conservatives back to power, and fought a long-running battle with them to be put on the circulation list for sensitive government papers. Civil Service officials were certainly unhappy about having her as a political adviser at the heart of government, but the reason they did not want her to see sensitive papers was that they did not think she could be trusted, not least because she had a political journalist as her lover. On her side, she felt that Wilson's personal staff were initially made to feel 'like intruders and squatters', and that the atmosphere at Number 10 was 'ice cold'. Her belief in a phallocentric conspiracy to thwart her was heightened by officials using the ground-floor urinal outside her study as a place to 'nab' the Prime Minister.

EDWARD HEATH: 1970-74

Edward Heath succeeded Alec Douglas-Home as Tory leader in 1965, the first Tory premier not to be educated at a private school, and the first to be elected by Tory MPs. On Wilson's defeat in the close general election of 1970, Heath became the first bachelor to move into Number 10 since Balfour. Heath was one of the more puzzling incumbents of Downing Street. Physically brave, as a sailor in international yacht races, and sensitive, in his love of painting and music, he could also be gauche and downright rude.

Women liked Heath and made a fuss of him. Two women in particular groomed him at Number 10: Sara Morrison and Araminta Low, the wife of his close friend Toby (later Lord) Aldington. There was no romantic attachment with either lady, but he enjoyed being pampered by attractive women. Prime ministers need partners to help with entertaining, and to talk over the pains and pleasures of the high-tension job. Ramsay MacDonald had been the last incumbent without a partner, but his daughter Ishbel fulfilled some of this role.

So too did Robert Armstrong, whom Heath selected as his Principal Private Secretary. Armstrong served throughout Heath's premiership, proving not only to be a masterly organiser of Number 10 business but also a loyal friend and companion to Heath, not least in helping to arrange some magical musical events (see Chapter 6). A 'Rolls Royce' among officials, and high priest of correct form, Armstrong restored to Number 10 its status after the erratic Wilson era, and set about raising the morale of the Garden Room girls, after the bashing they had received from Marcia.

▲ Edward Heath, art lover and Conservative Premier. He adored Number 10.

Heath adored Number 10. He used it not only as his office and town house, but also as a showcase for music, painting and sculpture. His personal space extended from the second-floor flat to the first-floor study and the White Drawing Room, where he placed his piano. His aim was to restore Number 10 to the appearance it had in Walpole's day, and the discovery of further dry rot became the occasion for having the State Rooms redecorated, and the Drawing Room walls covered in figured silk as well as the room being given a new carpet and table.

Heath was woken at 7.45 am (late for a Prime Minister) and senior aides, including Armstrong and Douglas Hurd, his Political Secretary, would go up to discuss the day's business. Heath was a remarkably good listener. The boxes would be the next call on his time – red boxes from the Private Office, a black box with political material from Hurd and, making its first appearance at Number 10, the *pièce de résistance*, a blue box with a red stripe (subsequently to be named 'Old Stripey') for extra-sensitive material. Heath would come down for his first meeting

◄ The Heath Cabinet lines up in August 1973. On the extreme right sits the Education Secretary, Margaret Thatcher. Such formal 'school' photos in the garden are a regular occurrence for Cabinet Ministers.

of the day at 10 or 10.30 am. Thereafter, he followed the usual weekly programme of Cabinets, preparation for Prime Minister's Questions, audiences with the Queen and receptions. In the early evening, he would try to fit in a swim, and would return to work in his private flat, listening to 'hi-fi' classical music rather than Wilson's pop, or relaxing over television, before turning in at around midnight.

Heath's measured lifestyle continued at weekends. On Friday afternoons he would leave Number 10, to go either to Chequers or to Cowes, on the Isle of Wight, to sail, and would not be seen again until Sunday evening. He was captivated by Chequers and filled it with stimulating and diverse house guests.

Heath brought order back to Number 10. But it was to prove the most traumatic premiership since the end of the Second World War. From 1971 until the bitter end in March 1974, the government appeared to be under constant challenge: industrial unrest, violence in Northern Ireland which led to the imposition of 'direct rule' from London, war in the Middle East leading to a quadrupling of oil prices, student unrest, extremist agitation from left and right, and the imposition of a 'three-day working week' over the winter of 1973/74. A government that began with high promise was ended with Heath calling an election in February 1974, posing the question 'Who runs Britain?' The inconclusive answer on polling day led some to conclude that no one did, and that Britain was becoming ungovernable.

HAROLD WILSON: 1974-76

The prospect of a Wilson government and the return of Marcia Williams filled some staff with horror. The Head of the Garden Room refused to join others upstairs to welcome the Wilsons back; she remained downstairs, comforted by Wilberforce, the Number 10 cat, who jumped up on her lap in a gesture of feline solidarity.

The fears were misplaced. Marcia had become a largely spent force. Wilson, meanwhile, had taken to heavy drinking on Prime Ministers' Questions days, and became prone to long bouts of reminiscing: some believe he was already suffering from the early symptoms of Alzheimer's disease which was to afflict him later in life. Wilson also began to show signs of what can only be described as paranoia, in his suspicion about British and overseas intelligence services tracking him. In March 1974, he told a friend, Harry Kissin, while they were talking in his study: 'There are only three people listening – you, me and MI5.' In his last year, 1975/76, his low and erratic work-rate was being shielded by the Private Office. Not since Churchill's final premiership (1951/55) had the Number 10 officials done so much to compensate for the Prime Minister's lassitude.

Mary Wilson was another who had dreaded the prospect of a Labour victory. She made it perfectly clear to her husband that she would not return to the Number 10 flat. Wilson, accordingly, became the first peacetime premier since Lord Salisbury in 1902 not to live in Downing Street. The Wilsons had sold their home in Hampstead Garden Suburb, and after the 1970 election defeat had bought a Westminster town house in nearby Lord North Street. From there, Wilson was driven each morning to Number 10, arriving by 9 am. The day followed a similar pattern to 1964/70, but at a more gentle tempo. There was lower wattage electricity, less excitement and much less of Marcia. Socially, Wilson performed less well: aides complained that receptions 'could be a real nightmare. You'd try to ensure he was talking to the most important guests and he'd be off in the corner chatting away to cronies about party business.' The evenings were spent gossiping, working and drinking in the study, before he was driven back to Lord North Street.

To the nation's surprise, and to the surprise of many of his MPs, Wilson announced his decision to stand down in March 1976. His government had had its successes, including restoring industrial harmony of a kind, some economic recovery and the holding of a nationwide referendum on whether Britain should remain in the European Economic Community, which Heath had taken Britain into in 1973. The nation decided it did want to remain in Europe, and many were sorry to see this unusual, pipe-smoking, kindly and intelligent Yorkshireman leave Number 10.

▼ Marcia Williams leaving Number 10 on 16 March 1976, the day Wilson announced his resignation.

JAMES CALLAGHAN: 1976-79

One of Harold Wilson's better jokes was that he had retired to make way for an older man. James Callaghan was elected at the age of sixty-four, in April 1976, and promptly moved into Number 10 with his wife, Audrey.

▲ Callaghan with US President Carter and West German Chancellor Helmut Schmidt, meeting for the G7 summit held in London in May 1977. They are surrounded by an assortment of bodyguards, necessary in the days when Number 10 was still open to the public.

Callaghan was one of the most experienced figures to become Prime Minister this century, having held all three great offices of state (Home Secretary, Chancellor of the Exchequer and Foreign Secretary). He exuded calm and experience, taking as his maxim a native Welsh saying, 'Byd ben: byd Bont' – he who would lead must be a bridge.

James and Audrey Callaghan spent most of their time in London in Number 10, but would sleep periodically in their Kennington flat south of the river, which they kept throughout their three years in Downing Street. Weekends were spent at their beloved farmhouse in Sussex, where they relaxed and thrived in the company of grandchildren and cows (both a great source of joy). Problems arose at weekends over accommodation for the support crew of detectives and Garden Room girls: the farmhouse was too small, so they slept at Shelley's Hotel in nearby Lewes. Audrey was an utterly loyal and supportive consort, and was the first wife of a Labour Prime Minister to enjoy life at Number 10.

Callaghan was formal in his daily routine. Visiting aides were not welcome in the second-floor flat and, unlike Wilson, he avoided conducting business in the car, in the corridor or in doorways. He cherished good order. His boxes were always meticulously handled; officials like a tidy prime minister. After breakfast, he would come down to work in the first-floor study, or occasionally the Cabinet Room. In the afternoons, he spent longer than many premiers talking to fellow MPs in the Commons tea room and other communal areas in the House. Dinner would often be taken in the Commons and he would wait until the 10 pm vote before being driven back to Downing Street. One official commented: 'It was all very prosaic. He would call in to the Private Offices to wish those still working "goodnight" and say, "I'm going up now". There was no gossip nor chat. There were no late night meetings nor cabals, no plots, nor talk of plots. There was also no drink, and he turned in early: he needed his sleep. As he told an aide, he considered that being Premier was 'like being an athlete: "he had a duty to be fit".'

◄ Margaret Thatcher with husband Denis, Ronald and Nancy Reagan, and James Callaghan, in the Blue (now Green) Drawing Room. President Reagan admired her greatly; so much so that Washington officials became very anxious about her influence over him when they were together.

MARGARET THATCHER: 1979-90

Callaghan's Labour government lost the general election in May 1979 after the industrial unrest of the 'winter of discontent' of 1978/79 had destroyed the impression of a sound government restoring economic order to the country. Margaret Thatcher moved in to Number 10 the next month, from her Chelsea home. She was not greatly impressed by the untidy flat and dullish official rooms, and when she left Downing Street eleven and a half years later, the house was much enhanced. On arrival, she described the Cabinet Ante Room as resembling 'a down-at-heel Pall Mall club, with heavy and worn leather furniture', while the rooms upstairs had a 'furnished house to let' feel about them.

Intense interest surrounded Britain's first ever woman prime minister: female monarchs had been not uncommon in British history, and a queen had been on the throne for over a quarter of a century. The idea of a woman presiding over Number 10, however, was something entirely new. How would she cope with power, with all the men around her? How would her husband, Denis, manage his role?

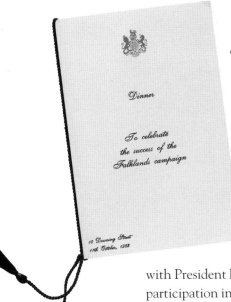

▲ A Downing Street
dinner was held on
11 October 1982 to
celebrate the success of
the Falklands campaign.
Controversy had
been aroused over
'celebrating' the victory
in the war.

Margaret Thatcher proved to be a formidable premier, and came to be compared to Churchill. No prime minister since him had been the subject of so many anecdotes, many complimentary. One such story, undoubtedly apocryphal, had Mrs Thatcher taking her Cabinet out to dinner. The waiter asked her for their order: 'Beef,' she replied. 'And the vegetables, madam?' enquired the waiter. 'Oh, they will have beef too.' It is to her credit that she rather enjoyed such caricatures. The nation admired her for her tenacity and courage, exemplified by her commanding role in the Falklands War of 1982, the defeat of the striking miners and militant trade unionism in 1984/85, and the personal courage and strength of will she displayed after the bombing of the Grand Hotel, Brighton, in 1984. Her close relationships with President Reagan of the USA and Mikhail Gorbachov of the USSR, and her participation in the ending of the Cold War, gave her an international standing of a kind no British premier had enjoyed since Churchill.

Her hard work, and ability to survive on just a few hours' sleep, were legendary. Rising at 6 am or earlier, she would begin by listening to BBC Radio 4, while working on papers in the flat, having her hair done, eating breakfast and getting ready for the day. One reason why Caroline Stephens, her Diary Secretary in the Private Office, was so valued by officials was that she would be their envoy, communicating with her in the second-floor flat while she was in the bath or dressing. 'Crawfie' (Cynthia Crawford) was her personal assistant throughout her time at Number 10, as invaluable to her in clothes and other personal matters as Churchill's valets had been to him forty years before.

Meetings began in the first-floor study at 9 am, with her Principal Private Secretary talking over the day ahead. A light lunch was often taken in the flat while she was working; if it was a Prime Minister's Questions day she would have aides helping her prepare. She liked to make her own meals (a quick salad or a poached egg on Bovril toast, for example). Afternoons were spent working in the Prime Minister's room in the Commons. The late evening was spent in the sitting room of the second-floor flat at Number 10, where she was often joined by close aides; kicking off her high heels, she would put her feet up and drink a glass or two of whisky. At 10 or 11 pm she would go into the kitchen to prepare a meal: eggs and cheese were the staple ingredients, or pre-prepared dishes from the deep-freeze; her ingenuity was greatly enhanced by the arrival on the scene in the mid-1980s of the 'microwave'. According to her daughter, Carol, 'One MP was so horrified to find his chain of thought constantly interrupted by the Prime Minister bobbing up and down to check on the simmering frozen peas that he read the riot act to her.' She kept her head clear for her boxes, which would always be completed before she turned in for the night at 1 am or later.

Mrs Thatcher left her mark on Number 10. Her most enduring contribution was to bring in the architect Quinlan Terry to make the three Drawing Rooms look more stately. She was guided in her quest by Carla Powell, the formidable wife of her formidable Foreign Office Private Secretary, Charles Powell. Mrs Thatcher brought contemporary British art to Number 10, including the Henry Moore Alcove on the main passageway between the Hall and the Cabinet Ante Room. The first-floor study was redecorated to her taste. She chose a light grey paper for the walls and cream-coloured damask for the furniture. She was intensely proud of her study (below): on one occasion a guest spilled coffee over the settee and carpet. Typically, Mrs Thatcher spent twenty minutes herself trying to remove any trace of a stain.

She called her domestic life 'living over the shop', recalling her early years living above her father's grocer's shop in Grantham, Lincolnshire. The large corner room overlooking Horse Guards Parade and St James's Park was converted from a bedroom into the main sitting room, and she decorated it with two settees covered in a floral pattern of red and blue on a cream background. The cushions, curtains and window seats all matched. In a recessed wall cupboard she arranged part of her large collection of Derby and Staffordshire china.

As she said of the flat, 'it quickly became my refuge from the rest of the world'. Unlike many of her predecessors, she shared a bed with her spouse. Denis proved the ideal partner, in her eyrie and outside. He played up to the popular image of him as an amiable buffoon, tipsy and nicotine-addicted, and dreaming of his next game of golf. In reality, he was both highly intelligent and a wise and calm counsellor. Mrs Thatcher realised how much she owed to him: 'What a man. What a husband. What a friend,' was how she touchingly described him. He remained her closest ally throughout her eleven and a half years, to an extent never fully realised by outsiders. The achievements of her premiership, which included strengthening the competitive base of the British economy and bolstering Britain's position as a world power, would not have been possible without Denis at her side, especially as in her first two and her last two years she had at best limited support from Cabinet colleagues. It was the ultimate loss of this support that led to her downfall in November 1990.

> '*I like things bright . . . but when I first came here the walls of the study were covered with heavy sage-green damask-flock wallpaper. It was oppressive . . . So I had it redone myself at my own cost.*'
>
> MARGARET THATCHER

▼ The first-floor study as it was early on during Mrs Thatcher's time. She would sit working at the desk in the background. Earlier, it had been used as the bedroom of prime ministers and their wives. Its style is more 'country house' than official prime ministerial room.

JOHN MAJOR: 1990-97

It has been common in British history for premiers to find difficulty following strong predecessors – Peel, Gladstone, Salisbury, Lloyd George and Churchill are the more obvious examples of great figures who were followed by lesser figures. After such a towering premiership as Mrs Thatcher's, the next prime minister would inevitably appear but a pale imitation. John Major suffered in part from this comparison. He was also serving at a time when the Tory party was less united than at any point in the century, with a small and disappearing majority after the 1992 general election. Furthermore, from 1994, he had to face the challenge of Tony Blair, Labour's most effective leader since Harold Wilson. John Major's premiership, sniped at from all sides at the time, is only now beginning to be reassessed as a largely successful juggling act at a very difficult time.

▲ John Wonnacott's portrait of Major in the White Drawing Room, which hangs in the National Portrait Gallery. Norma sits at the window, where Clementine Churchill is photographed taking tea (see page 143).

Major came to Number 10 in November 1990, aged forty-seven, and a comparative unknown. Three years before, he had not even been in Cabinet, and subsequent spells at the Foreign Office and Treasury were brief. He later acknowledged that the premiership had come to him too early; he was essentially a compromise candidate between two strong and more experienced rivals, Michael Heseltine and Douglas Hurd. His elevation to the premiership happened as in a whirlwind. Major's supporters gathered in Number 11 on the evening of 27 November 1990 to hear the result of the leadership election. Tim Bell, a friend of both Thatcher and Major, vividly recalls sensing 'power move across the room from her to him, as people left her side and gravitated towards him'.

John and Norma Major moved across from the Chancellor's residence at Number 11 into Number 10. Initially, Norma lived during the week at their home near Huntingdon, in their constituency, and admirably succeeded in shielding their two children, James and Elizabeth, from the glare of the media; she was determined that the public glare that fell on Mark and Carol Thatcher would not fall on her children.

► With Georgian President, Eduard Shevardnadze, signing an investment agreement.

Major rose each morning in the second-floor flat at about 6 or 6.30 am, listened periodically to the radio, and finished off his overnight boxes. Aides would begin to come up to the flat from about 7.30 am to discuss the day ahead. Shaving time was particularly prized by aides because, for a few minutes, their boss would be rooted to the spot. He would come downstairs at about 8.30 am and begin work, for the first few weeks in the first-floor study but thereafter in the Cabinet Room. The mornings and evenings would usually be spent at Number 10. On his return to Downing Street in the evening, he would go to the Cabinet Room, working through papers or holding meetings until about 9.30 pm, when he would go up to the flat to continue to work on his boxes, often with the television on in the background and with an aide or friend present, off whom he would bounce ideas. He would go to bed around midnight.

'Come on, how long have we been here now, three and a half years? When do we overtake Ted Heath?'

NORMA MAJOR, MARCH 1994

▼ The Majors invite South African leader Nelson Mandela to lunch in July 1996. Such was the excitement among Number 10 staff that they most unusually were allowed to greet him in the Hall.

Major's was a conservative Number 10. He left no mark on the fabric of the building, although he had always taken pains to ensure that it was attractively filled with works of art. He was also an exceptionally hospitable premier. Norma proved to be an exceptional wife. With little training, she showed herself, after an initial period of doubt, to be both an excellent hostess and a loyal supporter and adviser to her husband.

Major's fifty-first birthday was on 29 March 1994; this was also a day on which he had suffered a particularly humiliating reversal in the House.

When he returned in early evening, an impromptu birthday reception had been prepared by Number 10 staff in the Cabinet Room. Major's despondent air depressed those present, but Norma bustled around the room saying, 'Come on; how long have we been here now, three and a half years? When do we overtake Ted Heath?' One who was present recalls, 'She was absolutely magnificent . . . She made it clear that they were there for the duration and no one would budge them. It was one of the times we saw how sensible, acerbic and tough she really was.'

During the premiership, Norma became a steadily more powerful counsellor; it was her anger at the way her husband was treated by some senior Tory politicians that played a decisive part in his announcement that he would stand down immediately as leader of the Party, after losing the May 1997 general election.

Tony Blair: 1997-

Tony and Cherie Blair, and their three children Euan, Nicky and Kathryn, moved into Downing Street on 2 May 1997, following the Labour landslide of May 1st. They had already decided to move out of their Islington home and to move into the larger flat above Numbers 11 and 12, giving the second-floor flat above Number 10 to the Chancellor, Gordon Brown.

Blair is an early riser. He wakes at 6 am and works on his boxes, wandering down in his pyjamas and making calls on a cordless phone. He then has a bath. The first two aides to see him each morning will be Jonathan Powell, his Chief of

▶ Tony Blair shakes hands with Bill Clinton on the steps of Number 10 as the First Ladies talk in earnest.

▲ An informal moment – taking tea on the balcony outside the Cabinet Room.

Staff, and Alastair Campbell, Press Secretary. He comes across to Number 10 a few minutes prior to his first meeting, usually at 9 am. On Mondays, this is an-hour long 'office meeting', vital for establishing Blair's priorities and setting the tone for the week ahead. The principal attendees are Powell, Campbell, Anji Hunter, his personal secretary, Sally Morgan, the Political Secretary, and David Miliband, Head of the Policy Unit. Powell draws up a page of 'action points' and distributes it to members of the group and to other key figures at Number 10.

During his first year, Blair used the Political Secretary's office at the end of the Cabinet Room. He would sit on the couch and make phone calls, meet colleagues, read or give interviews. By 1998, however, he was finding it too small and moved his office to the Private Secretary's office at the east end of the Cabinet Room.

Receptions and official meals have been reduced in number during the Blair reign: in the evenings, he likes to see his family and at weekends, when not visiting his Sedgefield constituency or on any official business, he enjoys spending time with them at Chequers. Tony Blair enjoys a balanced lifestyle, and he has that at least in common with Number 10's first incumbent, Robert Walpole.

◄ In the first-floor study with Microsoft chief Bill Gates, October 1997.

Death of a Princess

On Sunday, 31 August 1997, at 1.15 am, the Duty Clerk at Number 10 received a call from the British Embassy in Paris. A car accident had taken place in which the Princess of Wales had been injured, and her boyfriend, Dodi Fayed, killed. The British Ambassador, he learned, was on his way to the hospital that very minute.

The Duty Clerk phoned Angus Lapsley, the Private Secretary on duty that weekend, who had to take the key decision on whether or not to wake the Prime Minister from his much-needed sleep. Lapsley had no doubt, and immediately phoned Blair's private number at his Sedgefield constituency to break the news.

An hour after the first Paris call came another to say that Diana had died. Tony Blair was devastated when he heard the news. He sensed immediately the enormous import of the news – Diana was the mother of the two young princes and a woman of unparalleled international fame. There was a personal dimension too. A few weeks earlier, Diana had visited the Blairs at Chequers with her children. The first great tragedy of his premiership, the Prime Minister felt her death acutely. He knew he would have to make a press statement within hours, and that he would have to hit the right note. He spoke by phone to his key Number 10 aides, including Alastair Campbell and Anji Hunter, neither of whom were with him in his constituency.

He thought through what he would say as he drove down to St Mary Magdalene Church that morning. The words were his own. Visibly upset and shaken, and on the verge of breaking down, he not only struck a chord with the nation, but also set the tone for the outpouring of grief in the days that followed. Later that day, he flew to London to meet her coffin, which was flown back that evening to RAF Northolt. 'I feel like everyone else in the country today,' he said, his voice broken with emotion.

'I am utterly devastated . . . she was the People's Princess and that is how she will stay, how she will remain in our hearts and our memories for ever.'

ART, ARTEFACTS & ENTERTAINING

Number 10 is more than just an office and family home; it is also a building full of rooms and works of great aesthetic beauty, and a showcase where the art of entertaining reaches the highest level.

Robert Walpole was not just the country's first Prime Minister; he was also the building's first art collector, and was proud to use Number 10 to show off his treasures. He acquired Van Dycks, a vast Poussin, and Maratti's portrait of the dying Pope Clement IX. His collection would have been a marvellous boon to the nation, but in 1779 it was sold by his grandson to Catherine the Great of Russia for £40,000.

▶ George Lambert's painting of 'St James's Park from the Terrace of 10 Downing Street', mid-eighteenth century. One still has uninterrupted views of the park from Number 10.

◀ An elegant dinner setting for the Prime Minister.

Since Walpole, it has been the tradition for each incumbent of Number 10 to bring his or her own pictures to grace the house. But when Ramsay MacDonald became Britain's first Labour Prime Minister, in January 1924, he lacked private means and owned no works of art that would have been considered appropriate for Number 10. So he approached the National Gallery and asked to borrow works from its considerable reserve collection.

This practice continues today. About half the art in Number 10 belongs to the Government Art Collection, which owns 14,000 works, available on loan to Whitehall departments and British overseas embassies. The remaining works of art are on loan from public galleries, including the National Portrait Gallery, the Tate, the Victoria and Albert Museum and the National Gallery.

When Edward Heath (1970-4) arrived at Number 10 he thought it looked drab, and took advantage of the redecoration forced on the house in 1970-1 by the latest round of dry rot to brighten up the Cabinet Room with lighter paint, curtains and carpet. The Prime Minister's study and State Drawing Rooms were treated in similar vein. Distinctive blue silk wallpaper was hung in the Middle Drawing Room, which was later to be redecorated by Mrs Thatcher in green. Heath loved the house. Works by eighteenth- and nineteenth-century artists, including four big Gainsboroughs, replaced undistinguished paintings and portraits of British 'heroes'.

Political Differences over Art

Heath borrowed French paintings from the National Gallery, and he was lent two Renoirs in succession by a private collector, which ruffled some patriotic feathers. Perhaps it was the blue wall coverings that upset her, but Mary Wilson planned to reverse Heath's changes and return Number 10 to how it had been in the 1960s. However, when the Wilsons returned in March 1974, she did no such thing, perhaps because the Wilsons chose to live in their own Westminster home. The Callaghans also left the house much as they found it.

Mrs Thatcher arrived in 1979 with definite ideas about art: it had to be British, and she wanted Number 10 to show off 'British achievers', an anathema to Heath. She felt there was too little recognition of those who by skill and courage had made outstanding achievements in their fields. As a former chemist, she took particular pleasure in devoting the small Soane Dining Room to a celebration of British scientists. Portraits of Joseph Priestley, who discovered oxygen, and Sir Humphrey Davy, who helped make mining safer, were hung there. In the State Dining Room she introduced John Shackleton's portrait of George II, the monarch who bequeathed the house to the First Lord and the only king whose portrait hangs at Number 10. A portrait of Admiral Thompson by Thomas Gainsborough, on loan from the Tate, was also hung there. 'Achievers' in the Pillared Room resulted in some rather dour and dark pictures, which added dignity but not life to the large room.

A NEW APPROACH

On his arrival in 1990, John Major surprised some people by the interest he took in the paintings at Number 10, and by his modern thinking. At his prompting, the first-floor Ante Room became a mini gallery of the best of modern art. Photographs of this room show selections from the Major years; they are certainly striking. Under Major, Constables were brought into Number 10 to be displayed alongside the Turners, so the house could boast paintings by Britain's two best-known nineteenth-century artists.

John Major introduced George Lambert's painting of *St James's Park from the Terrace of 10 Downing Street* (see page 171) to Number 10. It hangs in the Cabinet Room, facing the portrait of Sir Robert Walpole by Jean-Baptiste Vanloo, given by Viscount Lee of Fareham and hung over the mantelpiece above the prime minister's chair since 1921. (Viscount Lee was a generous benefactor: he also gave Chequers to the state so that prime ministers could find there a peaceful haven.) In the Prime Minister's study on the first floor, Major introduced two cricketing paintings, including a portrait of England's most celebrated batsman, W G Grace, by Archibald Wortley. His main selections were largely British and modern.

▲ 'Gillingham Bridge' by John Constable, which hangs in the White Drawing Room.

◀ Rachel Whiteread's 'Mausoleum under Construction', hung in the corridor off the first-floor Ante Room — a sample of Number 10's commitment to modern art.

▶ The front staircase, with paintings by Gary Hume. This staircase was created in the early 1960s by Raymond Erith.

New Labour, New Picture

Since 1997, Tony Blair's tastes have been reflected in some striking works by younger British artists, including Rachel Whiteread (above) and paintings by Scottish colourists on loan from the National Galleries of Scotland.

New prime ministers can indulge their preferences only up to a point. Paintings from galleries will be loaned only if they are not required for public showing or special exhibitions and not even Number 10 can always demand first choice from the Government Art Collection. They must also be returned after a period. Triumphalist war paintings, pictures of past imperial glories, or those demeaning overseas allies are ruled out, and the choices favour British artists. An annual turnover of about a dozen paintings a year has been established, which is accepted as the right pace for the building. Only some twelve paintings remain from the 1970s. At times the house has boasted paintings by Winston Churchill, the most accomplished artist among Britain's 50 prime ministers. His *Long River, Alpes Maritimes*, on loan from the Tate, now hangs in the first-floor study.

Some paintings have established themselves in Number 10, and would only be changed with a degree of institutional reluctance. In the Entrance Hall, John Chapman's *Horse Guards Parade* (1760) has become a familiar part of the scene, as have the portraits on either side of the door to the Inner Hall, of Walpole and

▲ William Marlow's 'View of St Paul's and Blackfriars Bridge', in the White Drawing Room. With windows on two sides, and with light walls, this room is deemed especially suitable for showing off landscapes.

Pitt the Elder. This Walpole, also (like the Walpole in the Cabinet Room) by Vanloo, is a half-length portrait, and was purchased specially for Number 10 by the Government Art Collection in 1985. The Chapman painting shows both Downing's buildings and Bothmar House behind, and there is a photograph of a painting of George Downing in the room (the original is at Harvard University). The Inner Hall has two portraits by George Watts: one of Gladstone, and the other of the glamorous actress Ellen Terry in a vivid turquoise dress. Above the fireplace hung, until Blair, another view of Horse Guards Parade, by Samuel Scott, dating from about 1755. Full of Breughel- or Lowry-like detail, it shows a man urinating against the back wall of Downing Street. Showing that one can eventually make money in politics, MacDonald bought the picture to hang in Number 10. The Cabinet Ante Room boasts another local townscape, *Whitehall From St James's Park* (1675), as well as *Longleat* by Jan Siberechts (1678). Since

1997, a telling portrait of Labour hero Clement Attlee has hung there (see page 139). He looks down benignly on Labour ministers as they assemble for Cabinet.

With the regular rotation of pictures, many of those described in this chapter will inevitably change in due course: only a snapshot in time can be given here.

The Green Drawing Room has tended to have portraits, such as James Ward's painting of Wellington, on loan from the present Duke since 1982, and Henry Raeburn's marvellous portrait of Graham of Gartmore (see page 179). The Pillared Room is hung with large, rather sombre portraits, such as George Romney's portrait of Pitt the Younger (see page 103), fitting the scale of this, the largest of the three inter-connecting drawing rooms. The paintings in this room would have been changed with greater regularity were it not for the difficulty of finding works of sufficient scale to fit the spaces on the wall. Number 10 has few paintings of women – the portrait of Mary Queen of Scots after Nicholas Hilliard, in the Small Dining Room, is an exception.

▼ 'East Cowes Regatta starting for Moorings' by J M W Turner, in the White Drawing Room.

◄ Horatio Nelson by Francis Lemuel Abbott, in the Green Drawing Room.

► Graham of Gartmore by Sir Henry Raeburn, in the Green Drawing Room.

The paintings add immeasurably to the impression of Number 10 as one of the most elegant houses in the land and reflect much of what is best about British art over the last four hundred years. They do not dominate, as paintings necessarily do in galleries, but blend into the rooms in a measured and natural way, creating a harmonious whole.

Sculptures and Busts

The aesthetics of Number 10 are further enhanced by the collection of sculptures and busts. The busts rotate according to taste but also the political complexion of the party in government. The bronze bust of Tory Prime Minister Harold Macmillan by Angela Conner may not survive long into the Blair era; a bust of the scientist Michael Faraday, by Matthew Noble, is likely to last longer. An established tradition is the display of a succession of sculptures by Henry Moore, Britain's great twentieth-century sculptor, in an alcove in the corridor connecting the Inner Hall and the Cabinet Ante Room. In 1984, at Mrs Thatcher's instigation, an arrangement was made with the Henry Moore Foundation to supply sculptures for the alcove, which Mrs Thatcher created from a space previously occupied by a phone booth and a cupboard for cleaning materials. The bronze sculpture displayed on a plinth illustrated below is *Reclining Figure: Open Pose* (1982). Behind it, on the wall, is a Henry Moore drawing; for conservation reasons, the drawings are changed every three or four months.

*The Moore alcove (**left**) and the bust of Isaac Newton in the State Dining Room (**above**).*

◄ The top of the grand staircase. John Major's photograph (and all the other portraits of prime ministers) will shuffle down the stairs when Tony Blair's image takes pride of place after he ceases to be Prime Minister.

PHOTOGRAPHS

Number 10 has a Jekyll and Hyde approach to photographs. For a variety of reasons, many of the non-public rooms have been little photographed. No photograph appears to exist of the Garden Room girls *in situ*, or of the kitchens in use, and very few of the Private Secretaries' and other office rooms. Only a handful of photographs have been taken of the Prime Minister's private flat on the second floor, and, disappointingly, none appear to exist of Churchill working in the flat's master bedroom, propped up in bed with papers spread over the counterpane. There are very few, mostly poor quality, early photographs of the rooms inside Number 10, or of prime ministers in Downing Street, before Balfour (1902-5).

Official posed photographs, on the other hand, exist in Mississippi proportions. Prime ministers on the doorstep, greeting or bidding farewell, or receiving guests by the fireplace in the Entrance Hall or in the State Rooms, choke photographic libraries. But informal photographs of prime ministers at work (or play) at Number 10, and unstaged photographs of their aides doing anything other than bustling them into cars, are rare.

There are two main locations where photographs are displayed in Number 10. One is on the main staircase, where portraits of the fifty prime ministers are hung, from Walpole at the bottom of the basement stairwell to Major at the top, just before the first-floor landing. The sequence was the brainchild of Sir Edward Hamilton, Treasury Permanent Secretary, who assembled the collection of prime ministers' images and donated them to Number 10 in 1907. Since then, every prime minister, after his (or her) departure, has donated a portrait of themselves, which Number 10 frames and hangs. Up to and including Lloyd George (1916-22), the images are engraved prints, but from then on they are black-and-white photographs. Often taken by distinguished photographers, such as Karsh of Ottawa, they are highly formal portraits, revealing the public face but often leaving the spectator to surmise the personality.

The immediate outgoing prime minister holds pride of place at the top of the stairs, but has to shuffle down when his successor's portrait arrives. John Major's portrait was taken by Sarah King, who had toured the country with Major's entourage during the 1997 general election campaign, taking literally thousands of photographs. 'The fact that we knew each other well was a big advantage,' she said. 'He takes time to relax, and you have to wait for the optimum moment. I felt the earlier photographs on the staircase conveyed all the weight of the prime minister's office, but little else. I wanted to show Major's official side, but also his inner personality and his integrity. He has such a subtle and interesting face.'

The other, and less well-known, sequence of photographs is on the basement corridor leading out past the Garden Rooms to the back garden. Here, shut away from public view, are the large group photographs of prime ministers and their cabinets, and also the frozen-in-aspic formal photographs of leaders at all the great Imperial and Commonwealth meetings that have been held in London.

▼ State Dining Room wall sconce.

FURNITURE AND ORNAMENTS

Number 10 contains some exceptional items of furniture, owned either by the house, or on loan. One of the most striking of these greets the visitor on arrival in the Entrance Hall – the Chippendale hooded chair, in black leather, with a pull-out drawer under the seat. To the left is a gilt table in the style of Kent and a long-case clock by Benson of Whitehaven. A similar clock, but without a third bauble on its top, is in the Cabinet Ante Room; this is by Samuel Whichcote of London.

▶ The long-case clock by Samuel Whichcote which stands in the Cabinet Ante Room.

◀ The Chippendale hooded chair which greets visitors inside the Entrance Hall.

▶ The books in this collection, housed in the Cabinet Room, have all been presented to the Prime Minister of the day by retiring Cabinet Ministers.

▼ 'Randolph Churchill' signed by Winston Churchill. 'In Place of Fear' signed by Aneurin Bevan.

The Cabinet Room is dominated by the wooden boat-shaped table covered in brown baize, which Macmillan introduced in the early 1960s. The chairs all have brown leather backs; only the Prime Minister's seat has arms. Two high bookcases on the end wall behind the double columns are the only ones remaining from the time the room was also a library and map-room, when bookcases lined most of the walls, containing Hansard reports of parliamentary proceedings and other reports. Each Cabinet Minister, on retirement, typically presents a book to the Prime Minister's library in a tradition that began with MacDonald in 1931.

The Cabinet Room is sparsely furnished, which lends even greater focus to the all-dominant table. Each Cabinet Minister has a brown leather blotter in front of his or her chair, inscribed 'Cabinet Room 1st Lord'. The silver on the table includes a William IV wafer box, William-and-Mary and Georgian candlesticks, and a single candlestick with a unique history, which has passed through the possession of five prime ministers or their children. Owned by one of the Pitts and later by Disraeli, the candlestick was given in 1901 by Peel's daughter to Rosebery (1894-5), whose son gave it in 1957 to Macmillan for the Cabinet Room. The room is lit by three central brass chandeliers, each with a cluster of individual electric candles.

The first-floor Ante Room has a set of six chairs and a settee in the Chinese style, made by Thomas Chippendale for Clive of India, and used to have three cabinets of Spode services lent by the Victoria and Albert Museum. The White Room contains elegant Adam furniture, gilt armchairs, a bombé commode (chest of drawers) in satinwood and walnut with ormolu mounts, and an oval mirror with decorated metal surround. The furniture and window seats have been covered in striped material to match the white and red colours of the room. Staffordshire figures of prime ministers and other senior figures decorate the room. The Waterford glass chandelier is paired with one in the Green Drawing Room, visible through the usually open double doors. There are two gilt armchairs by the windows, but the green covered settees are modern. The rest of the furniture is mainly Chippendale, including a card table also made for Clive of India. Other items include two George II commodes, a Georgian backgammon and card table, and a desk which was once thought to have belonged to William Pitt and used by him during the Napoleonic wars. Rococo-style mirrors grace the walls and reflect the glass chandelier.

◄ The bombé commode in the White Drawing Room.

▲ Detail of the inscription on the large carpet in the Pillared Drawing Room.

▼ William Pitt's mahogany desk in the Green Room.

▲ Green Drawing Room Chippendale card table.

The most striking feature in the Pillared Room is the large carpet, which is a copy of a sixteenth-century original in the Victoria and Albert Museum. The inscription is translated as 'I have no refuge in the world other than this threshold. My head has no protection other than this porchway. The work of a slave of the Holy Place, Maqsud of Kashan in the year 926' (the Muslim year corresponding to AD 1520). The carpet is a splendid testament to a more multi-cultural Number 10 as it enters the new millennium. Again, there is an array of fine furniture, mainly by Kent: a marble-topped table against the wall between the pillars; twelve gilt chairs and two matching settees covered in red fabric; and a pair of Chippendale mirrors. The chandelier is the largest in the house, and is also cut glass.

▲ (above and left)
Kent marble-topped
table in the Pillared
Room. The painting is
of Nelson's second-in-
command, Admiral Sir
Thomas Graves.

The oldest piece of furniture in the State Dining Room is the large mahogany sideboard by Adam. The central rectangular table and chairs are modern, the latter made originally for the British embassy in Brazil, but deemed too traditional in style when the capital moved from Rio de Janeiro to the modern embassy in Brasilia. On the table is silver by modern British artists, collected by the Silver Trust, a body set up in 1987 to commission a national collection of silver. The arresting candlesticks, inscribed plates and goblets are all part of their collection. The modern silver took the place of the 200-year-old Belton collection loaned to Mrs Thatcher.

▲ The Adam sideboard in the State Dining Room.

▲ Silver plates by modern
British artists, collected by
the Silver Trust.

◀ Modern goblet bearing the
Prime Minister's name and an
image of Number 10's front door.

Gifts to Number 10

Prime ministers are frequently given gifts by fellow heads of government, heads of state and others at home and abroad. Few of the large number of offerings, however, remain permanently at Number 10. Gifts received in this official capacity must be handed over to the state: they are not for the prime minister personally to keep. Two unusual exceptions are the large globe in the staircase, presented to Mrs Thatcher by President Mitterrand of France, and the piece of moon rock, presented to Harold Wilson by one of the lunar astronauts on behalf of President Nixon, following the successful moon landing by the Apollo spacecraft in 1969.

*Harold Wilson receives a photograph taken on the moon from Colonel James Irwin, the Apollo 15 Moonwalker. The Union Jack was taken on this mission to the moon (**left**). The particles of moon rock were a gift from President Richard Nixon to Number 10 (**above**).*
*Looking down the well of the grand staircase from the first-floor landing by the State Dining Room, the Mitterrand globe is at basement level (**opposite**). The door leads through to the Cabinet Ante Room.*

▶ Balfour's music and study room. This is now the White Drawing Room.

▶ Balfour's music and study room. This is now the White Drawing Room.

MUSIC AND MUSICIANS AT NUMBER 10

Number 10 probably saw more music in the Heath years (1970-74) than at any other time before or since. One of the happier images from Heath's Number 10 is of his Steinway piano being manoeuvred into the front hall on 2 July 1970, shortly after he became Prime Minister. Bought with money given to him as a personal gift by the City of Aachen, he chose it in the company of the celebrated pianist Moura Lympany. Pianos have not been common at Number 10: one can be seen in the 1940 blitz photographs, and also during Balfour's administration in the early 1900s. Heath's was placed in the corner of the White Drawing Room, by the windows looking out over Horse Guards Parade. Heath would slip off and play his beloved piano in snatched moments of solitude – after a quick tray lunch, in the early evening, or after returning late at night from the Commons or an official function. Robert Armstrong, Heath's devoted Principal Private Secretary, said the Private Office would heave a sigh of relief when they heard Heath's playing drifting down the stairs, as they knew they would have a few minutes' respite.

Upstairs, in the private flat, Heath also placed a harpsichord in the Small Soane Dining Room. In his den, he had his own music stereo system. He had selected the speakers, amplifiers and record turntable separately, taking great trouble to ensure the purity of the sound was optimised, and even insisting that chromium coverings replace the wood surround of the speakers. In all matters, Heath was meticulous. One of the most memorable moments of his life took place in this private sitting room. On 28 October 1971, the House of Commons passed, with a large majority of 112, the motion that Britain should join the European Economic Community – a prize towards which Heath had laboured for ten years. It was a personal triumph. Here, surrounded by his closest friends and associates, champagne glasses in their hands, he played Bach's *First Prelude* on his harpsichord, symbolising the mood of pan-European harmony.

Heath wanted to celebrate music in the public rooms, too. He introduced sung graces before and after meals when official guests were being entertained. Of Soane's State Dining Room, he said, 'acoustically it is excellent – clear and not too resonant'. Martin Neary, then organist of Westminster Abbey, would be responsible for arranging many of the sung graces. Sensing he was on to a rich vein, Heath hit on the idea of using Neary to devise a programme of madrigals and part-songs for guests to enjoy while drinking after-dinner coffee and liqueurs. The music could be selected for amusement – a choral arrangement of *Waltzing Matilda* was sung when Australian Premier Gough Whitlam came to dinner – or for more serious purposes: folk songs were sung when Heath brought together over a surprise dinner representatives from both Northern Ireland and the Republic of Ireland at a key stage in talks on the future of the Province. By the end of the evening, all the guests were singing together in true Irish style.

Heath would also use Number 10 for chamber music concerts; the large Soane Room was deemed the ideal venue. In November 1972, the Amadeus Quartet played a Mozart Quartet and Schubert Quintet to the eight EEC ambassadors as part of the celebrations of Britain's imminent entry into the Community. Renowned musicians would also be invited to Number 10 for hospitality: Herbert von Karajan came to supper at Number 10 after conducting the Berlin Philharmonic Orchestra in a celebrated concert of Beethoven's Fourth and Fifth Symphonies at the Albert Hall, as part of the 'Fanfare for Europe' concerts.

▲ Heath's grand piano being moved into Number 10 from his Albany flat after his 1970 election victory.

◄ Music lover Edward
Heath settles down at
his grand piano. Heath
placed his piano in the
White Drawing Room
looking out over Horse
Guards Parade.

The most illustrious musical gathering at Number 10 in Heath's time,
perhaps ever in its history, was the celebration of William Walton's seventieth
birthday in March 1972. The guests included some of the world's great musicians:
Georg Solti, Benjamin Britten, Peter Pears, Yehudi Menuhin, and Sir Arthur
Bliss, Master of the Queen's Music. The celebratory dinner opened with a special
grace composed by Herbert Howells to words written by Robert Armstrong.
After dinner a special 'Ode to William Walton' was sung, followed by Walton's
own *Song of Solomon*. Then the guests came through to the Pillared Room where
a surprise awaited them: a performance of Schubert's B Flat Trio, played by John
Georgiadis, the Leader of the LSO, Douglas Cummings, its first cello, and John
Lill on piano. The three had never played together before, and the audience,
which included the Queen, Queen Elizabeth the Queen Mother and Laurence
Olivier, listened spellbound.

Robert Armstrong, Secretary to the Board of Covent Garden from 1966–88,
was a key ally in Heath's mission to bring music to Number 10. Heath had known
his father, the musician Sir Thomas Armstrong, when Heath had been Organ
Scholar at Balliol College, Oxford. Armstrong's omnicompetent style was

evident in the smooth running of many of the musical events at both Number 10 and Chequers; Heath was lucky to have had such a soul mate and such a sympathetic counsellor by his side.

Heath used music to spectacular effect, enriching not just state occasions, but helping to add style and distinction to public entertaining. It is a notable lost opportunity that so few of his fellow prime ministers have elected to tap the unparalleled musical potential at their disposal to enhance Number 10.

Another premiership to take music seriously was that of John Major (1990-7). Though Major himself enjoyed music, it was Norma, his opera-loving wife, who was mainly responsible for music again becoming so prominent. 'Opera interludes' would be organised both at Number 10 and at Chequers, often for charity. At a birthday dinner for Sir Georg Solti, Kiri te Kanawa and Placido Domingo sung an impromptu 'Happy Birthday'. In July 1996, the Majors invited Heath back to Number 10 for his eightieth birthday. As well as the Queen, musicians Yehudi Menuhin, Mstislav Rostropovich and Moura Lympany were guests. The Martin Neary Singers returned to sing grace, part-songs and madrigals.

Churchill, not normally known for an interest in music (he seems to have lacked an ear for it), nevertheless presided over a celebratory musical dinner held by 'Number 10 at Potsdam', at the conclusion of the Second World War. This unique event bequeathed the signed card displayed here, with the names of many of the most prominent military and political leaders from the war.

▲ The seating plan for 'Number 10 at Potsdam', a unique occasion during the famous conference between the 'Big Three' (the USA, USSR and Great Britain), which took place at the end of the Second World War.

▶ The music programme and signatures for 'Number 10 at Potsdam'.

The Government Hospitality Fund

The Government Hospitality Fund (GHF) was set up in 1908 to provide hospitality on government and state occasions for all ministers. Before then, ministers used their private servants, but by the beginning of the twentieth century, a more uniform service was considered necessary. The GHF, which is divided into two sections – functions and visits – now has 28 staff, including 5 butlers, but uses a number of selected outside caterers to provide the food. Since 1982, the GHF has been linked to the Foreign and Commonwealth Office. The GHF arranges most prime ministerial functions (and elsewhere for other ministers), checks guest lists, prints invitation cards and menus, receives acceptances and regrets, and prints the all-important table plans.

It co-ordinates the hospitality of foreign guests of the government – a huge task, involving travel, transport and entertainment arrangements, which has to be carried out with exceptional tact and thoroughness. To avoid the embarrassment of errors, the GHF will check and re-check arrangements four to five times. GHF are very conscious of hygiene, mindful of the need at all costs to avoid food-poisoning. They even take samples of all dishes at important meals and keep them in freezers for two weeks after an event, as a check in case a guest claims to have eaten bad food.

*Hospitality menu cover with a painting by Hugh Casson (**above**). Menu cover with a painting by former Tory Secretary of State for the Environment, Nicholas Ridley (**left**).*

The Prime Minister

requests the honour of the company of

at Luncheon at No. 10, Downing Street,

on Friday, the 22nd May, 1942, at 1.30 p.m.

Please reply by telephone to—
The Secretary, Government Hospitality,
Telephone: Whitehall 1481.

The GHF's earliest
surviving dinner
invitation to Number
10, dating from
1942 *(left)*.
Accompanying
seating plan *(below
left)* and wine list
(right).

Amontillado

Grand Chablis, 1934

Charmes Chambertin, 1933

Grand Fine Champagne, 1864

Liqueurs

Gulls Eggs
Smoked Salmon

Lamb Cutlets
Spinach
Lettuce Salad

Rum Charlotte

Coffee

Luncheon at No.10 Downing Street on Friday, the 22nd May, 1942.

TABLE PLAN

Air Chief Marshal
Sir Charles Portal

The Rt.Hon. Sir James Grigg

The Rt. Hon. H. V. Evatt

The Rt. Hon. Sir John Anderson

His Excellency
the Soviet Ambassador

THE RT. HON. THE PRIME MINISTER

His Excellency
Monsieur Molotov

The Rt.Hon. Sir Stafford Cripps

Monsieur Pavlov

The Rt.Hon. A.V. Alexander

General Sir Alan Brooke

Colonel Sir Eric Crankshaw

Mr. J.M.Martin

The Hon. Sir Alexander Cadogan

The Rt.Hon. Sir Archibald Sinclair

The Rt. Hon. Oliver Lyttelton

Brigadier R.C.J.G. Firebrace

Major-General Ismay

The Rt.Hon. C. R. Attlee

His Excellency Monsieur Sobolev

The Rt.Hon. Anthony Eden

The Rt.Hon. Ernest Bevin

Admiral of the Fleet Sir Dudley Pound

Sir Orme Sargent

Commander C. R. Thompson

Dinner

In honour of
Their Royal Highnesses The Prince and Princess of Wales

10 Downing Street
16th November 1989

Dinner invitation
for the Prince and
Princess of Wales,
November
1989 *(right)*.

An elegant dinner
setting for the Prime
Minister *(above)*.

ENTERTAINING AT NUMBER 10

Entertaining at Number 10 is an art, and is important not just for promoting the Prime Minister's image at home, but also for advancing Britain's international standing. Traditions have been built up over many years, and those involved in hospitality at Number 10 take pride in the meticulous professionalism of their work. Increasingly, too, Number 10 is used for charity events. Entertaining usually takes the form of lunchtime or evening receptions and meals. Very occasionally, breakfasts are also held at Number 10. The Blairs prefer to entertain over lunch or dinner, and also prefer smaller receptions of 50 to 100, as opposed to 200, the traditional number at Number 10, and the maximum number considered possible to accommodate and look after in comfort.

▲ Mr and Mrs Clinton were invited to dine with the Majors in November 1995.

The Social Secretary compiles the initial invitation lists and co-ordinates the setting up of functions. This involves close liaison with the Number 10 Private Office, and also with the Government Hospitality Fund. Arrangements for US visits are run rather differently to those for any other country. For President Clinton's visits in 1995 and 1997, his own car was flown over from the USA, and while some of the incredible number of eighteen cars in the convoy came from the US embassy in London, others were hired from the UK. The convoy includes two hospital cars. The American scale often bemuses the British; the Prime Minister's convoy, as he travels around Britain, is a quarter or less in size. The President's advisers are naturally very concerned about security. US presidents usually bring with them two food and beverage advisers, who are in fact 'tasters', although no one calls them that. They stay in the Number 10 kitchens while the food is being prepared, keeping an eagle eye on all stages. It is not uncommon for visiting heads of state and government to be concerned about the risks of poison – with the idea of 'tasters' harking back to the days of medieval kings.

Number 10's supply of wine comes from the GHF wine cellar under Lancaster House; the cellars currently hold some 45,000 bottles. In a normal year, 9,000-10,000 bottles are drunk at official functions. A wine committee, set up in 1922 to oversee the wine and make recommendations for the purchase and the optimum drinking times, meets four times a year. There are four members and a chairman, currently Sir Ewen Fergusson, a former diplomat and chairman of Coutts Bank. Members are all Masters of Wine – there are only 200 in the world (140 are British)! There are no women on the committee at present, but this may change. Members of the committee are unpaid, but not surprisingly, places on the prestigious committee are in high demand and the Government Hospitality Fund receives several applications every year.

Much of the wine drunk at Number 10 receptions is inexpensive: Colombard is a much-served white, Château Tour de Mirambeau a popular red. The cellars also contain grand wine for use on special occasions, but the very finest vintages are often withheld for a really prestigious occasion, when the Queen or a visiting head of state is guest of honour. The oldest wine in the cellars is a Château Latour (1955) and there are also very good 1961 clarets and a spread of good vintages from the late 1960s. The oldest fortified wine is a port – a 1931 Quinta do Noval; the oldest cognac is Grands Fins Bois (1878). The oldest champagne in the cellar are the two magnums of 1964 Krug, while the Pol Roger Sir Winston Churchill Cuvée (1985) is a popular choice for special occasions. At some receptions, champagne is served; at others, still wine and a selection of mixed drinks (spirits, mineral water, freshly squeezed orange juice and English apple juice).

A WELL-OILED ROUTINE

For receptions at Number 10, rather more invitations are sent out than the optimum number of guests desired, though few people would decline an invitation to Number 10, and usually only do so if they are unwell or abroad. The GHF allows six weeks to prepare for a reception and send out invitations. For commercial and business receptions the time frame is shorter. It is GHF's responsibility to double-check each guest's correct style and title, and great care is taken to ensure that names are correctly handwritten on the invitations, in the correct form of address. The invitations are then sent back to Number 10 to be checked by the Social Secretary. By the time of the reception, all the butlers and staff should be acquainted with the guest list, and the Prime Minister is informed in advance who is coming. Guests arrive at the front door, hand in their admission card, and are invited to give their coats to two ladies who hang them on racks in the Inner Hall. The ladies are very experienced and have needle and thread at the ready to sew on buttons and medals. They also have spare black bow ties lest someone arrives incorrectly dressed. The guests are shown along the corridor and up the Grand Staircase to the Ante Room. A butler may ask for their names so that the Prime Minister can welcome them personally.

Receptions before Tony Blair began formally with the Prime Minister greeting guests inside the door of the Green Drawing Room, before they were ushered into the Pillared Room. Evening receptions usually start about 6 pm and last an hour to an hour and a half. All three State Rooms are used on such occasions, and the Dining Rooms are also open. The receiving line is in place for the first 30 minutes or so and the Prime Minister then circulates. Crudités, crisps and olives are available on the Pillared Room tables, and staff serve both hot and cold canapés. GHF estimate eight bite-sized pieces for each guest, and these include triangles of smoked salmon, goujons of sole, and filled pastry puffs. They try to avoid using cocktail sticks or skewers; they also take care to ensure that the canapés will not shatter into crumbs and that they leave no mark on the fingers.

▲ Cherie Blair chats to actors John Thaw and Sheila Hancock at a Number 10 reception.

Food and drink continue to be served as long as the Prime Minister is present; he usually retires at about 7.30 or 8 pm, when the waiting staff will begin to collect empty glasses, and soon after this the guests disappear. It is very rare that guests have too much to drink or are truculent; most feel a sense of honour and privilege to be in such surroundings. The Number 10 and GHF staff help ensure that guests are introduced to others, especially if they see someone stranded in a corner. Circulation is encouraged so that the Prime Minister, who is often accompanied by his wife and other hosts, can be introduced to as many people as possible.

Lunches and dinners are more formal affairs. The Small Dining Room will sit a maximum of 12, and the State Dining Room can cater for up to 32 people on the central rectangular table, or up to 65 if a special U-shaped table is erected for major occasions. To accommodate 65, 'gunners' are put onto the 'sprigs', (i.e. guests are seated on the ends of the table). In a well-oiled routine, Number 10 staff disassemble the rectangular table, which is removed by section and stored, and they then erect the U-shaped table. The silver-gilt Silver Trust pieces, full picture menus, flowers and candles (if it is a dinner) are always placed on the table for these grand occasions. Seating plans are given to lunch and dinner guests in the Cabinet Ante Room before they go up the stairs, so everyone can see where he or she will sit, and who else is present. The seating plans on the reception table remaining are a quick way of checking who has not yet arrived.

Lunch invitations are for 12.45 or 1 pm. Guests assemble in the Pillared Room and are ushered into the dining room smartly at 1 pm; lunches often have to be over by 2.15 pm. Razor-edge decision-making takes place if a guest has not arrived by 1 pm, especially if he or she is to sit near to the Prime Minister. If the starter is a hot dish, or the Prime Minister has to get away smartly, a delay is unlikely. There are usually three courses for lunch and food is normally served by butlers. Until the Blairs, fish was avoided as a second course because it meant only one main wine can be served (red is never served with fish and GHF does not like to serve two different white wines for starters and main courses). When fish is served, a second wine might be served with the dessert.

The food is always carefully prepared, and trouble is taken to ensure it is suitable for all the guests. Special dietary needs, for religious, cultural or reasons of personal taste or health are researched beforehand. If there are guests from African countries, chicken will be avoided because it is perceived to be common. Similarly, lamb is not served to German and Japanese guests. Vegetarian courses are always available. The whole point of the menu is to make the guests feel welcome. The art of entertaining at Number 10 is not just practical, but also aesthetic. Changes are made in contrast, colour and texture between courses. A further consideration when choosing a menu is to avoid repetition with other meals, especially for the hosts. Although the Prime Minister might not always be aware of it, records of the meals and wines consumed are carefully kept to ensure repetition is avoided.

▲ Comedians Eric Morecambe and Ernie Wise filming with Sir Alec Guinness outside a mock-up of that famous door.

Dinners are usually more formal. On average, two dinners will be held a month, although they have become less frequent under the Blairs. Some are black tie but lounge suits are more common. White tie events have been abandoned at Number 10; not even the visit by the Queen in 1985 on the 250th anniversary of the house, when one current and five retired prime ministers were also present, was white tie. Full evening dress (white tie and tails for men) is now only expected at Buckingham Palace, military messes, the Guildhall, livery companies, society balls and some Oxbridge colleges. It could well be that when the Queen dies, white tie dress may disappear entirely. Ladies often telephone beforehand to clarify their dressing arrangements: whether to wear long gloves is one concern (it is no longer *de rigueur*). If it is black tie, ladies will wear long dresses, and if lounge suits, cocktail dresses or the business clothes they have worn during the day. Clergy and military figures will dress in their own version of black tie or lounge suit. Foreign guests may well arrive in their own national ceremonial dress, which means that kilts may be worn.

Dinner is Served

Dinners last for around two hours and guests are ushered into the Dining Room from pre-dinner drinks in the Pillared Room when the butler knocks loudly. Each guest then stands behind his or her place at the table, and then the Prime Minister and guests of honour walk in, occasionally to the accompaniment of clapping by the other guests. When a cleric or bishop is present at dinner, he will often be asked to say Grace before the meal begins, but Grace is not normally said (or sung). The butlers offer the guests wine as well as bread rolls. Every effort is made to avoid having food already on the table, and the food is offered to everyone from the left, while plates are removed from the right. The courses are presented on silver trays, from which guests help themselves, and the butlers divide the table into groups of eight guests. Each serving tray contains nine portions, so the last to be served does not feel they are taking the final item, and the butlers try to avoid a lady being the eighth to be served. The Number 10 style is 'understated elegance'. There are no 'oohs and ahs' as the waiters remove the silver covers from the main course; Number 10 does not like silver cloches: 'that is for hotels like the Ritz'. Guests rarely take too much food, though on one memorable occasion a guest of honour over-indulged. A visiting monarch renowned for his large appetite, took a whole tray of quails, not realising that they were meant as individual servings. Fortunately, the kitchens had prepared extra food. It is all part of the art of entertaining at Number 10.

For dessert, wines may be offered, notably Château Filhot (a Sauternes) and Doisy Dubroca (a Barsac). At state occasions, a toast will be given by the Prime Minister to the Queen, then to the guest of honour or visiting head of state. Coffee will then be served, from the right, along with petits fours on silver trays. Port will follow, and sometimes brandy and liqueurs – Crème de Menthe, Drambuie and Cointreau. Malt whisky tends to be offered if it is a military or commercial event, especially if Japanese guests are present. Cigars and cigarettes have been traditionally provided on request, but the Blairs prefer people not to smoke.

Towards the end of the evening the butler will knock and say, 'Pray silence for the Prime Minister', who will then make a speech or say a few words – followed by some words from a guest of honour. Women no longer leave the room while men drink port and discuss business; the custom seems to have died in the 1960s. Mrs Thatcher had developed to a fine art the subtle hint on when to leave, 'Mr President, I expect you have got a busy day tomorrow,' she might say. She, as much as any prime minister, used dinners and hospitality for diplomacy and would be in no hurry to terminate the evening if further business had yet to be conducted. The Prime Minister, sitting at the end of the table, will have the most influential guests nearby and can conduct conversations with up to ten people. This is important because, once the dinner commences, there is no further opportunity to talk to a guest not in one's immediate vicinity. At the end of the dinner, the guests stand and leave; it is rare for hospitality to continue in the drawing rooms, and the Prime Minister will have red boxes waiting to be processed before the morning. The Prime Minister will see his or her guests down the stairs to the front door. For the guests, it is the end of a memorable evening; for the Prime Minister, it is time to get back to work.

▲ Tony Blair with Noel Gallagher of Oasis. The Blairs have become renowned for inviting the best of Britain's 'bright young things' into their home.

BELOW STAIRS

Number 10's prime ministerial inhabitants have filled the pages of the nation's history books. The attention has naturally been focused on the man (or woman) at the top, rather than on those who have worked at Number 10 at less elevated levels. But this chapter will endeavour to reveal more of the life and work of the very considerable support staff in Downing Street, without whom the prime ministers and Number 10 would be unable to function.

▶ Doorman Bob Jordan on 30 October 1997, the day of his retirement. Jordan was a fitting successor to John Berry, in whose arms Prime Minister Campbell-Bannerman died in 1908. It was said that to be saluted by Berry 'added to the stature of even a Cabinet Minister'.

◀ Humphrey, the famed Downing Street cat.

THE FRONT DOOR

An attendant had been on duty inside the front door at Number 10 since the earliest days. It was not always clear to visitors that he was the doorman. At the instigation of Lord Rosebery (1894-95), the attendant was put into uniform – a blue frock coat, with the crown wrought in crimson and gold on the lapels.

A policeman became a regular feature outside the front door during the First World War and has remained *in situ* thereafter. A wooden wall was built during the Irish Troubles that arose during the war, but it was soon taken down. In 1981 a temporary barrier was erected at the entrance to Downing Street, but as car bombs, laden with high explosives and driven by suicide bombers, became more of a threat, the present security gates were installed in 1989. The final go-ahead for this controversial move came after an Arab extremist was killed in a London hotel that August while strapping a bomb to his body. Sceptics within Number 10 were converted at the time of the 'poll tax' riots of 1990, when the gates kept out the enraged protesters: 'That was when they really earned their keep,' said one.

In 1997, when doorman Bob Jordan retired, a new era began: security guards now man the inside of the door, in the Entrance Hall.

> *'This necessary attendant, standing at the fireplace, might have been mistaken for anybody: peer or commoner, member of the Cabinet, or chairman of a deputation.'*
>
> A VISITOR, CITED IN PASCOE (1908)

THE GARDEN ROOM GIRLS

Very little has been written about the Garden Room girls, the *crème de la crème* of Britain's secretaries working for the Prime Minister and the Private Office in the garden basement of Number 10. The girls work in two inter-connecting rooms under the Cabinet Room – an inner and outer office – which are on the same level as the garden at the back of the house. The secretariat was set up during the First World War, and has been run since by a series of remarkable women. One of the early heads was 'Mags' Stenhouse, who had worked for Lloyd George. She was succeeded by Sheila Minto, who joined when Baldwin was Prime Minister, and who retired in 1968 after 33 years. Her two longest-standing successors have been Jane Parsons (1968-81) and Janice Richards (1985–99).

Fourteen secretaries are currently employed in the Garden Rooms, 12 of whom cover the shift system which ensures a secretarial service at any time of day or night, 365 days a year. There are usually two, and sometimes three, on duty overnight; bedrooms are available for their use on the third floor. Before 1968, the secretaries were hand-picked by the Treasury from secretarial colleges and the public and private sectors: since then, they have been recruited from within the Civil Service. Working conditions were cramped and uncomfortable before the 1960-63 rebuild added several inches to the height of the rooms.

◄ The inner Garden
Room (**left**) and outer
Garden Room (**below**) as
they were in the 1940s.
During the Second World
War these rooms were
vacated by the Garden
Room girls and used by
Churchill as a sitting
and dining room.

The girls do not work only in Downing Street. They accompany the Prime Minister when he travels – both abroad and within the United Kingdom. Rotas for overseas travel are organised by the Garden Room head. Trips cover 'one to three nights', 'over three nights', and 'holiday visits'. Most prime ministers like to dictate on aeroplanes, though less dictate while travelling by car, and few since Churchill have dictated while in bed! Usually two secretaries accompany the Prime Minister abroad (on occasions it may be more) and the aim is to keep the same team until the end of a visit. One secretary accompanies the Prime Minister on visits outside London. The girls may also be asked to run the office and to communicate back to Number 10. A Garden Room girl always goes to Chequers with the Prime Minister over the weekend or during holiday periods.

A secure communication system is provided for the Prime Minister whenever necessary. For a long time, the only secure link with Chequers was a huge teleprinter, encrypted by the secretaries at each end of the link to Number 10 by inserting short wires in holes in two small boxes. Known as 'knitting', it was rather like a miniature version of a plug-in switchboard. For secure speech, there was a piece of equipment known as 'Pickwick', encrypted by an even slower method of sliding keys up and down with an instrument like a small crochet hook. Today's encryption methods are rather more 'user-friendly'!

Office technology has changed enormously during the life of the Garden Rooms. For many years, manual typewriters with a large typeface were used, with secretaries taking several carbon copies. During the Second World War, Churchill had been given two Remington silent typewriters by an American friend and was intrigued by the new machines. The girls hated them, but found that telling Churchill that 'the gadgets needed a new battery' would suffice to prevent him asking for them. When Janice Richards arrived in 1971, she was surprised to find the Garden Rooms still using manual 'Imperial 66' typewriters, when other government departments, still more the private sector, were using electric models. It was not long after this, however, that the first electric typewriter was introduced – an Olivetti (not a popular machine) – replaced by a succession of more modern electric typewriters, culminating with the first Rank Xerox 'golfball' typewriter in the late 1970s. Photocopiers also arrived in the 1970s, and transformed the girls' lives, reducing the need for carbon copies. The first word processor, an ICL, came into the Garden Rooms shortly after, and was used alongside the electric 'golfballs'. During the 1980s, the girls moved over to word processors, eventually networked one to another, but it was not until 1996 that the whole of Number 10 was computerised and networked. Slow to catch up with technological change, today Number 10 boasts equipment that is second to none.

The area of greatest growth in activity in the Garden Rooms since its founding has been in the volume of correspondence. Staff numbers have stayed fairly static for some time, but the Prime Minister's mailbag has risen from 12,500 letters a month in the early 1980s, to over 30,000 a month by 1999. A separate Correspondence Section was created to take over the responsibility of opening the mail and processing letters which needed to be forwarded to other government departments. When there was a glut of mail, or when emotional issues hit the news, such as the white-seal cull when Mrs Thatcher was Prime Minister, or the death of the Princess of Wales, all available hands in Number 10 are called on to help sort the letters into appropriate

> *'Please thank all your staff who worked so hard on my speech, whether personally for me or for anyone in my private office engaged on the speech.'*
>
> CLEMENT ATTLEE TO GARDEN ROOM HEAD, SHEILA MINTO.

categories. Great care is needed: among a clutch of letters from children might lurk a letter of major state importance, written to the Prime Minister. Letters are first screened to ensure they are safe to open. By hiving off the work of opening the mail and some of the processing, the Garden Rooms can concentrate better on providing their core secretarial function to the Prime Minister.

The Garden Room girls have always had a special place in the affections of prime ministers and their spouses. After helping him type a particularly difficult speech to the House of Commons during the economic crisis in the summer of 1947, Clement Attlee wrote the letter of thanks shown opposite. In similar vein, in September 1963, Harold Macmillan, wrote to thank Jane Parsons for typing a long draft on the Denning report into the Profumo affair. He wrote, 'the Garden Rooms have never yet failed to carry out the tasks thrust upon them. Once again they have met the challenge and have done a magnificent job. To produce, at short notice and in a few hours, thirty copies of a document of 203 pages is a splendid achievement.' Elizabeth Douglas-Home, a particular favourite with the girls, would come down and might give the girls chocolates and flowers.

A fair, if charmingly dated, view of the Garden Room girls was given by Sir Harold Evans, Macmillan's ebullient Press Secretary: 'A Garden Room girl is a very special person. Not only does she have to be totally competent at her job, but also the possessor of poise and personality. Moreover, it always seems to happen that she is delightful to the eye. Collectively and individually, they adorn the Number 10 scene. So, too, when the Prime Minister travelled overseas two or three of the young ladies would be in the party, working very long hours in conditions which were often makeshift and onerous, but never losing their poise.'

SWITCHBOARD AND DUTY CLERKS

Telephones arrived at Number 10 in the late nineteenth century, and a small switchboard was introduced early in the twentieth century. When the Second World War broke out, the telephonists (or 'switch', as they are popularly known) remained for a time in Downing Street, but when the staff moved into the Number 10 Annexe overlooking St James's Park, 'switch' moved too. Outside calls would be connected to a particular individual by inserting a plug into the relevant socket on the vertically mounted 'switchboard'; if the Prime Minister, or anyone else, wanted to make a telephone call, he would call the telephonists and ask to be put through. Muriel Williams, who joined the team of seven telephonists in early 1943, remembers how grumpy Anthony Eden, the Foreign Secretary, would be when she woke him in the early hours to say, 'The Prime Minister is on the line.' She forgave Churchill the demanding hours because she found him so convivial; he would always call in to say 'good night' before going to bed in the early hours. 'Thank you, girls,' he would say, 'I am sorry for working you so hard.'

After the war, 'switch' was housed in a small room on the third floor of Number 10. Only in the 1970s did modern vertical keyboards replace the horizontal ones. The girls (no men!) who have manned the telephones have been of the highest quality, and were trained by the GPO and then, after privatisation, by British Telecom. The Number 10 telephone number is confidential and is circulated to only a limited few. Callers find it never rings more than a few times before an alert and friendly voice responds. The telephonists' ability to connect the speaker with the Prime Minister, wherever they are in the world, is legendary.

The team of Duty Clerks, like the Garden Room girls and 'switch', also maintain a 24-hour, 365-day duty roster. The Duty Clerk, who might be the most senior figure awake at Number 10, is often the first point of contact between the outside world and senior Number 10 staff. The job is an exceptionally demanding one, requiring not just stamina but also judgement: whether or not to disturb the Prime Minister in the middle of the night being one of the most difficult decisions. One 1990s Duty Clerk, who always seemed to be *in situ* when bad news came in, earned himself the nickname, 'the grim reaper'.

▲ 'Switch' at work during wartime.

COOKS AND CATERING

Ever since the Government Hospitality Fund was set up in 1908, catering at Number 10 has been hived off to this specialist organisation. Official business occasionally demands an 'in-house' meal, such as lunch before Parliamentary Question Time for the Prime Minister and aides. On these occasions, catering staff are hired to provide a meal. Prime ministers, however, have to pay for their own catering for private occasions and, aware of an eagle eye constantly upon them, they are meticulous in paying for any private domestic help in Number 10. As a result, it has been traditional for prime ministers to leave Number 10 poorer than when they entered it.

Senior Number 10 staff, such as the Private Office, repair to the Cabinet Office canteen for meals, though many bring sandwiches to eat at their desks. 'Below stairs' staff, the Garden Room girls, other secretaries, 'switch' and the messengers have to fend for themselves. The Garden Room girls can go to a room in the basement under Number 11, which has a refrigerator and a cooker.

Cars

Balfour (1902-5) was the first prime minister to bring a car to Number 10. Thereafter, prime ministers either drove themselves or were driven by their wives or, from the 1950s, by government chauffeurs.

Churchill's limousines were large enough to accommodate himself, pets and secretaries in the passenger compartment. Attlee was often driven by his wife, Vi, in their 14 hp Humber. During general elections she drove him stolidly around the country in their small car, covering 1,300 miles in the 1950 election alone. By contrast, Churchill drove around in a cavalcade accompanied by a massive entourage, with detectives following in an unmarked car. Macmillan was driven by government drivers when on official duty and by Lady Dorothy on holidays. One aide recalls, 'it is amazing the Prime Minister survived. She loved driving around at some speed, pointing out the view. Contact with the road seemed entirely coincidental'.

All Number 10 cars, hired on long loan from the government car service, had for patriotic reasons to be British made. The first post-war car was a Humber Pullman, with a sliding central glass partition but no heating, nor radio. In the late 1950s, Rover Saloons and automatics began to replace the Humbers.

In the 1970s, fears of terrorist attack or kidnap grew, so in the 1980s came specially built bomb- and bullet-proof cars. Drivers had to be specially trained in anti-terrorist techniques, including the skills of driving unusually heavy cars at speed. 'Outriders' were also introduced, for security and speed. Many prime ministers have liked these special policemen on motorbikes, but Mrs Thatcher did not and was even heard to say that Hitler had used outriders.

Churchill with his Humber in October 1931 (above). On the way to the Commons in May 1945 (left).

By the late 1980s, the Number 10 fleet had settled at two Jaguars, two Rovers and a 'run-about' car, a Ford, used for errands, but never by the Prime Minister.

Routes that the Prime Minister is going to take are never broadcast in advance, and are constantly changed for security reasons. Nevertheless, when the Prime Minister's convoy sweeps across west London en route to the airport, passers-by gawp as the head of government is whisked effortlessly through the traffic congestion.

Cats, Dogs and a Budgerigar

Lloyd George's Number 10 was home to a small menagerie. His daughter Megan had a black pug called Zulu, which would be adorned with a red ribbon when she came back from boarding school for the holidays. Zulu died while on active service at Number 10 and was buried in the garden.

Olwen, another daughter, owned a Pekinese called Ching. One morning, Lloyd George spotted Ching sleeping on a ministerial chair just as the Cabinet was about to meet. 'I see,' he said, 'that we have a new member of the Cabinet.' When Lloyd George's own dog, a Welsh terrier called Cymru, was sent away to his home at Walton Heath, it mysteriously reappeared at Number 10 two or three days later. A fourth animal, a Chow called Chong, would sit with him while he worked.

Winston's friends

Churchill was another animal lover. When he became Prime Minister in May 1940, he inherited a cat from Chamberlain, and dubbed the hapless animal 'Munich Mouser'. However, Nelson, a black cat which had been wounded in an air raid at Admiralty House and brought to the relative safety of Number 10, quickly pulled rank on the cat which had previously had the house to itself. According to Churchill's daughter, Mary Soames, Nelson was 'rusticated' to Chequers when Number 10 moved to the Annexe, and lived out his days 'getting crosser and crosser'. At Chartwell, Churchill kept Mr Cat and Tango. Tango died the week Tobruk fell in 1942. Lady Soames recalled, 'No one could bear to tell

Papa until the war news got better. He loved cats and took his relationship with them very seriously.'

When Churchill returned to power in 1951, a poodle, Rufus, and a budgerigar, Toby, moved in along with the cats. Toby was allowed to fly free in Churchill's bedroom; the Prime Minister would sit up in bed with a large flat sponge on his head in case Toby had an accident – a luxury the secretaries did not enjoy. Both Toby and Rufus would join Churchill on car journeys, with resulting mayhem; but cats remained his chief love. Margate was a small black kitten found on the steps of Number 10 in 1953 as Churchill was preparing his speech at the annual Conservative conference at Margate; Smokey and Orlando occupied Number 10 during Churchill's 'Indian Summer' years as Prime Minister in the early 1950s. When he retired in 1955, the cats, to Clarissa Eden's horror, stayed on. She took Margate to the Churchills' flat at Hyde Park Gate; a duty clerk opted to look after Orlando, while Smokey was adopted by the Garden Room girls.

Wilberforce

The Wilsons introduced their Siamese cat, Nemo, and a Labrador, Paddy. Nemo was taken to the garden each morning by Mrs Wilson. He quickly worked out that if he stood by the lift door in the basement, the doors would eventually open and he could return upstairs to the second-floor flat. Nemo was a casualty of Labour's defeat in 1970 and departed without ceremony. The result of this rightward swing in the political mood of the nation was more rats, and a skewbald, Wilberforce, who quickly made friends with Lady Howe's terrier at Number 11, Budget. Wilberforce evoked strong feelings: 'He was a miserable, unfriendly animal. I never got any warmth out of him,' said one senior Number 10 figure, for whom the emotion of rejection was clearly still raw.

Humphrey

The Pitt, Gladstone or Churchill of the late twentieth century was undoubtedly Humphrey (named after Sir Humphrey Appleby in the television comedy *Yes, Minister!*). The black and white tom has even been the subject of two biographies, *Humphrey: The Nine Lives of The Number Ten Cat* by Willy Rushton and *A Day In The Life of Humphrey, The Downing Street Cat*. Not everyone was pleased by the glamour Humphrey brought to the workaday Number 10: 'I never thought of Humphrey as a Number 10 cat at all,' said one insider. 'He was really just a Cabinet Office cat who was overpromoted.'

Churchill with his horse, Colonist, from whose exploits he derived much solace during the 1950s **(opposite)**. *Lord Hailsham arrives at a Cabinet meeting in June 1980, with his dog, Mini* **(above)**. *Humphrey collects the morning papers* **(left)**.

4 Departures & an Arrival

No western country has a more brutal system for the transfer of power than the UK. Overnight, the incumbent becomes *persona non grata*. It is as if the occupant is being slung out for not paying the rent. To leave by the front door, with one's possessions, is made all the more awkward by the booing crowd and zoom lenses, eager to lap up every drop of discomfort. Some premiers have left by the back door into Horse Guards Parade, but the media have quickly become wise to even that bolt hole.

▶ 2 May 1997. John Major, his family behind him, bids farewell as Prime Minister.

◀ 2 May 1997. Minutes later, Tony Blair arrives on the same doorstep with his family.

An outgoing prime minister does at least have the right to a brief occupancy of Chequers, but this may be scant comfort. Several less affluent premiers in the twentieth century had no permanent home into which to move back. As the chauffeur-driven cars, the red boxes and the ever-present aides are withdrawn, the deposed prime minister is left with little but the realisation that he is no longer the centre of attention, but must still endure a lifetime of security men intruding on his privacy. Many former premiers seize on the opportunity of writing their autobiographies – Macmillan has been the most prolific, with six volumes of two million words – partly as a source of revenue but also as a way of occupying the mind and body in the long years that stretch ahead.

Here we focus on four 'departures' – two following defeats at general elections and two mid-Parliament – and one 'arrival'.

▲ Balfour's worldly goods are removed after his departure in 1905.

WINSTON CHURCHILL'S DEPARTURE: 1955

Churchill's role as Leader of the Opposition had been an issue even before he took over again as Prime Minister, aged seventy-six, in October 1951.

As early as 1947, groups had met to discuss how to induce the 'old man' to retire. Churchill's conduct as Leader of the Opposition from 1945-51 could be at best described as lackadaisical – shadow Cabinet meetings consisted of liquid lunches at the Savoy Hotel. Reforming Tories, younger Tories, right-wing Tories, were all anxious to see him go, in favour of someone more in tune with the post-war world and the fight against Clement Attlee's Labour policies.

Churchill told intimate friends initially that he intended to stay in office for only a year after the 1951 general election, but George VI's death, in February 1952, provided an unshakeable reason to stay on: he could not possibly go before seeing the young Queen Elizabeth crowned the following year. Then Stalin's death, in March 1953, gave him a new and more personal reason for staying on: as the sole survivor of the wartime 'Big Three' (Roosevelt, Stalin and Churchill), he felt that he was uniquely placed to end the Cold War and usher in a new era of peace, free from the horrors of nuclear bombs. Churchill's stroke in June that year failed to provide the chance for his critics in Cabinet to prise him from office, as Anthony Eden, the heir apparent, was himself incapacitated for six months, following a botched abdominal operation.

With Eden back in harness at the Foreign Office from the autumn, and Churchill visibly weaker, the heat was on again. But he clung on, limpet-like, to office. In July 1954, the plotters decided to enlist the help of Clementine Churchill: Harold Macmillan was delegated to tell her that several Cabinet colleagues thought Winston should retire. Really? Well they had better tell him themselves. Hopes rose on November 30th, at the party in Westminster Hall to celebrate his eightieth birthday, when Churchill announced, 'I am nearing the end of my journey.' But in December, at a meeting with senior staff in the Cabinet Room, he thundered the words below.

Were they to force him out, he told stunned colleagues, an election would be inevitable – and he would tell the country what they were up to.

Realisation dawned with the New Year in 1955 that his hope of bringing about a new rapprochement between East and West, of adding the Nobel Peace Prize to his Nobel Prize for Literature, was not to be. His will was broken. He set his retirement date for the first week in April, though some final flutters of regret, as when President Eisenhower promised to come to Europe to celebrate the tenth anniversary of VE-Day in May 1955, threatened a last-minute volte-face. The US Ambassador in London had his ear bent: could he tell the White House to ease up on the visit until Churchill's departure became irrevocable? Officials helped arrange a dinner at Number 10 for the Queen and the Duke of Edinburgh on April 4th, Churchill's last night as premier. It was a glittering success. Churchill chaired his last Cabinet on the morning of April 5th, before being driven to Buckingham Palace. He was insistent that, in accordance with royal prerogative, the monarch should select her own premier, and that Eden should wait a full day before going to see her, to be formally installed as Prime Minister.

> *'I know you are trying to get rid of me . . . but I won't do it. But if you feel strongly about it you can force my hand by a sufficiently large number of ministers handing in their resignations.'*
>
> WINSTON CHURCHILL, JULY 1954

▲ Churchill leaves for the Palace to hand in his resignation, on 5 April 1955. Behind him stand his two most loyal aides, Christopher Soames and Jock Colville.

ALEC DOUGLAS-HOME'S DEPARTURE: 1964

Alec Douglas-Home received politics' equivalent of a 'hospital pass' in rugby when he succeeded Harold Macmillan as premier in October 1963. The Tory party had already been in office for twelve years, and the next general election could not be more than twelve months away. The country, and the media, were growing tired of the Tories, their strongest policies had been enacted and their most able lieutenants burnt out.

Yet Alec Douglas-Home brought the Tories back to within a whisker of beating Harold Wilson's Labour party in the October 1964 general election. He battled hard for a year, preparing his party for the election, and he worked tirelessly during the campaign. Party apparatchiks, deciding that his aristocratic appearance and oddly shaped head were a liability on television, saw that he would best serve the party by travelling around the country in person. Face to face, few could resist his charm.

Unpublished diaries, from which come the quotations opposite and

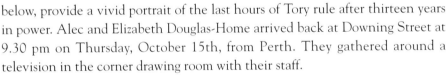

▲ Alec Douglas-Home faces the press after the 1964 election defeat.

below, provide a vivid portrait of the last hours of Tory rule after thirteen years in power. Alec and Elizabeth Douglas-Home arrived back at Downing Street at 9.30 pm on Thursday, October 15th, from Perth. They gathered around a television in the corner drawing room with their staff.

A moment of belief that they could win came with the retaining of Billericay: immediately 'everyone rushed for the drink'. The Garden Room girls were following the news two floors below, all dressed in blue and all fed up: 'They were glued to the television damning Harold Wilson for all they were worth, as were the drivers, messengers and detectives.' But as the night wore on, the news worsened. Elizabeth Home, ever thoughtful, went up in the lift to the third floor to give the switchboard girls a drink.

Before dawn, and believing they had lost, the Homes retired to bed. Yet the news that greeted them on Friday, October 16th was not discouraging: Labour had still to secure the magical figure of 316 seats needed for a majority, and the morning's results were going less well for Labour. A lunch party for a dozen, including Cabinet ministers Ted Heath and Reginald Maudling, was held on the first floor.

'It was rather like a wake with lots of flowers, food and drink and an awful feeling of dread. The lights were rather dim which didn't help . . . Things started off not too badly, then worsened.'

DIARY, 16 OCTOBER 1964

In the early afternoon, after a tantalising period when Labour remained on 315 seats, the target was passed, and Labour finished up with an overall majority of four. As our diarist wrote, 'Many spirits fell again when Sir Alec had to go off the Palace. As he went out [into Downing Street] everyone booed. Poor Lady Home was taking photos out of the window – it must have hurt her horribly and I hate them for it, especially as loud cheers accompanied Mr Wilson's arrival at 4 pm. As if defeat was not enough, in the middle of the afternoon we heard China had exploded her first atom bomb.' News of the fall of the moderate Soviet leader, Khrushchev, also began to circulate. To the stunned and exhausted figures in Number 10, it must have appeared as if a brave new socialist era had truly dawned.

Pinned upstairs, with Wilson now ensconced in the Cabinet Room believing that his predecessor had left, the Homes decided to make their getaway by the back door. Slipping down the grand staircase like furtive refugees, they passed the Cabinet floor, now in the hands of the enemy, and at the door to the garden were met by some of the staff. It was customary for the outgoing prime minister to write a letter of good wishes to the incomer. Sir Alec, having written in his own hand 'To the Prime Minister', handed the letter to Jane [Parsons], which nearly finished her. In the room directly above, the official team which only hours earlier had ministered to Alec Home, were now helping plan Harold Wilson's new government. The Homes stole across the Number 10 garden to the gate in the back wall.

> 'There was no official send off, no private secretaries, no anything. All the Garden Room girls lined up at the window to watch them go. It was absolutely miserable. That was the most agonising moment of the whole thing – slipping surreptitiously out the back way and handing a letter addressed to the new Prime Minister for someone to give to Mr Wilson later.'
>
> DIARY, 16 OCTOBER 1964

So rushed was their departure, that Elizabeth Home and her secretary, Lorne Roper-Caldbeck, had to return to the flat on Monday, October 19th, after a weekend at Chequers, to complete the packing. It was a race against the clock, but they were helped by the Number 10 staff; the affection the Homes had inspired after only a year in Number 10 was extraordinary. Lady Home saw their enforced departure as a 'splendid opportunity to throw out unvalued possessions', including a large store of her husband's medicines. While she was doing so, Mary Wilson, although still living in Hampstead Garden Suburb, was asked up to the flat by Lady Home. She looked 'very miserable and was on the verge of tears. What a prospect it must all be for her!'

The building was already bubbling with gossip, above all about Marcia Williams seizing the room adjoining the Cabinet Room for her office. In a final act of defiance, the Homes' secretaries left their Tory posters in the room in the flat that they had used as their office. Of all transfers of power since 1945, the 1964 transition was the most polarised and aroused the most mutual animosity.

MARGARET THATCHER'S DEPARTURE: 1990

The Conservative victory of June 1987 gave Mrs Thatcher a third successive general election win, a feat unprecedented in the twentieth century for any premier. Yet, in little over three years, she had fallen from power, pushed out of office by the very people, her Cabinet Ministers, who owed their political preferment to her.

The economy, which had been booming in the mid-1980s, went into decline following the Stock Market crash of October 1987. Concern was compounded by the unpopular introduction of the community charge, or 'poll tax', differences over entry into the European Exchange Rate Mechanism (completed in October 1990), and Geoffrey Howe's resignation from his Cabinet post on November 1st. Poor by-election results unnerved Tory MPs, as did Howe's bitterly anti-Thatcher resignation speech on November 13th, described later by her as his 'final act of bile and treachery'. When Michael Heseltine, who had walked out of her Cabinet in 1986 over the Westland dispute, announced his intention to stand against her, on November 14th, many began to wonder whether she could survive.

> 'You can find Heseltines wherever you go. But there is only one Mrs Thatcher. Handle with care. This valuable object is irreplaceable.'
>
> THE 'SUNDAY TELEGRAPH',
> 18 NOVEMBER 1990

The first ballot of Tory MPs, in a Byzantine electoral process, was to be held on November 20th. Proposed by Douglas Hurd, her Foreign Secretary, Mrs Thatcher was seconded by John Major, her Chancellor, despite the fact that, as one of his aides wrote in her diary, 'I get the feeling he isn't that keen'. On the afternoon of Sunday, November 18th, she flew to Paris for a European conference, assured by her courtiers she would beat Heseltine in the first round. As she flew across the English Channel, she was not comforted to read that day's newspapers, with many saying it was time for her to go.

That weekend, even ardent Thatcherites sensed things might be slipping away from them. If she failed to win the first ballot, who would be best placed to challenge and defeat the arch anti-Thatcherite, Heseltine? Hurd was deemed by many to be too European. Major emerged as the figure best placed to carry the Thatcherite torch forward and the man most likely to unify the party. On Monday, November 19th, Jeffrey Archer drove to Major's Huntingdon home, where he was recuperating in bed from a wisdom tooth operation. Archer spread a copy of every newspaper over Major's bed and set about persuading Major that there was broad backing for him, should a second ballot be necessary.

Voting took place all day on Tuesday, November 20th. The result, announced at 6.30 pm, gave Mrs Thatcher insufficient votes, according to the rules, for an outright victory over Heseltine: she had 204 votes to Heseltine's 152. The news was broken to her in her private rooms in the British Embassy in Paris, and she fell silent. A second ballot would be necessary, called for a week later. She returned to London just before midday on Wednesday, November 21st, fired up to beat off the

▲ Mrs Thatcher announces that the time has come for her to go.

challenge. But by now even ultra-loyalists realised the game was up. That afternoon, she toured the Tea Room and corridors of the House of Commons to drum up support. It was a pathetic scene. Even Denis, her husband, told her, 'Don't go on, love.' But she was not yet ready to listen. She called Hurd. Would he nominate her for the second ballot? Good. She phoned Major. You'll second me? There was a long pause – 'it was a very long period of silence,' he later recalled. He agreed to back her, 'but I resented the way she didn't ask, but presumed on my support'.

She now set herself the task of stiffening support among her senior ministers. One by one she saw them in her room in the Commons on the Wednesday evening. Almost to a man, they conveyed their view that though they personally supported her, they did not believe she was in a position to win: 'weasel words,' she wrote, 'whereby they had transmuted their betrayal into frank advice and concern for my fate.' She returned to Number 10, confused and upset, and at 7.30 pm on November 22nd phoned Andrew Turnbull, her Principal Private Secretary, to tell him that she had decided to resign. At Cabinet that morning, with tears in her eyes, she announced her decision to go, in the interests of party unity, and she urged her ministers to unite behind the figure best placed to defeat Michael Heseltine. It was a sombre affair. Expressions of appreciation were intoned; she sensed that they were relieved she was going, yet everyone pretended otherwise.

Tuesday, November 27th saw the second ballot, in which Major defeated Hurd and Heseltine. Mrs Thatcher was delighted by the result and danced a jig of joy at the top of the stairs of Number 11, where the Majors were living. Mrs Thatcher had the luxury of five days to compose herself before she left Number 10 for the last time on the morning of Wednesday, November 28th. Over a thousand bouquets had

> *'We are leaving Downing Street for the last time after eleven and a half wonderful years. We are very happy that we leave the United Kingdom in a very very much better state than when we came.'*
>
> Margaret Thatcher,
> 28 November 1990

◀ A tearful Mrs
Thatcher bids a final
farewell as Prime
Minister.

poured into Number 10 from the public over the previous five days, and she was in sparkling form at a farewell party for 200 guests in the Pillared Room on the Tuesday evening. Her personal staff presented her with a first edition of Rudyard Kipling's poetry; 'Life begins at sixty-five,' she quipped in her speech. At 9.30 the next morning she left Number 10. At 9.35 am, her chauffeur-driven Daimler arrived at the gates of Buckingham Palace and she stepped out to tender her resignation as Prime Minister.

JOHN MAJOR'S DEPARTURE: 1997

John Major's departure as Prime Minister six and a half years later was just as traumatic, and a much more rushed affair than Mrs Thatcher's; leaving after a general election is more fraught than departing mid-Parliament.

Major's premiership, we can now see with hindsight, was holed below the water when Britain was forcibly ejected from the ERM on 'Black Wednesday' in September 1992. From that moment on, little went right for him. His bid to re-establish his authority in the summer 1995 leadership election resolved nothing. From mid-1996, he realised that victory in the general election would be highly unlikely. Choosing a date for the election was agonising, and squabbles broke out with senior advisers over the election manifesto and the style of the election campaign. Not even Saatchis, to their chagrin, could pull it round for the Tories.

Major set the election day for May 1st, with an unprecedented six-week long campaign. Number 10 duly emptied, as was the custom during general elections.

Civil servants kept the Private Office and other essential services manned, but political activity shifted to party headquarters, Central Office in Smith Square. It was a bleak time. On one of the final weekends, George Bridges, a young political aide, became aware that he was the only person in Number 10. His sense of isolation, of being surrounded by hostile forces, was heightened by the film he was watching that Sunday on television. *Zulu* portrayed the last-ditch battle for survival of a garrison of vastly outnumbered British soldiers.

In the last few days of the campaign, Major's staff found themselves lingering in the building, dimly aware that they might never enter it again. It was a hard time for both John and Norma Major personally. Norma's mother was dying and needed constant attention, while Norma herself was suffering from a bad cold she could not throw off, and deep anger about the way her husband had been treated by some senior Tories. One cheery soul tried to lighten his mood: 'Never mind, Prime Minister, it will be like 1945. The party will lose, but the party, not you, will take the blame: you yourself will be no more blamed than Churchill was in 1945.' He went white. 'Oh, my God,' he said, 'you don't think it will be that bad, surely?'

The hope he clung onto, that sustained him, was that they might avoid a Labour landslide. In 1945, the Tories has been reduced to just 213 seats. If he had to lose – and he had already decided to resign after a general election defeat – he wanted to bequeath his successor as large a number of MPs as possible, to optimise the prospects for winning the subsequent general election from Labour. Major awoke on the morning of Thursday, May 1st, still hoping he could keep Labour's lead down to 80 or 90 seats. He spent the day touring his Huntingdon constituency, cheering everyone up with an ebullience that did not seem forced. At 5 pm, a phone call came through to the Prime Minister's car from Central Office in London. Their initial estimates of a medium-sized majority had been revised after exit polls during the day. The party, he was told, faced electoral disaster. Major went very, very quiet. 'Shell-shocked' and 'very, very bleak' were two of the epithets used to describe his mood. At 6.30 pm, Arabella Warburton, Major's close personal assistant, arrived at his Huntingdon home in a car festooned with balloons and flowers. As they walked round the garden, he confided: 'It will be a very bad night for us.'

▲ When the curtain falls . . . John Major bows out.

An aide was dispatched to buy fish and chips to fortify the growing party for the long night ahead. No one in the house knew whether or not to mention the election. Major himself ate in almost total silence. Seventy miles away in London, the three most powerful officials of the British state – Robin Butler, Cabinet Secretary, Robert Fellowes, the Queen's Private Secretary and Alex Allan, the Prime Minister's Principal Private Secretary – finalised details of the bloodless *coup d'état* that would unfold the next day. At 10 pm, as the polls closed, the tight-knit party in Huntingdon put on ITN's *News at Ten*: 'It was like death,' said one present. At midnight, Major withdrew to a quiet room and made a telephone call to Tony Blair at his Sedgefield constituency, congratulating him on his undeniable victory. Blair thanked him. It was a dignified five-minute conversation between two men who clearly had profound reservations about each other.

At 2.30 am on Friday May 2nd, Major's motorcade moved off to his count in Huntingdon. Knowing his appearance at his local constituency would be broadcast nationwide, he wanted to put on a good show. At 3.15 am, the motorcade set off down the A1. The roads were virtually empty. While Norma dozed, Major stared into the middle distance, tensing himself for the ordeal of the next few hours, his final test as Prime Minister. The car radio droned out with each passing mile the list of Tory fatalities, including some of the seven Cabinet Ministers who lost their seats. At 5.20 am, the convoy arrived at Smith Square, where Major spent an hour in discussions and in trying to cheer up the party faithful. But no words, he knew, could bring solace.

By 6.30 am he was back in Number 10, and went up to the second-floor flat for breakfast with Norma and their children, Elizabeth and James. They kept each other's spirits up as they ate and talked, but below all was the emotion, the deep fatigue and the pain of terrible defeat. While the others rested, Major busied himself thinking through his next few hours.

At 10.30 am, after showering, and having make-up applied to disguise his fatigue, he came down to the Pillared Drawing Room where 60 staff had gathered in clusters for coffee, orange juice and croissants. He moved from group to group, chatting and thanking each member of staff individually, and addressing them by their first name. Clearing his throat, he moved to the middle of the room and spoke to his staff in a quiet but steady voice. Number 10, he said, had been not just an office but also his and Norma's home for six and a half years, and he would miss each and every one of them.

By now, everyone in the room, except Major himself, either had tears in their eyes or were openly crying. He had just one request. He knew it was the custom for staff to line the front hall to clap out departing prime ministers, but would they mind foregoing the practice this time? He feared that if he caught anyone's eye he would lose his composure and he knew, as soon as the black front door was opened, that the eyes of the world would be scrutinising his every reaction.

At 11.25 am, he emerged onto the spot where 2,347 days and one hour before he had announced that he had accepted the Queen's invitation to form a government. With his family by his side, he congratulated the incoming Labour government, and said that they would inherit the most benevolent set of economic statistics since the First World War. There was also a final matter he wished to clarify: he would be advising his parliamentary colleagues to select a new leader. With words recalling the theatrical tradition of his parents, he said, 'When the curtain falls, it is time to get off the stage and that is what I propose to do.'

With this most dignified of exits, he boarded the car which would take him to the Palace to resign as Premier, and then on to watch cricket at the Oval – a luxury, he told Sue Lawley on 'Desert Island Discs', that he would like to take with him to his faraway island.

TONY BLAIR'S ARRIVAL, 1997

Tony Blair, too, spent election day touring his constituency in Sedgefield, County Durham, with his wife, Cherie. He was surprised and gratified by the phone call at midnight from John Major, two hundred miles to the south in Huntingdon: 'There was no real need for him to [phone] but it was a nice gesture and he just wished me well.' The Blairs left their home shortly after midnight and went to the Sedgefield count. Only when they arrived did Tony Blair and his team begin to realise that victory would be theirs, and by such a margin. They called in at Trimden Labour Club before driving on to Teeside airport, where the small party – Tony and Cherie Blair, Jonathan Powell, Alastair Campbell and Anji Hunter – boarded a jet for London's Stansted airport.

Arriving at 4.30 am, three cars led by a police escort vehicle whisked them off to the Royal Festival Hall, where the victory celebration was in full swing. En route, a call from President Clinton was taken in the car: it was still evening in the US but dawn in the UK.

Once inside the Festival Hall, the Blairs mounted a specially constructed podium to euphoric acclaim. They stayed for 45 minutes before being driven to their north London home in Islington. As they snatched an hour or two to freshen up, key Labour figures repaired to the party headquarters in Millbank Tower, a mile away on the opposite bank of the Thames, to make arrangements for the immediate future. Shortly after the Majors' Daimler had disappeared down Whitehall at 11.30 am, aides entered Downing Street and handed out 200 Union Jack flags to the crowds who were being let in to line the street, awaiting the arrival of the Blairs. Children were given

▼ The smile of victory.

special T-shirts emblazoned with 'BRITAIN JUST GOT BETTER', echoing a Labour campaign slogan.

At the same time, the Blairs were being driven by motorcade from their Islington home en route to the Palace. After only 10 yards, they asked the car to pull up, and joined a crowd of cheering local residents. Security officers soon bundled them back into the car, with Mrs Blair looking visibly disconcerted. For those few minutes, between the departure of John Major from the Palace and the arrival of Tony Blair, Britain was without a Prime Minister. Then, the royal audience with the Queen over, the Blairs' Daimler swept into Downing Street. Just inside the iron gates, Tony Blair ordered the second stop of the day. He and Cherie emerged, and walked towards the front door, greeting the cheering crowds with both hands – his first 'walkabout' as Prime Minister. Outside the house, Blair jumped up on the front doorstep and turned to the crowd with Cherie by his side. She clung to him in an affectionate and informal embrace that delighted both crowds and cameras.

> *'Most of the team had fought together through the previous two elections: part of us refused to believe that this time we had really done it.'*
>
> DEREK DRAPER, 2 MAY 1997

Blair paid warm tribute to John Major for 'his courage over the last few days and the manner of his leaving – the essential decency which is the mark of the man.' He concluded with the unambiguous statement and signal, 'We were elected as New Labour and we will govern as New Labour.'

The Blairs gathered up their three children and went in to be greeted by the applauding staff lining the corridor. The front door closed. Blair felt a rush of emotions: a sense of 'I am here!', an awareness of the contrast between the noisy, enthusiastic scenes outside and the subdued applause within, a concern for the staff, some of whom had tears of emotion in their eyes. It was a moment of history that would remain with him all his life. He was shown into the Cabinet Room at the end of the corridor, where Robin Butler, Cabinet Secretary, greeted him. 'You are in charge,' he said. 'What do you want to do?'

> *'For eighteen years – eighteen long years – my party has been in opposition . . . Today we are charged with the deep responsibility of government. Today, enough of talking – it is time to do.'*
>
> TONY BLAIR, 2 MAY 1997

The meeting with Butler was brief. Blair was surprised to find a letter of congratulation and a bottle of champagne from John Major on the Cabinet table. The children, the Blairs' parents and other close relations were upstairs awaiting him for a family buffet lunch; after weeks of being on the move during the campaign, it seemed incredible to be having a civilised, unhurried meal. Awake for nearly 36 hours already, but with his mind sharp with the adrenalin and excitement, he appreciated the sustenance. Cherie was taken on a tour of the building by Carol Allen, the House Manager: bar a state occasion the year before, it was the first time the Blairs had been in the house, and most of it was new to them. Cherie wandered around intrigued, and when

photographers, massing in the Cabinet Ante Room and the well of the stairs, were ready for a final promised photograph, Cherie could not be found. Tracked down, the Blairs posed at the top of the grand staircase, with the Prime Minister standing behind his wife and placing his right hand on her right shoulder: a more composed image than the jubilant images on the doorstep two hours before. In the background were the black and white photographs of Harold Wilson and James Callaghan, Old Labour, while at the bottom of the staircase was the portrait of Robert Walpole, the first prime minister, where the story of the house, and of this book, began.

▲ The Blairs, happy in their new home. The Prime Minister's predecessors look on.

227

PICTURE CREDITS

Page 13 London Aerial Photo Library; pages 15 (top), 17 (right), 113 Mary Evans Picture Collection; pages 17 (left), 22 (top), 24, 25 (top), 26 (top) 30, 31 (left), 62, 63, 67 (top), 69, 70, 71 (bottom), 76, 86–7, 89, 105, 115, 118, 121, 128, 129, 132, 133 (bottom), 137 (bottom), 146 (top), 149, 150, 155–6, 192–3, 201, 213 (top), 211, 218 Getty Images Ltd; pages 19 (top), 22 (left), 25 (bottom), 60, 81 Mansell/Time Inc; pages 3, 20, 26 (top), 108 London Metropolitan Archive; page 27 courtesy of the Public Record Office; pages 28 (top), 67 (bottom), 78, 79, 80, 82, 83, 117, 138,

210 Imperial War Museum; pages 28 (bottom), 114, 151 The Illustrated London News Picture Library; pages 33, 119 Associated Press; page 35 Peter Jordan/Network Photographers Ltd; pages 61, 65, 73, 132 (left), 135, 137 (top), 143 (right), 146 (bottom), 169, 217 Popperphoto; pages 71 (top), 92, 93, 94, 125, 153, 167, 168 (top), 200, 203–5, 212, 213 (bottom), 215, 227 PA News; pages 77, 84, 131, 132 (right), 140, 195 The Master and Fellows of Churchill College Cambridge; pages 90, 148, 159, 160, 161, 162, 164, 166 (top), 183 (right), 190 (left) Stockwave/COI; pages 97, 116,

216 Westminster City Archives; pages 96, 99 British Museum London, UK/Bridgeman Art Library; page 98 The British Library; pages 110, 165 by courtesy of the National Portrait Gallery; page 142 reproduced by permission of Punch Ltd; page 143 (left) courtesy of Sothebys, London; pages 152, 154 Express Picture Library; pages 158, 214, 221, 225, 223 UPPA; pages 123, 171 Museum of London; page 178 National Maritime Museum London; page 194 Srdja Djukanovic/Camera Press; endpapers and page 207 Jane Parsons; page 222 Mirror Syndication International.

SELECT BIBLIOGRAPHY

Adams, Ralph James Q, *Bonar Law* (1999)
Archer, Lucy, *Raymond Erith* (1985)
Asquith, Margot, *The Autobiography of Margot Asquith* (1920)
Attlee, Clement R, *As It Happened* (1954)
Avon, Anthony, *Full Circle* (1960)
Benn, Anthony, *Out of the Wilderness: Diaries 1963–67* (1987)
Benn, Anthony, *Against the Tide: Diaries 1973–76* (1989)
Blake, Robert, *Disraeli* (1966)
Charlton, John, *No 10 Downing Street* (1977)
Cockerell, Michael, *Live from Number 10* (1988)
Colville, John, *The Fringes of Power: 10 Downing Street Diaries 1939–1955* (1985)
Crossman, Richard, *The Crossman Diaries* (1979)
Draper, Derek, *Blair's 100 Days* (1997)
Egremont, Lord, *Wyndham and Children First* (1968)
Egremont, Max, *Balfour* (1980)
Ehrman, John, *William Pitt: The Years of Acclaim* (1969)
Englefield, Dermot; Seaton, Janet; White, Isobel, *Facts about British Prime Ministers* (1995)
Evans, Harold, *Downing Street Diary – The Macmillan Years, 1957/63* (1981)
Farr, *Six at Ten* (1985)
Feely, Terence, *Number 10: The Private Lives of Six Prime Ministers* (1982)
Gash, Norman, *Mr Secretary Peel: The Life of Sir Robert Peel to 1830* (1961)

Gash, Norman, *Sir Robert Peel: The Life of Sir Robert after 1830* (1972)
Gilbert, Martin, *Churchill – A Life* (1991)
Gray, D, *Spencer Perceval* (1963)
Haines, Joe, *The Politics of Power* (1977)
Harris, Kenneth, *Attlee* (1982)
Home, Lord, *The Way the Wind Blows* (1976)
Horne, Alistair, *Macmillan 1894–1956* (1988)
Horne, Alistair, *Macmillan 1957–1986* (1989)
Howe, Geoffrey, *Conflict of Loyalty* (1994)
Hurst, Simon Conway, *The Reconstruction of Downing Street and the Old Treasury 1960–64* (1998)
Jenkins, Roy, *Gladstone* (1995)
Jolliffe, John, *Raymond Asquith – Life and Letters* (1980)
Jones, Christopher, *No 10 Downing Street: The Story of a House* (1985)
Jupp, Peter, *Lord Grenville* (1985)
Lucas, Scott, *Britain and Suez: the lion's last roar* (1996)
Macmillan, Harold, *Riding the Storm 1956–59* (1971)
Marquand, David, *Ramsay MacDonald* (1977)
Matthew, Henry Colin Gray, *Gladstone 1809–1898* (1986)
Middlemas, Keith and Barnes, John, *Baldwin: A biography* (1969)
Minney, Rubeigh James, *No 10 Downing Street: A House in History* (1963)
Moneypenny, W F and Buckle, G E *The Life of*

Benjamin Disraeli, Earl of Beaconsfield (1910–20)
Moran, Charles Wilson, *Winston Churchill: The Struggle for Survival, 1940–1965* (1966)
Morgan, Kenneth O, *Callaghan: A Life* (1997)
Nicolson, Harold, *Diaries and Letters of Harold Nicolson* (1966–68)
Pascoe, Charles Eyre, *No 10 Downing Street, Whitehall* (1908)
Pimlott, Ben, *Harold Wilson* (1992)
Riddell, Lord, *Lord Riddell's Intimate Diary of the Peace Conference and After 1918–23* (1933)
Seldon, Anthony, *Major: A Political Life* (1997)
Soames, Mary, *Clementine Churchill* (1979)
Sylvester, Albert James, *The Real Lloyd George* (1947)
Thatcher, Carol, *Below the Parapet: The Biography of Denis Thatcher* (1996)
Thatcher, Margaret, *The Downing Street Years* (1993)
Vansittart, Robert, *The Mist Procession* (1970)
West, Algernon, *Recollections 1832 to 1886* (1899)
Williams, Marcia, *Inside Number 10* (1972)
Wilson, Harold, *A Prime Minister on Prime Ministers* (1977)
Ziegler, Philip, *Melbourne* (1976)
Ziegler, Philip, *Wilson: The Political Life of Lord Wilson of Rievaulx* (1993)

INDEX

With
Every Good Wish
for Christmas
and the New Year
from

C. R. Attlee Violet H. Attlee

10 Downing Street,
Whitehall, S.W.1

WITH ALL GOOD WISHES
FOR CHRISTMAS
AND THE NEW YEAR
FROM

Mary and Harold Wilson

10 Downing Street,
Whitehall

With All Good Wishes
for
Christmas and the New Year
from

Harold and Dorothy Macmillan

HM

10 DOWNING STREET

WITH ALL GO
FOR
CHRISTMAS AND THE NEW YEAR
from

Alec & Elizabeth Douglas Home

added in for good measure!

With Best Wishes
Christmas and the New Year

Edward Heath

With Best Wishes
for
Christmas and the New Year

*Audrey and Jim
Callaghan*

10 Downing Street,
Whitehall

The Cabinet Room

With Best Wishes
Christmas And The New Year

Margaret Thatcher

10 Downing Street
London SW1

With Best Wishes For
Christmas And The New Year

John Major

"The Green Room" 10 Downing Street.